WHERE TWO OR THREE ARE GATHERED

D1369387

Where Two or Three Are Gathered

Liturgy and the Moral Life

Harmon L. Smith

The Pilgrim Press
Cleveland, Ohio

4 -29 -06

The Pilgrim Press, Cleveland, Ohio 44115

© 1995 by Harmon L. Smith

Biblical quotations are from the New Revised Standard Version of the Bible,
© 1989 by the Division of Christian Education of the National Council
of the Churches of Christ in the U.S.A., and are used by permission

Printed in the United States of America on acid-free paper

00 99 98 97 96 95   5 4 3 2 1

Library of Congress Cataloging-in-Publication Data
Smith, Harmon L.
Where two or three are gathered : liturgy and the moral life /
Harmon L. Smith.
p.   cm.
Includes bibliographical references and index.
ISBN 0-8298-1024-2 (alk. paper)
1. Liturgics.   2. Christian ethics.   I. Title.
BV187.S56   1995   94-39961
264—dc20   CIP

FOR DONNA

CONTENTS

PREFACE

I was not born in a parsonage, but like many others of my generation, I literally grew up in church. As a Methodist preacher's kid in rural northern Mississippi, it was not uncommon to begin a Sunday with my father's congregation and end it several hours later with the local Baptist, Presbyterian, or Episcopal youth group in their evening service. There were times in my boyhood when I thought that my entire life was being spent in the churches and revivals of my hometown, church-sponsored community projects, summertime Bible schools, and camp meetings in brush arbors across the rural deep South.

Our family quartet, composed of my father and his sons, was regularly invited to sing at services, to my mother's piano accompaniment. Our busiest season was revival and camp-meeting times. In my late adolescence I had memorized the lyrics and music of more than 250 hymns; and in due course I was invited to be the song leader before the "main event" in evangelistic meetings. This was a vocation which, however brief, netted me a substantial income during high school and college years, in no small part because I was privileged to "lead the singing" for some of the outstanding evangelists of that time.

In retrospect, I find it unremarkable that on more than one occasion I wondered aloud why there were several Christian denominations, because interests and activities were hardly distinguishable from one church to another. In fact, apart from the eleven o'clock service on Sunday morning, when we went to "our church," folks in my several hometowns tended to attend services at *all* the churches. Nobody, however, was able to explain the differences to me.

I was beginning to recognize that with notable exceptions—like Hazel Brannon Smith, who edited and published the Lexington, Mississippi, *Advertiser*—many, if not most, of the folks who so faithfully attended the churches on Sunday simply did not connect what happened in morning and evening worship services with the conduct of their everyday affairs. Sunday rituals clearly marked the first day of the week; but during the other days, conventional Mississippi culture presided.

It is clear to me now that this book was aborning in that kind of prescience.

There are some who say that liturgy is not "ceremonial clothing for doctrinal teaching,"[1] that it ought not *teach* the faith but *celebrate* it. But I believe it arguable that liturgy ineluctably reflects—indeed, that it must mirror and mediate—what we believe to be true and good and beautiful if it is to be an authentic celebration. The classical phrase is *finitum capax infiniti*, the finite carrying the infinite. Liturgy, as the church's prayer, expresses a theology; and it is this, I eventually learned, which explains and accounts for the differences among the forms of liturgies which I observed as a youngster. It is these particular forms, rather than some others, which help these particular worshipers to adore and praise and love God.

The fact is that prayer always expresses a theology of some sort; otherwise it becomes merely an exercise in egocentric psychobabble. William Temple rightly observed that the gospel does not begin by asking of our needs and then trying to meet them, but by announcing God's truth and inviting us to live by that.

So there is actually no need to bifurcate teaching and celebration, or even make that division attractive or desirable. Truth be told, they go together. Liturgy both reflects and teaches us the kind of people we are and are meant to be. It is both catechesis and celebration. And it is the divorce of these two, their separation into virtually vacuum-sealed compartments, which is liturgy's (and the church's) undoing. The technical word for the result is *hypocrisis*—hypocrisy—which means appearing to be what you are not.

This project was begun as an introduction to Christian ethics when my friend and colleague Stanley Hauerwas joined our faculty and the two of us undertook to team-teach a section of this course. Because both of us were concerned about the extent to which Christian ethics had become more or less conventional cultural ethics, and about the ways in which the theological encyclopedia had tended to isolate aspects of theological education which belong together, we conceived the course in terms of "Liturgy as Ethics/Ethics as Liturgy." It was (and is) our contention that the separation of liturgy from ethics, of moral theology from worship, is artificial and contrived and mistaken—and recent! I would like to think that this book is only one of the fruits of that shared labor; meanwhile, he alone will know of my thanks and how much this book is indebted to our collaboration.

Ethically significant issues typically arise in the presence of competing, frequently conflicting, values and neighbor-claims; and it is only in contexts where persons encounter other persons that humanly important moral matters appear. Moreover, it seems to be inevitable that where two or three of us are gathered together the ingredients are present for engaging, and often challenging, our most cherished commitments. How those commitments ought to get appropriately expressed in interpersonal relationships is the work of moral philosophy and moral theology. It is clear that a shared conviction of purpose and identity holds the best possibility for yielding constructive resolution of moral conflict; and I believe that worship and the church's liturgy is the principal resource for that commonality and community between and among Christians. Dissonance in the commitments of those gathered denies them the means for peaceful resolution of their moral disputes.

One way to characterize what I have undertaken to do here would be to rehearse Claude Levi-Strauss's attention to linguistic structures as part of the process of imposing form upon content. Another, perhaps more familiar, way would be to recall Marshall McLuhan's discussion of the relation between "medium" and "message." I mean to claim that there is a universe of discourse for Christians between the languages of worship and the moral life; and as one way to do that, I have sometimes conflated in this book elements of the liturgy which otherwise tend to get treated separately. I have tried to show how Christians are a people whose moral life is formed by gathering for worship and engaging in prayer, adoration, thanksgiving, confession, offering, and the rest. I want to display the character of the church's liturgy and illustrate how moral indicatives can get displayed by liturgical themes. In a word, my aim is to show how worship and sacrament are meant to engender personal and social holiness.

The literal meaning of liturgy is "the people's work"; and in the pages which follow, a community's liturgy serves as one of the principal ways in which we do our work of prayer. Understood as a form of prayer, the liturgy throughout adores and praises and petitions and worships God. Indeed, prayer is the language of worship; so that as we participate in the liturgy we are actually taught how to pray. Read from this perspective, the entire book is an exercise in prayer.[2]

When my sister and brothers and I accompanied our mother to view our father's body in the "slumber room" of the local funeral home, I noticed that his hair had been parted on the wrong side. Because my father had always been careful about his appearance in life, my mother thought that we should inform the mortician of his mistake. But we children suggested that, in view of the sermons he had preached about life and death, and indeed in consideration of his life itself, it would be his final commentary on conventional morality to be buried with this mistake. And he was. For better or worse, I take responsibility also for whatever errors are discovered in what follows.

I know that the use of the masculine pronoun to refer inclusively to both women and men, while customary with me for years, is either problematic or unacceptable for many readers nowadays. So I want to acknowledge that there are valid reasons for this, and where I could I have used both feminine and masculine pronouns comprehensively. This remains an imperfect accomplishment, and I have only partly succeeded; but enough, I hope, to show that I am not entirely morally delinquent in this matter.

ACKNOWLEDGMENTS

This book, as my whole life, is deeply indebted to more people than can be named here. All the same I have to say my special thanks to some folks in particular, and plainly among them are my former students in Christian Ethics 33 who worried about these matters with me. The distinguished Israeli teacher Haim Ginott, reflecting on his experiences in the classroom, is reputed to have said on one occasion, "I fail to detect any similarity between that which I teach and that which they learn"; my friend Murray Struver, clearly in order to chasten vanity in my own teaching, takes occasional delight in reminding me of this comment. I am happy to say that the days when I would embrace Ginott's observation are many times outnumbered by the days when I would not; and, of course, large credit for that has to go to my students, to whom I say "thank you."

Whether the result of providence or blind luck, my graduate teaching assistants have been one of my greatest joys. Their criticisms of my lectures have been both sympathetic and trenchant, and I have valued highly their collegiality. St. Titus Episcopal Church, where I am sometime interim rector, provided a laboratory for testing—and proving—most of the hypotheses which I offer here; and I hold its communicants in special affection. The Reverend Pamela L. Porter provided needed help with many of the technical materials; and Mr. and Mrs. James M. Goodmann were kind enough to read the entire manuscript and make useful suggestions, both stylistic and substantive. The Duke University Divinity School, and especially its library staff, has been consistently supportive of my research and teaching; and I gladly express my deep appreciation to the faculty secretaries, Sarah Freedman and Gail Chappell, who helped bring this project to visible expression. I hope that the editorial staff of The Pilgrim Press will know the many ways in which I am in their debt; and I thank them particularly for their attention to my project as a whole and to tedious detail, both of which have made this a much more accessible book. My dear wife, Donna, to whom I dedicate this book, is my *ultra non possit*.

THE SHAPE OF THE LITURGY

It is clear to the point of almost universal acceptance in contemporary Christian scholarship that, before anything else we have come to know as Christian faith or practice, the earliest Christians *worshiped* Jesus as God's anointed. Before the very first formulation of doctrine, before there was any orthodox teaching, before there was church or sacraments, before there was anything identifiably "Christian," the earliest disciples adored and reverenced Jesus as God's Christ.

In fact, one prominent line of New Testament interpretation argues that the evidence clearly shows that the use of the Hebrew Scriptures by authors now canonized in the New Testament is a retrospective accounting for their having already acknowledged Jesus as Messiah.[1] The New Testament writers did not begin with a checklist of messianic identifiers from the Hebrew Scriptures and proceed to measure Jesus by them. Jesus' authority and presence were real enough to these early disciples; so their questions had to do with whether there could be a viable connection between the messianic expectations of the Hebrew Scriptures and the early Christian experience of the messiahship of Jesus.

Following this argument, we could say that, instead of the Hebrew Scriptures judging Jesus, Jesus judges the Hebrew Scriptures for these earliest Christian writers—or, to put it plainly, Jesus validates the Scriptures and not vice versa. This is an important claim, and one to which we must return when we examine the place and function of Scripture as canon in the liturgy. For now, this helps to explain why *lex orandi est lex credendi*; why the law of prayer is the law of faith; why we believe as we worship; why a Christian's moral agency and action are tied deeply and intimately *and antecedently* to prayer and worship.

This way of viewing how worship shapes religious imagination is also, I suspect, why some modern theologies stretch credibility; why it seldom if ever occurs to us to incorporate their rhetoric and conceptual apparatus into

1

devotions; and why our intellectual love of God does not always seem synchronized or even coherent with the language of our prayers.

How did this come to be? My own, not at all cynical, view is that a few hundred years ago, for reasons neither time nor space permits us to rehearse here, most churches effectively abdicated the task of "doing theology," relegating this function to the academy. And academicians, in pursuit of scientific credibility through the "academic study of religion," distanced themselves further and further from the generative community of the faithful at worship. It happened (dare we say, "naturally"?) that the tradition, the *paradosis*, the receiving of something handed over and passed on, was thus interrupted and in large measure eventually forgotten or explicitly rejected. What became important to the scholars of religion were artifacts—principally texts of various sorts—which, it became widely believed, were amenable to careful scientific scrutiny as the means of understanding both them (i.e., the texts) and the people who had composed them.

Understanding this process helps to make clear how Christians and churches have come so readily to make two important—and, in my opinion, disastrous—moves. One of these moves has been to reduce vital Christian piety to propositions; the other has been to suppose that decision-making is the *sine qua non* of the moral life. In addition, both of these moves are widely believed to be autonomous and largely severed from serious consideration of the kind of people Christians are meant to be.

I believe that these moves are serious mistakes, because no more than Christian faith can be reduced to doctrinal formulae can Christian identity be comprehended apart from prayer and worship within community. Until we recover the awareness that our Christian life is derived from a succession of faithful witnesses upon whom we are dependent, and that prayer and holiness are essential marks of our moral life, we will continue to suppose that Christian responses to the human situation—to war, to sexuality, to racism, and to all the other "moral issues" which require our urgent and faithful attention—are equivalent to Aristotle's understanding of politics as "the art of the possible."

Christians are a people whose vision of the moral life is formed by adoration and praise, by penitence and pardon, by thanksgiving and offering, by petition and intercession, by revelation and confession . . . and by all of these ascribed and supplicated to the God whom we know through

Jesus. When our vision of the moral life is formed in these ways, we Christians will know that we worry about war and sexuality and racism and the rest *soli Deo gloria*.

Over centuries of pious devotion, the liturgy has changed (and it continues to change) in order to accommodate the purpose of worship and various senses of "decency and good order." The Reformation considerably altered the ancient shape of the liturgy by removing the offertory and emphasizing penitence at the expense of thanksgiving. The Reformation also concentrated so much on the cross and a *theologia crucis* that Nativity, Resurrection, Ascension, Second Coming, and the like got obscured or received only peripheral attention.

From earliest Christian times, the essential shape of the liturgy has remained largely unchanged in the Catholic churches. The principal themes of the liturgy are common, and its structure is generally well known: adoration and praise; penitence and pardon; thanksgiving and offering; petition and intercession; revelation and confession (here meaning to bear witness, as in saying the creed); ascription and supplication.

Of course, it is not enough that we perpetuate these themes and this structure as a tribute to their antiquity: they are not authenticated by age. All the same, there are good reasons why we ought to retain these themes and this structure; and why we should do so can be illustrated by reflecting on one or two other aspects of cherished tradition. For example, if we believe in the *communio sanctorum* and apostolic succession, as we ought, we do so not because they are parts of some grand ecclesial encyclopedia which we learn for the sake of knowing them, but because they are required by and derive from our worship. It is in honoring and worshiping God that *communio sanctorum* and apostolic succession make Christianly believable sense, because it is preeminently here that we get our first glimpse of why it is at all important for us to understand ourselves to be in the company of all the saints, and to participate in an unbroken historical succession of the faithful. The later, embroidered explanations of these two pieces of the tradition depend upon the church's worship, because it is in worship and liturgy that we learn that *the Christian life is something received.*

Another metaphor illustrates the same claim. In quite the same way that a marine navigator cannot determine a course without knowing the current position of the ship, it is necessary for us to know where we are before undertaking to chart our full course as disciples of Jesus Christ. Where we are, as Christians, is within a *tradition*, "What have you that you did not receive?" Paul asks rhetorically in 1 Corinthians.[2] What we have received is a tradition, something handed over or passed on. Actually, the Greek word for it—*paradosis*—appears very often in the New Testament; and the "tradition of men" or the "tradition of the Hebrew fathers" is frequently contrasted with what is handed over from Jesus and his apostles.[3] And Paul, speaking explicitly about the meaning and manner of celebrating the Holy Communion applies this principle to his entire message: "For I received from the Lord what I also delivered unto you."[4]

Among the first things to understand about the Christian life, then, is that it is something received. It is something like an inheritance bequeathed to us. We may reject it, or ignore it, or disown it. But in the measure to which we have it, we receive it; and we are therefore debtors both to the tradition itself and to all those who have preserved it for us. Our Christian life and our anticipated ministries, in quite profound ways, derive from a succession of ministries upon which ours are dependent.

It is this sort of perspective, this way of looking differently at ourselves, at our life and work, that assists us in knowing and comprehending where we are. We have an inheritance. We participate in a tradition which is handed over to us. We stand in a continuous line of Christian faith, life, witness, and ministry, and this continuous line of Christian faith, life, witness, and ministry supplies us, in turn, with an inkling of the meaning of the word "church." In part, "church" signifies this unbroken line of Christian faith and life, which has extended across the centuries, and through which our own Christian experience has been engendered and nourished. In part, "church" is unmistakably institutional in its incarnate form, and this is an indispensable part of its bifocal identity.

Concomitantly, the historical reality is also emphatically and substantively *corpus mysticum*. The Christian life always has a historical grounding or rootage; it is something that has come to be in time and space, and it is something that has been extended through time and space. It is also more than the naked eye can discern, and not merely one more alternative lifestyle or empirical reality among many, many others. So, in order to get our bearings, and from there chart our course as Christians in our own time and place, we need to understand our inheritance. Without it, we don't know who we are, where we have come from, or where we are destined to go.

When we understand where we are, and that our Christian life is a late link in a long chain of successive Christian ministries, we understand that *our Christian experience is not self-constituted*, that it is not simply a private transaction between ourselves and God, and that it is really and only constituted in a worshiping community. The palpable historic church is the partly comprehensible and identifiable earthly sign or symbol of that community; but the community extends beyond, and embraces more than, the earthly church. It includes "the communion of saints"; it is the *corpus mysticum*. So where Christians are is in the church. Within the church, within some particular portion of it, we have come to have our being as Christians.

To this point, I have suggested a definition of the church as that unbroken line of those in whose lives the ministry of Jesus Christ has worked redemptively. Thus far I have suggested that Christians come to life as Christians in a worshiping community, in a tradition, as inheritors of something received. This approach, I believe, conforms to one of the distinctive rediscoveries of twentieth-century theological, biblical, and ecumenical studies: namely, the rediscovery of the corporate conception of the Christian life—that it is engendered in a worshiping community, that it is nourished in that community, that it expresses itself in perpetuation and extension of such a community . . . and that this community is the church.

A seemingly opposed line of thought in Protestantism (maybe most apparent in, but certainly not limited to, the United States) takes the view that the Christian life is an intensely personal, even private, realization and experience. Protestant Christian hymnody is one of the great reservoirs of this view, and even a cursory look through the hymnals of "mainline" denominations will reveal titles and full stanzas which display it. There is little doubt that this attitude was rooted in the Protestant revolt against the medieval Roman establishment, and in the notion of the "priesthood of believers." But it deserves noting that this perspective was not a repudiation of the communal basis of the Christian life so much as it was a revolt against the domestication of grace in special vehicles, persons, and agencies. Indeed, Protestantism may be said to have reaffirmed even more emphatically the community of believers by refusing to acknowledge a hierarchy of persons who exercised exclusive (and, they believed, despotic) hegemony over the means of grace.[5]

The communal, corporate feature and the personal, realizational aspect are properly seen as two complementary and reciprocal dimensions of one reality—namely, the Christian life. So an adequate and authentic understanding of the Christian life maintains as its basis these two aspects in reciprocal relation and dialectical tension. The church cannot be said to exist without the aggregate of faithful individuals, just as faithful individuals cannot exist without the church. The church can be defined only in relation to individual believers, as individual believers can be defined only in relation to the church.

These are the reasons why I believe it is important to establish clearly where these priorities lie. Both theologically and historically, prayer is the form of worship, and worship is the form of doctrine. Theology and creeds and catechisms emerge from the church's life of prayer, from its liturgy, from its pious devotion. Indeed, prayer and liturgy are historically anterior to Bible, ecclesial polity, and all of the accoutrements of institutional Christianity. Of this we must say more later.

According to the Gospels, the only thing the disciples asked Jesus to teach them was how to pray. His response was to give them a common liturgy, which begins "Our Father." He did not give his disciples *instructions* on how to pray; he gave them *a form*. That he gave them a form suggests that they, and we, learn how to pray by praying this form.

The central and fundamental importance of the Lord's Prayer may surely be assessed in many ways; but four aspects claim our attention just now:

1. This prayer does *not* begin with "My Father."[6]
2. This prayer is the single indispensable ingredient in all Christian worship, from the most ceremonial and stylized to the least tectonic and most extempore traditions of Christian liturgy.[7]
3. This prayer serves as the model for what is essential in Christian liturgical action.[8]
4. This prayer presents to us the prototype of the Christian life.

My experience is that most Christians generally have little or no difficulty acknowledging and understanding the first three of these aspects. The fourth one, however, is something of a stumbling block. It is also one of the prominent reasons why I have written this book. Some excerpts from a commentary on the Lord's Prayer by Theodore of Mopsuestia speak eloquently to this point; and I offer them here as further argument for the intimate points of contact between a life of prayer and a life of holiness:

Every prayer contains teaching of good works. . . . He who cares, there-fore, for perfection and is anxious to do the things that are pleasing to God, will pay more attention to prayer than to any other thing. . . .

He {i.e., Jesus} made use of these short words as if to say that prayer does not consist so much in words as in good works, love and zeal for duty. . . . Prayer is by necessity connected with good works, because a thing that is not good to be looked for is not good to be prayed for. . . .

This is the reason why here also He uttered the above words to the disciples who had asked Him how to pray, as if He had said to them: If you care for prayer know that it is not performed by words but by the choice of a virtuous life and by the love of God and diligence in one's duty. If you are zealous in these things you will be praying all your life.[9]

CHAPTER ONE

LITURGY AND LIFE

ANCIENT LINKS BETWEEN LITURGY AND LIFE

When Evelyn Underhill formulated a general definition of worship as "the response of the creature to the Eternal," she acknowledged that there are powers greater than ourselves to whom we wish to relate.[1] If this is so, as theists plainly believe it to be, it will not be surprising that the rites and ceremonies and symbols and liturgies which we employ in worship are very ancient indeed, and in fact have their roots in the earliest recorded evidences of human activity. To be reminded of this may help to set the stage for talking about particular features of Christian liturgy and the close relation it shares with Christian ethics. To remember that these roots are in point of fact very deep may further assist us in seeing that it is not at all odd that a particular people's self-understanding of who they are and ought to be also corresponds with how they express that self-understanding in the kinds of things they do. Consider, for example, that among the oldest rituals of which we have any record are those connected with obtaining and eating food.[2] We are told that evidence from prehistoric hunters in alpine caves, especially in the Drachenloch cave of the eastern Swiss Alps, dates from the third interglacial period (ca. 180,000–120,000 B.C.E.) and contains clear evidence of ritual activity in connection with hunting of cave bears.[3] The bear skulls and long bones are unbroken, signifying that brain and bone marrow had not been removed. Moreover, these artifacts have been found in protected niches or in an altarlike stone chest.[4]

The distinguished paleontologist Johannes Maringer suggests that, inasmuch as these delicacies were not eaten but were the votive offerings of successful hunters, this practice has religious significance. To suggest that these hunters were making such sacrifices further implies that they must have believed in a supreme being of some sort. Perhaps these gifts "were offered to the divine dispenser of hunting fortune in token of thanks for the benefits received and to entreat success in future expeditions."[5] At all events, writes Maringer, "here for the first time we find a human group emerging from the darkness of the remote past with its specific religious beliefs and practices—the cave-bear hunters of the last inter-glacial, whose sacrifice of the skull and limb bones of their quarry bears witness to their faith in a divinity."[6]

We can only guess whether Maringer is correct; but the fact that it is the present practice of primitive arctic hunters similarly to preserve the skulls and long bones of their prey, and to consider the brain and the marrow to be sacrifices to the "dispenser of hunting fortune," makes his hypothesis plausible.

Ice-age paintings (ca. 30,000–10,000 B.C.E.) in the great cave at Lascaux, France, present further evidence that the ice-age hunter believed that there was more to hunting and eating than merely physical phenomena. These paintings are, for the most part, of large animals—such as bear, reindeer, bison, elk, horses, and mammoths—but more important for our interests, most of the paintings depict the animals mating, giving birth, or at the point of death, which suggests that these paintings have ritual, and perhaps even religious, significance.[7]

These paintings connote this intimation of ritual and religion by acknowledging the bond between the hunters and their prey: the hunters knew that when their game supply was exhausted, they would face starvation and death, and so it was of great importance to them that the animals mated and produced offspring and that they as hunters were able to kill them. Out of similar concerns, these ancient ecological and environmental themes have been repristinated in the late twentieth century, although usually without appealing to religion or sorcery. Maringer believes that "[ice-age hunting] art was essentially in the service of hunting magic . . . and the pictures were executed in the belief that the image gave the hunter a mysterious power over the animal portrayed." In fact, these pictures have a magical function which borders on, if indeed it does not frankly express, a religious sensibility. Certain portions of caves were reserved for ritual and painting and "Those places were consecrated, so to speak as 'sacred nooks' and were the sanctuaries of the ice-age hunters. . . . Impotent, as he was, to cope with the powers of nature, and inadequately equipped to confront the great beasts of his day, ice-age man derived from his magical faith a mysterious power and a sense of security."[8]

A religious interpretation of these artifacts would tend to view them as tokens of worship—sacrifices made to the source of life in thanksgiving for the abundant supply of game, and in intercession for a continuing abundant supply, and maybe even in petition for permission to kill or thanksgiving for already having that permission.

It is virtually certain, as Mitchell contends, that the ritual form which we call sacrifice developed from the milieu of the ritualized hunt. The hunt itself was part of a ritual; and the killing almost surely evoked recognition that the sacred life of the animal was connected with its blood. Indeed, some centuries later our ancestors observed that humans also grow steadily weaker as they lose blood; and they concluded, quite logically but erroneously, that human life—in all its experiences, strengths, and characteristics—was contained in the blood. Following such reasoning, Pliny's *Natural History* recommended that epileptics might benefit from quaffing the fresh, warm blood of gladiators not yet dead. Both Jews and Christians should also be familiar with the interdependency of life and blood, inasmuch as this appears in a number of biblical passages.[9]

Animal fertility, success in hunting, the discovery that blood is preconditional to life, sacrifice, thanksgiving, intercession—all of these appear in our earliest evidences of human activity; and they appear also to conform to Underhill's general definition of worship as "the response of the creature to the Eternal."

Together with the ritualized hunt, there is early and continuing evidence of intiatory rites for both boys and girls. These rites, as Mircea Eliade put it, produced "a decisive alteration in the religious and social status of the person to be initiated . . . the novice emerges from his ordeal endowed with a totally different being from that which he possessed before his initiation; he has become *another*."[10]

These primitive rites typically consisted of three parts, not always equally important but each of them essential: rites of separation, rites of transition (liminal rites), and rites of incorporation. The patterns for boys and for girls were comparable and consisted, roughly, in the following stages. The children were taken away from the larger community to a "sacred ground," to a site where they were isolated. Then the liminal or transitional stage got under way, sometimes violently. For example, boys were required to undergo certain ordeals and to be instructed in tribal lore, and they usually were physically marked in some way (by circumcision, or by knocking out a tooth) so that thereafter they could be identified as adult males; and girls, typically at the onset of menstruation, were taught the rituals and skills appropriate to women in the culture, following which there was sometimes a ritual bath and then a "showing" of the former girls to the community as adult women. This second phase was the transition from child to adult. Finally, these former children, now full adult members, were reincorporated into the community.

In our modern western European traditions and customs, we perpetuate precisely the same patterns of initiation in several instances. Perhaps nowhere is this clearer than in marriage: the engagement signifies the separation or setting-apart; the marriage rite itself occasions the transition from one status to another; and, when the couple sets up housekeeping in the community, the final action is reincorporation. In our culture, childbirth, funeral rites, and the like show similar patterns.

Particularly for Christians, Holy Baptism, Holy Matrimony and Holy Orders display the basic patterns of these very primitive rites. Think for a moment about baptism, where the pattern is followed with what may seem to be a striking correlation: the child is taken from the parents, a transition is signified by baptism and chrismation, and the child is reincorporated into the community.

It is important to remember that the point of this excursus is to elaborate several claims about ritual, symbol, ceremony, and liturgy: that they are indispensable to and consubstantial with human existence; that a measure of mystery and ineffability attends them; and that before those of us in the modern situation can talk intelligently and in the same breath about worship and ethics, sacrament and social action, or liturgy and a life of holiness, we will need to look differently at the natural world. What is minimally clear to anybody not entirely infatuated by modernity and seduced by immediacy is that Christian liturgy and ritual, for all of their particularity and historical contingency, are connected to ancient patterns of human action which we have inherited from the lush imaginations and fertile discernment of our ancestors. To acknowledge this fact does not detract, in the least, from God's action in hallowing these rites for our instruction and formation; indeed, theists will see God present and projected in the full range of these actions.

So blood, water, a sacred meal, an initiatory rite—all of these, and more—are ancient symbols and rituals and did not spring into being *de novo* in the first century C.E. From the life-supplying blood of animals exsanguinated from the wounds inflicted by hunters to the life-supplying sign of menstrual blood, blood is a *natural ritual image*. Indeed, this notion is so deeply rooted in antiquity that from biblical times orthodox Jews refused to ingest blood because blood is life and life is sacred.

Blood symbolizes life, not death, and the pagan gladiators who drank the still-warm blood of their victims in the circus, believing that they would thereby acquire their victims' courage and bravery and strength, shared this ancient view. Blood is life; again, it is a *natural ritual image*.

Similarly, water dissolves and destroys, and symbolizes both death and rebirth. At the dawn of creation, the Spirit of God "broods" over the formless waters. Later we learn of ritual washings of initiates, or great cosmic events like the Flood of Genesis 6–8, or the souls of the departed crossing the River Styx, or Moses and the Israelites passing safely through the parted waters of the Red Sea; or of Isaiah's and Jeremiah's portrayal of the dawn of the new age in terms of the fertility of an oasis; or of the demonic powers of Leviathan. In every case, water provides a natural ritual image. It purifies by washing away; it regenerates by cleansing; it transforms by sustaining.

The point I wish to iterate is that these very natural images—which can, of course, be seen as nothing more than physical phenomena—are transformed by supernatural meanings. But being transformed, they do not lose their "natural" aspect; and grace, far from destroying nature, in this way perfects it.

RITUAL IN EVERYDAY LIFE TODAY

It is frequently suggested nowadays that we have lost our ability to deal with ritual, that symbols no longer communicate to us, that liturgy is just so much baggage from an archaic past which is unintelligible in the present. Indeed, Mary Douglas has argued that "One of the gravest problems of our day is the lack of commitment to common symbols" and that there is a "wide-spread, explicit rejection of rituals as such."[11] Among the reasons she gives for this circumstance, and borrowing from Robert Merton, Douglas defines a ritualist as "one who performs external gestures without inner commitment to the ideas being expressed."[12]

We can bracket for the moment consideration of whether "ritualist" is the correct identifier for the kind of attitude Douglas means to address. As a matter of fact, she recognizes that we are handicapped by vocabulary and terminology, and part of her project is to provide a lexicon which is anthropologically and sociologically more accurate and precise. To that end, for example, she argues that

> *it is fair enough that "ritualized" ritual should fall into contempt. But it is illogical to despise all ritual, all symbolic action as such. To use the word ritual to mean empty symbols of conformity, leaving us with no word to stand for symbols of genuine conformity, is seriously disabling to the sociology of religion."*[13]

So we need to worry about words, and I find that there is fairly wide agreement on this point.

All the same, and without denigrating the importance of terminology and vocabulary, more urgent just now is the fact that in our present scientific and technological age, with sociological and psychological structures very different from those of preindustrial and prescientific cultures, many people share the view which Mary Douglas describes so well. Lots of modern folk suspect that not only do we not need ritual and ceremony and symbol but that, beyond this, we are no longer capable of engaging in action that is liturgically intelligible.

Of course, these people are mistaken in this suspicion, as a large number of anthropological and sociological studies show. Virtually all of us act in ways which are deliberately symbolic; and many of these actions are liturgically significant as well. Symbols and ceremonies and rites, both secular and religious, are not accidental, or merely incidental, to the ways our lives are put together; on the contrary, they are of the *esse* of human reflection and communication. They are, in point of fact, the material transmitters of culture. So, however unconscious the development of these forms, they are the brick and mortar—or perhaps better, the heart and soul—of human communities.

Insofar as performing liturgies, rituals, ceremonies, and rites is merely "going through the motions," repeating inane actions made sacrosanct by antiquity, we are right to repudiate them. My guess is that all of us have our own storehouses of illustrations that would support this judgment; and I imagine, moreover, that the examples we could cite are not limited to the hocus-pocus and mystification of religious services and church meetings.

Among the obvious, and one of my favorite, colloquial examples is the casual, customary greeting which is exchanged as two people hurriedly pass each other, going in opposite directions: "How are you?" Its variants include phrases like "How're you doing?" and "What's happening?"—and a typical response goes something like, "Fine; how are you?" Now on a scale of one to ten, this example is probably a one, or at best a two; it is a trivial, maybe even frivolous, illustration of how a banal action (in this case, speech) suggests, if taken seriously, a kind of human and syntactical misfire.

When we greet one another in this way, ordinarily we do not really want to know "how the other person is" in all the complexity and richness and intimacy such a question could evoke. We really mean to do no more than extend a salutation. We emphatically do not intend this to be an invitation to autobiography. But this, of course, is not what we say when we ask, "How are you?" So sometimes, when greeted in this way, I have stopped dead in my tracks, looked the other person straight in the eye, and said something like, "Wow! Gee whiz! This has been some kind of remarkable day! Let me tell you about it." Almost without exception, the response to this verbal flourish has been complete astonishment, followed by some clear though unspoken message that, however much the other person might be willing (not eager, mind you—just willing) to listen to whatever I would want to say about my "remarkable day," this chance meeting was neither the time nor the place for it. Now, after several decades of experiencing this sort of thing, I've concluded that altogether it's usually better just to say "good morning" and let it go at that

In a similar genre of social setting, remember the last time you were introduced to somebody who said, after your name was called, "Pleased to meet you." Well, maybe they were, and maybe they weren't. This is another one of those moments that we ordinarily do not dissect. It is just another social convention, a ritual, that is polite however insincere. On balance it is, in Mary Douglas's words, one of those "external gestures without inner commitment to the ideas being expressed."

The ante gets significantly raised, however, when we move from these simple circumstances to others more sublime. If a lover says, "I love you," and doesn't mean it; or a preacher says, "I believe in God," and doesn't mean it; or a physician says, "You're quite healthy," and doesn't mean it— now we feel as though we have made quantum leaps in deceit and fraud and hypocrisy. In these kinds of circumstances we think we have every right to be offended, even outraged, because we feel betrayed and exploited and lied to. So, with a heaping helping of righteous indignation, we may say (with expletives deleted) something like, "If you don't mean it, don't say it" or "Say what you mean, and mean what you say."

The fact of the matter is that, however desirable a high level of lexical precision and definition may be, it seems only seldom achieved in human affairs. Among the reasons for this state of affairs is that ritual and symbol are indispensable in human intercourse. Beyond this, however, a genuinely ineffable (not just indescribable, but quite frankly unutterable) aspect attaches to actions that are ceremonial and liturgical. It is as though, in some measure, we acquire them by a kind of human osmosis: we just absorb them. In addition, close examination reveals that both indispensability and ineffability attach to actions that are earthy and commonplace as well as to actions which are arcane or even esoteric.

So let us agree that there is a sense in which the critics are correct to challenge some of our too-comfortable and too-casual and too-cozy ways of being in the world and with one another. But that we agree "in a sense" suggests also a boundary, a limit on the extent to which the modern fascination for rationalizing and intellectualizing and verbalizing virtually *every* action of human actors can usefully proceed.

The sense in which these symbolic and ritualistic actions are indispensable seems to me to go far beyond the case against them so often made in terms of their religious aspects. What I mean to claim is that *whatever is conventional corporate activity is indispensably symbolic.* So standing for the national anthem, serving turkey at Thanksgiving, buying presents at Christmas, paying taxes, blowing out candles on a birthday cake, and voting—all of these conventional corporate activities are indispensably symbolic, ritualistic, ceremonial, liturgical actions.

Part of what certifies their standing as special events and occasions is that *there is a broad cultural understanding of their meaning; but it is a meaning that is also finally inexpressible.* I have tried sometimes, for example, to imagine the long chain of ideas and the commitments being expressed when I stand for the national anthem. And I discover that it is not that the inventory of patriotic ideas and commitments is inexhaustible so much as that some (perhaps many) of them are just finally beyond my capacity to articulate in cogent and coherent ways.

It may be even more telling to attempt such an exercise with religious devotion, with prayer, with loving God. Marianne Micks, in *The Future Present*, makes this point succinctly by comparing worship with love:

> *People who worship and people who love generally suppose that they know what they are doing. They assume that other people are doing something similar under the same name. But worship, like love, is a curiously difficult activity to talk about. If one asks worshippers, "What, precisely, is it that you are doing?" no one can say very clearly."*[14]

My experience is that if we go further, and ask not only "What are you doing?" but "Why are you doing it?" the problem gets confounded. I recall a postulant who was asked by his examiner during a psychological examination, "Why do you want to be a priest?" and who responded (with only scant impertinence), "I intend no disrespect, but the fact of the matter is that you couldn't understand if I explained it to you."

The temptation is great, I suppose, to answer in a similar vein when asked what one is doing in worship, and why one is doing it. But in this instance it is precisely these questions of "what?" and "why?" that need answers. Otherwise, religious ritual and ceremonial and symbol may be mere formalism—empty gestures performed without the vaguest idea of, or commitment to, what is being expressed. When this happens, religious ritual becomes not only empty but actually demonic. Of course, the corresponding error at the other extreme is the supposition that worship, and in our case Christian worship, is discontinuous with all other human experience—a kind of liturgical Gnosticism and snobbery. We will try in what follows to steer a course between the Scylla and Charybdis posed by these unhappy alternatives.

The proper question about all this is not whether we can do without it, because plainly we cannot; the proper question is rather whether we can embrace and employ the rituals, liturgies, ceremonies, and symbols we have inherited from our past, both Christian and human, and with a measure of integrity and understanding be formed by them.

Symbolic thinking, which is principally the kind of thinking that goes on in liturgies, "is consubstantial with human existence," said Mircea Eliade; "it comes before language and discursive reason."[15] Eliade asserted this claim in the context of an extended account of the "surprising popularity" of psychoanalysis in the mid-twentieth century, but his point applies with equal force to our interests in and for liturgy, and it reinforces the notion that we cannot dispense with or be rid of symbolic thinking.

Why this is so is addressed in *The Sacred and the Profane*, another classic by Eliade, in which he shows a marked contrast between primitive and modern sensibilities. Primitive peoples, according to Eliade, viewed the world as sacred, as filled with manifestations of the holy, which Eliade calls "hierophanies." In contrast, modern Westerners look at the natural world and see only physical phenomena, but no hierophanies or epiphanies.[16] Eliade's agenda is to show contrasts and comparisons between these two modes of being-in-the-world, to exhibit the differences between living in a sacralized cosmos and living in a desacralized cosmos. To a limited extent, this is my agenda also; and the limitation is exhibited by the measure to which understanding of this kind of perceptual schizophrenia helps to illuminate both the difficulties and the possibilities of embracing liturgy and ethics as one.

An obvious implication of Eliade's work is that religious persons will perceive an indissoluble connection between the natural and the supernatural. A further implication for modern religious men and women is that, before we can talk intelligently about worship and ethics or sacraments and social action or liturgy and the moral life, we will need to look differently at the natural world.

Part of this "looking differently at the natural world" will mean that we "see" the water of baptism and the bread and wine of eucharist as other than *only* or *merely* natural, physical phenomena. These elements *are* natural, physical phenomena, to be sure; and I want to say more later about why it is of bedrock importance that Christians honor these things as part of God's very ordinary creation. Beyond that, however, these things are also appropriated by the church as bearers of special grace; that is, they function as hierophanies, as epiphanies.

I suggested earlier that we Christians will need to alter our conventionally modern way of looking at the natural world if we hope to be able to talk intelligently about worship and ethics, about liturgy and the moral life. To look at the natural world in a different way means, simply, to acknowledge another set of meanings than those commonly associated with the presiding scientific, technological, perhaps even pagan, or *merely* natural perspectives of the late twentieth century.

It is not, of course, as everyone who has reflected seriously on Lockean empiricism knows, that no meaning at all derives from and attaches to physical phenomena. The environmental and ecological concerns with which we are nowadays so familiar have reinforced our awareness that natural phenomena have, in a sense, a life of their own. Nor is it the case— as Descartes mistakenly believed, and these same environmental and ecological concerns attempt to correct in our modern discernment—that the meaning, purpose, and value of physical things are merely the products of mentation, the projection of human mind.

What Christians look for, then, is a "point of view," a perspective from and within which we can make some coherent sense of what we know and believe. And beyond, or perhaps alongside, that perspective we look for symbols, liturgies, rites, and ceremonies which help us give expression to what we know are finally ineffable mysteries.

In this respect, what principally and chiefly distinguishes us from our paleolithic or ice-age or other primitive ancestors is the meaning which we attach to our liturgical actions—that is, how the rites and symbols of natural phenomena are specifically reinterpreted according to our understanding and intending of ourselves as disciples of Jesus Christ. We do not understand in order to believe; rather, like our primitive ancestors, we believe in order to understand. *Credo ut intelligam* is the necessary foundation of intelligibility in a world profoundly invested, as theists believe it to be, with theophanies and epiphanies.

The Romans and other persecutors of the early church rightly surmised that if they could prevent Christians from assembling together, they could destroy Christianity root and branch. The reasons why these tormentors were correct in this assumption are complex, but among them is the evidence that what brought the early Christians together was not some private, individual, insular longing for fellowship with God. Nor, so far as we can tell, were primitive Christians simply yearning for social companionship with a group of like-minded people who shared some mutual likes and dislikes, interests and disinterests. The apostolic church does not appear to be a kind of first-century civic or social club where community is reduced to congeniality and conviviality, where "the more we get together the happier we'll be."

What brought these people together, by their own testimony, was the very nature of Christian faith itself. The gospel of God's redemptive work in Jesus was not given to isolated individuals but to those who were, as their heirs were later to say, "very members incorporate in the mystical body of Christ" himself. An organic conception of the church, as one body of many interdependent members, is a consistent New Testament teaching. Destroy that organism (the worshiping community), if you can, and you will destroy Christianity. [17]

To talk this way in a time of rampant individualism and intoxicating autonomy doubtless sounds very strange indeed. Nowadays we would more likely incline to say that if people miss the church's worship, they don't hurt anybody but themselves. Were I to be painfully honest, I would have to admit that I have said this on occasion; and I would want to add that I believe there is a grain of truth in this claim. But the fact of the matter is that, although the statement is partly true, it is not the whole truth or even an essential piece of the whole truth. Separation from the common worship, being quarantined from the rites and liturgies and ceremonies of the community, is also separation from the body of Christ. With fractured participation, that body is further dismembered, fragmented, broken.

Now and then I observe theater or basketball ticket stubs which carry the legend "Not Valid If Detached." This phrase strikes me as an ecclesial paradigm which is, of course, neither new nor novel for Christians; in fact, it is explicit in quite early teachings of the church. Consider this excerpt from the fourth-century *Didascalia*:

> *Since therefore you are the members of Christ, do not scatter yourselves from the Church by not assembling. Seeing that you have Christ for your head . . . be not then neglectful of yourselves, and deprive not our Saviour of His members, and do not rend and scatter His body.*"[18]

It is surely no less true now than in apostolic times that the assured destruction of Christianity comes by way of destroying Christian assembly. It is not the absence or falsification of doctrine and dogma, but the nullity and nonoccurrence of corporate worship, that is the church's undoing. In contemporary America we tend to eschew the violent incorporations of former times and welcome assimilation, not through political edict or police action, but by acquiring and embracing the pagan philosophical ideology of the environing culture. Among other distinguished forebears, Thomas Jefferson helped set this aspect of the agenda for American Christianity when he asserted that "God will not save men against their wills." With this and similar aphorisms, the issue of sovereignty, of who is in charge, was apparently settled for bona fide Americans. In a culture marked by autonomous individualism, the imperial self is in charge. And alongside this commitment is another of equal importance: the self-sufficiency of individual persons is a normative belief in such a society.

These notions get enhanced in a populace which believes that it can, and should, separate church and state; because what separation does, far from espousing equality between them, is to guarantee the subordination of one to the other. The "one" in this case is the church, and the "other" is the state. Separation "of," in point of fact, means separation "from"; and the popular construction which follows is that life also gets separated into a "real" sphere—which consists of politics, economics, and the like—and a "spiritual" sphere—which has to do with religious, and therefore non-material, matters. Perhaps this is why religious people in this country have tended to value "religious liberty" over the separation of church and state; religious liberty posits an ultimate limit to the power of the state and refuses to recognize the state's sovereignty as absolute.

All of us have learned the formula: the church ought to stay out of politics because the Gospel deals only with "spiritual" things. And while these spiritual things are surely important *in their place*, we are taught that the really important and significant matters of our life and times are decided by politics, economics, social philosophy, and the like. Some of the crippling, if not devastating, effects of treating the separation of church and state in this way are that the church's moral and liturgical life gets separated from life in the world, that moral agency gets sundered from moral action, and that the formation of who we are gets divorced from decisions about what we are to do.

So, as any casual observer can testify, the commonality in the modern world concerning secular rituals is much larger than the commonality concerning religious ones. I observe that people who are not particularly enthusiastic about basketball games, or the Super Bowl, or presidential inaugurations, are nevertheless able to empathize with the true basketball junkies, football fanatics, and political zealots. Or, perhaps more to the point, many of us can recall the great coalescence of national sentiment in the quite astonishing ritual which was planned and executed at the unveiling of the restored Statue of Liberty. When we reflect on it, there appears to be a close correlation between the decline of religious ritual and the increase of secular ritual.

This phenomenon is attributable to some aspects of relatively recent social and political philosophy—from, let us say, the Enlightenment onward—and about which I want to say more later. But for now we can identify an example of the impact of this feature of modernity by observing that liturgical solutions (usually conceived as aesthetics) cannot remedy or solve our present liturgical problems because our problems consist in the social meanings associated with who we understand ourselves to be.

Another way to put this is to say that the community which gathers nowadays to celebrate religious liturgy is frequently not a real community so much as it is an aggregate of individuals. If this is so, as I believe it to be, an urgent task of the church is to re-create a social life within which commitments more profound than congeniality and gregariousness preside. In fact, the testimony of twenty centuries of Christian witness is that the church can do this simply by being itself; and this is why the first social task of the church is simply to be the church.[19]

Maybe it is true that "the more we get together, the happier we'll be"; but this is thin gruel for folks who want to feed on holy mysteries. What we want is not the celebration of lovely liturgies which, however aesthetically pleasing, leave our day-to-day lives largely unaffected—or, let us say, no more affected than they would be by the spectacle of a New Year's Day football bowl game or an impressive concert. What many of us are desperate for is the restoration (and notice that the word is "restoration," not "creation") of a community so bound to each other by Christ's love for them—and thereby by their love for one another—that they want to celebrate the liturgy as the sign of their unity and the mark of their identity.

Maybe it will appear trivial to say, but the motto on U.S. currency has this point right: e pluribus unum—out of many, one. This suggests that there is diversity in unity, not the other way around. Indeed, there is no unity in diversity, except perhaps as we agree to disagree. But to claim that we are united by a difference seems to me to be nonsense.

St. Augustine has written many wonderful and beautiful homilies, but none more wonderful and beautiful than an instruction to neophytes on how they are to participate, and become one, in the holy sacrament of the Lord's table. It turns out to be not a long homily, and I want to quote most of it here because it states so beautifully and cogently how we, being many, are made one:

Listen to me, especially you who are now reborn to a new life and for that reason are called infants, while I explain . . . what it is that you see before you here on the altar. . . . The food you see here on the Lord's table, you are accustomed to see on your own tables at home, as far as outward appearances go. It has the same appearance, but not the same worth. You, the newly baptized, remain the same individuals you were before; at any rate you do not present different faces before this assembly. Nevertheless, you are indeed new men. Your outward form is the same as before, but you are made new beings through sanctifying grace.

And so this food is likewise something new. Until now, as you see, it is simply bread and wine. But once the Consecration takes place, this bread will be the body of Christ and this wine will be the blood of Christ . . . and even though it looks like it was before, yet its worth is not what it was before. Had you eaten thereof before {the Consecration}, it would have supplied food to the stomach, but now when you partake, it gives nourishment to the soul.

At your baptism . . . we spoke to you about the mystery of the font. . . . Hear, then, in short what the Apostle, or better, what Christ says by the mouth of the Apostle concerning the sacrament of the Lord's table: "We, being many, are one bread, one body." That is all there is to it. . . . One bread, the Apostle said. No matter how many breads were placed before Him then, still they were only one bread. No matter how many breads are laid upon the altars of Christ throughout the world today, it is but one bread. . . .

The Apostle has shown us briefly what this bread is. Now consider the matter more carefully and see how it comes about. How is bread made? Wheat is threshed, ground, moistened, and baked. By moistening the wheat is purified, and by baking it is made firm. . . . You also underwent a form of threshing, by fasting, by the Lenten observances, by night watches, by exorcisms. . . . But moistening cannot be done without water; as a consequence, you were immersed. . . . {But without fire bread does not exist. What, then, does the fire signify? The chrism. For the sacrament of the Holy Spirit is the oil of our fire. . . . Therefore, the fire, that is, the Holy Spirit, comes after the water; then you become bread, that is, the body of Christ. Hence, in a certain manner, unity is signified.}

As one loaf results from combining the individual kernels and mixing the same together with water, so also the one body of Christ results from the harmony of love. And as the body of Christ is represented in the grains of wheat, so also is the blood represented in the grapes. For wine pours forth from the wine press out of what were formerly many individual grapes, now flowing together as one liquid to become wine. Hence both in the bread and in the chalice the sacrament of unity is present."[20]

The unity of which St. Augustine speaks has its roots in baptism and eucharist, and its branches in liturgy and holy living, in sacrament and social action, in prayer and politics.

So while the water of Holy Baptism is surely H_2O, it is seen by Christians also to be a sacramentally significant gift from God. As the "thanksgiving over the water" in the Book of Common Prayer puts it:

Over it the Holy Spirit moved in the beginning of creation. Through it you led the children of Israel out of their bondage in Egypt into the land of promise. In it your Son Jesus received the baptism of John and was anointed by the Holy Spirit as the Messiah, the Christ, to lead us, through his death and resurrection, from the bondage of sin to everlasting life. We thank you, Father, for the water of Baptism. In it we are buried with Christ in his death. By it we share in his resurrection. Through it we are reborn by the Holy Spirit."[21]

Water, for Christians, *is* a natural phenomenon the meaning and purpose and value of which are shaped by an orientation whose focus and direction are located in the beliefs and symbols and sacraments of Christian faith.

Similarly with the bread and wine of the Holy Eucharist, our prayer is that the holy and gracious God will

> *sanctify them by your Holy Spirit* to be for your people *the Body and Blood of your Son, the holy food and drink of new and unending life in him.*"[22]

Extending this way of looking differently at the natural world is limited only by imagination, since it is possible in principle to see literally everything in and from this perspective. Indeed, this is one way to describe the goal of the Christian life: to learn to see *everything* within the interpretive frame of Jesus' life, ministry, death, resurrection, and ascension—that is, to see with the eyes of faith. Thomas Talley put it this way:

new frame

> *Religious ritual is* serious. *Those who cannot take joy seriously may find this a gloomy observation and so may try to make worship fun or cute or something else inappropriate. The fact remains that ritual in general and religious ritual in particular is concerned with life in its seriousness and, especially for us Christians, with a serious experience of joy. Ritual is a life-and-death matter because it is a matter of Death and Life.*"[23]

We will consider later, for example, the difference it can make to view human friendship, or having babies, or going to war, or sexual intercourse, or working for social justice, or struggling for a fairer distribution of goods and services—or abortion, or capital punishment, or lying, or stealing, or marriage—as matters which are (or can be) hierophanies, occasions for the manifestation of God, and thus matters of Death and Life. Indeed, if we mean to be Christian, and if being Christian means being shaped and formed by a vision of ourselves and the world which is focused and directed by Jesus Christ, then we are *obliged* to perceive and talk about these matters within this orientation, from that point-of-view.

Of course, the pervasive tendency nowadays is for Christians and the church to speak of these matters in ways which are calculated to be congenial and comfortable in the presiding secular environment. This is merely another evidence for why the single largest problem with so much of Christian ethics these days is the extent to which "Christian" fails to control "ethics." My clear impression is that among Christians of all sorts and conditions the supposition is widespread that *Christian* ethics is either impossible or irrelevant: impossible, because the powers which preside in modern pluralist societies will not consent to be governed by such an embarrassingly particularistic religious outlook; or irrelevant, because whatever is special about "Christian" ethics is comparable to other special claims by other particular groups, and finally dispensable in the search for a congenial social policy which not only tolerates well, but even undertakes to incorporate, acutely dissonant points of view.

For a people who venture to understand and intend themselves as disciples of Jesus Christ, the modifier in the phrase "Christian ethics" is essential and determinative for the shape of the moral life. When "Christian" qualifies and norms "ethics," external gestures get connected to inner commitment, because our vision of ourselves and the world gets focused and directed by the beliefs and symbols and sacraments of Christian faith and life.

This way of talking suggests that we best comprehend the moral life as an identity, an orientation, a definition of who we are which norms and orders our will and desire and action. Moreover, this way of talking (together with the predicates of what is good and right, which rest upon that foundation and its qualification of our moral agency), strikes me as a viable exegesis of Matthew 13:10–17.

Jesus answered his disciple's question about why he spoke in parables, why he told stories and used metaphors, with a reason a modern teacher who is serious about a subject and wants students to understand would honor: I speak in parables and tell stories, said Jesus, because "seeing they do not see, and hearing they do not hear" (v. 13). The purpose of Jesus' teaching in story and parable is to equip his disciples with a way . . . a different way . . . his way of viewing themselves and the world. When this view was adopted, he told them, "Blessed are your eyes, for they see, and your ears, for they hear" (v. 16).

This would suit as well as an interpretation of John 9:35b–39. Jesus had restored sight to a man blind from birth, and the neighbors brought him before the Pharisees to account for how he had received his sight. The Pharisees questioned the formerly blind man about how he had gotten his sight; and after receiving unsatisfactory answers to their questions, they "cast him out," which probably means that they threw him out of the assembly.[24] When Jesus heard about this, he sought out the man and found him. Then Jesus asked him, "Do you believe in the Son of Man?" The man answered, "And who is he, Sir, that I may believe in him?" At this, Jesus identified himself as the one, and the formerly blind man exclaimed, "Lord, I believe."

That exclamation, in Christian parlance, signifies salvation. If the doctrine of original sin means to acknowledge a contradiction between our essence and our existence, between the people God created and called and a people who insist on writing their own story, and if it means that we become our own worst enemy when we make ourselves the center of the universe, then "blindness" is a striking metaphor for that perverse condition. And if salvation signifies that condition corrected, wherein the natural order and meaning of life are restored under the sovereignty of God, having eyes which in fact *see* characterizes that altered state of affairs wonderfully well. The natural and original purpose of eyes is seeing. What salvation offers us is a means of repentance, and a complete turnabout, so that we are directed away from ourselves and toward God. This is why the whole work of salvation entails the restoration of all of nature to its original and created purpose; and, in turn, this is why the church, imitating the Lord, uses *things* like water, bread, ashes, and wine to extend sacramental signs.[25] But more of this later.

The story of the blind man who was given his sight by spittle and clay, and washing in the pool of Siloam, ends with this declaration: "For judgment I came into this world, that those who do not see may see, and that those who see may become blind." It is precisely this reorientation, this ability to see things differently—indeed, the capacity to see things as they are meant to be and really are—that Jesus accomplishes for us. He allows us to see what formerly was blinded to us, hidden from us. That is his mercy. And his judgment upon us is that *any other way* of seeing ourselves and the world is wrong, mistaken, not true, or is, as he suggests, both here and elsewhere in the Gospels, a confusion of sight with blindness.

For the instruction of Roman catechumens, three Gospel readings were traditionally employed over the last three Sundays in Lent. These were John 4 (the Samaritan woman), John 9 (the man born blind), and John 11 (the raising of Lazarus). In the Book of Common Prayer, these are the Gospels appointed for these same Sundays in Year A. In the lectionary of the Greek church, readings from John 4 and John 9 are similarly appointed during the last three Sundays in Lent, while John 11 is replaced by John 5 (healing the paralytic). Raymond Brown has written persuasively of the baptismal imagery in John 9, and believes that John used that imagery deliberately. For example, two of Jesus' gestures, anointing and the use of spittle, later became part of the baptismal ceremony; the blind man was healed only when he washed in the pool of Siloam; and the narrative stresses the fact that the man was *born* blind, born into a condition which could be altered only "by washing in the waters of the spring or pool that flows from Jesus himself."[26]

Brown further observes, continuing with metaphors for being sighted, that "'enlightenment' was a term used by New Testament authors to refer to Baptism" and that this linguistic and conceptual connection was sustained by the church Fathers, who employed enlightenment as a favorite theme in both theological and devotional treaties.[27] All together there is considerable evidence that the church found a significant baptismal lesson in John 9 and the healing of the blind man; and, given Christian belief about the radicality of the transformation wrought by God in baptism, there is every reason why it should have done so.

By baptism one is received into the community of those who believe and profess God's salvation in Christ; by baptism one is incorporated into a socially and institutionally constituted people whose lives are meant to mirror the holiness of God; by baptism one is gifted with the sight which enables one to see the world aright. The first and most immediate effect of Christian baptism, and the foundation of Christian existence, is that one is initiated into the church by being washed in the waters which flow from Jesus himself. This washing cleanses us from sin which has plagued us from birth, just as Jesus' healing of the blind man relieves him of a condition into which he was born. So being baptized into the church is not trivial.

Nor will it do merely to say that one is initiated into "the family of God" or into "the people of the eschatological age," or some other euphemism, if such a phrase is meant somehow to ignore or immunize us from engagement in the church as a historical institution. If the church is the "body of Christ," one thing is plainly not possible without the church, and that is the grace of God palpably present as an ongoing event with historical reality and incarnational corporeality. Anyone who receives the grace of baptism therefore receives also a share in, a capacity for, a mandate to participate in, the church as the historical tangibility of God's grace in the world.

In this sense, baptism creates the church; baptism is the crucial rite by which the church gets born and comes into being; baptism is the sacrament, the sign and instrument by which the church becomes the church, and not something else. And this further suggests that baptism is the church's rite; that it is the church's duty; that it is the church's response to God's command to go into the world and make disciples, to baptize them, and to teach them to observe all that Jesus has commanded (Matt. 28:19–20). Of course, all of this implies that <u>baptism is a liturgical action over</u> which we exercise no control whatsoever.

THE MORAL GRAVITY OF THE LITURGY

Like the other sacraments, baptism is an action in which we believe that God is present. In fact, we believe that if we celebrate these sacraments as Christ commanded us to do, there is nothing we, or anybody or anything else, can do to prevent God from indwelling them and doing what God has promised to do in them. We are, in this circumstance, profoundly and decidedly out of control. Moreover, God is doing things here which we cannot fully explain or describe, and which are clearly not discernible to the naked eye of natural reason. To be sure, the newly baptized do not appear to be any different from what they were before. All the same, we believe that we have been gifted in baptism, as Thomas Aquinas put it, with a new agency and a new capacity: specifically, now we can be friends of God, and thereafter be friends to others and to ourselves. But this is something, as we should have learned by now, that is invisible except to eyes of faith.

So I want to invite us to a way of doing theological ethics which, it seems to me, is both more generous than some other ways and clearly more commensurate with our confession that God is finally a mystery beyond our comprehension. This way of doing theological ethics rests upon and employs a number of postulates which set the terms and tone for proceeding with this method and design; and I can identify several, but not all, of them. For example:

- Although the Christian claim is that Jesus has communicated the plenitude and fullness of God's grace and presence, we do not suppose thereby that we comprehend God fully or perfectly; until the Parousia we continue to see through a glass darkly.
- Although it is immodest and pretentious, and an offense against the sovereignty of God, to suggest that we know everything, it is

the faithful and pious confession of Christian faith that we know all that we need to know for salvation; and all that we need to know is that God loves us and has reconciled us to himself by the grace extended us in Jesus Christ.

- We may be silent about what it is not given us to know, out of respect for both divine sovereignty and the human limitation which is commensurate with it. We may speculate, but we may not confuse our speculations with the church's *confessio fidei*. The rule of faith is therefore not the Bible, and biblical theology is not Christian theology; but saying this does not, of course, exempt the rule of faith or Christian theology from accountability to the gospel of Jesus Christ where and as it is displayed in Holy Scripture.

- About matters not addressed in and by the church's *confessio fidei*, we may be silent and/or agnostic. So, for example, to the question "what is the ultimate fate of the unbaptized?" we may have no precise answer. The most that we can say about the unbaptized is that they are not part of the church, they are not incorporated into the "outwardness" of the body of Christ. The unbaptized are unchurched or not churched.

- This is not to say that the unbaptized are also unsaved, or not saved, or destined for hell or "outer darkness." It is only to say that the unbaptized are not baptized; and by virtue of this fact, they are neither initiated into Christ's holy church nor given "new birth through water and the Spirit."

- Christ's atonement is the presupposition for Christian baptism, and the practice of baptizing infants and children is a potent reminder of that priority. The baptism of those who cannot deliberately and intentionally respond to this rite reminds the whole church that God both initiates and completes this sacrament. Again, we are profoundly out of control. God acted in Christ to reconcile us to himself "while we were yet helpless" (Rom. 5:6).

- Christ's atoning work is God's doing for us, a "gift offered to us without price," what we plainly could not do for ourselves. That we continue to insist upon effecting our own reconciliation and at-one-ment with God, and on our own terms, is our original and continuing sin.

- What the entire creation had long awaited in travail and hopeful expectation has been accomplished *pro nobis* in Jesus' life, death, resurrection, and ascension. All the same, some of God's reconciled creatures continue, in either ignorance or willfulness, to exercise their freedom not to believe the Gospel's good news, not to acknowledge that God was in Christ reconciling the world to himself. Belief (on our part) has nothing effectively to do with whether God loves us and has, through Jesus, accounted us as righteous, as heirs of the kingdom, as beneficiaries of Christ's atoning work. Similarly, baptism is the church's acknowledgment that God has forgiven our sins and reconciled us. Baptism is the rite by which God constitutes, and reconstitutes, the church as that congregation that is already in this life participant in the life to come.

- Because baptism is indelible, an action which we perform because we are commanded to do so, and an action in which we are powerless to prevent God from doing what he has promised to do in it— and because the efficacy of baptism does not depend or hinge upon the belief of the recipient—we sometimes encounter the "baptized unbeliever." We say about such a one as this that he or she has been incorporated into the "outwardness," but not the "inwardness," of the body of Christ, the church.

Baptism, these postulates suggest, is initiation into a community which helps us to want the right thing(s), for the right reason(s), and in the right way(s). Alasdair MacIntyre has persuasively argued that the coherence and cogency of community are the presuppositions for rationality and reasonableness. For in the absence of common traditions and shared commitments—in the absence of com-unity—there is and can be no rationality; and in the absence of rationality, there can be no reasonable resolution of moral dispute or agreement about moral goals. Thus, while baptism conveys a number of discrete meanings, one notion which is plainly prominent among them is that baptism means to create the conditions for that kind of rationality and coherence in the church's life.

It therefore has to appear awkward, if not downright embarrassing, that Christian piety is obliged to acknowledge that baptism has also served to divide instead of unite God's people, both within and without the Christian family. Without shrinking the least bit from this painful awareness, I want to suggest here that what appears to be a contradiction is in fact a complementary juxtaposition of truth claims.

F. D. Maurice,[28] the nineteenth-century Anglican theologian and reformer, proposed that the kingdom of God comprises many realms, including the realms of Jesus, Moses, Muhammad, et al.; that Holy Baptism initiates us into the kingdom of Jesus Christ; and that the church is not an end in itself, but aims toward the kingdom of God, which transcends and comes after it. It is therefore particularity, not universality, which marks us in this world; the Church is our family; the community of baptized Christians is our commonwealth.

But Maurice's further point was that this scandalous (and sometimes embarrassing) particularity need not, and does not, deny the legitimacy and authenticity and even appropriateness of other particularities. I think that he meant this claim to be more profound than a vapid notion of tolerance; I believe that he intended it to recognize and acknowledge finitude, creatureliness, and the limits of human boundedness.

To illustrate his point differently, I can imagine Maurice acknowledging that your marriage and mine share some things in common in order to be called "marriage" (otherwise, we should call it something else) and simultaneously recognizing that there are also distinctive marks and characteristics which reflect an individuality and specificity and particularity which permits me to claim mine as "my marriage" and you to claim yours as "your marriage."

Richard Norris, writing about Maurice's theological method, put it this way: "[E]very system opposes the reality which it seeks to define, and does so precisely because it is not so much an attempt to enter into and appropriate that reality as an attempt to control it."[29] The "reality" is a mystery which is beyond every particular history, every particular story; yet every particular history and every particular story participates in the "reality" because the "reality" is the presupposition of everything that is.

Christian baptism is like that. It is particularizing because it participates in, but does not exhaust, the reality which is universally presuppositional. Christian baptism creates the church, and initiates us into the kingdom of Christ; and we thus enter into, but do not control, the kingdom of God.

For another example of how particular commitments fail to issue in universal coherence, consider the plight of those thirty-seven million Americans who have no medical insurance, together with those millions more who are underinsured or for whom certain health services are inaccessible. If medical care—not health, mind you, just basic medical care—is an entitlement of U.S. citizenship, how is it that year after precious year we, as a nation, can provide a tolerant and even fertile environment for continuing the disadvantage of those who lack the means, and therefore the power, to enter the health care system in this country? A short answer is that the centrifugal forces in this society appear to be stronger than the centripetal ones, and we are simply unable (because we are unwilling) to agree on the policies and programs which would change and correct this condition.

Of course, Ivan Illich[30] may well be right that some medicine is dangerous to our health; yet this provides little comfort for those who need the most basic kinds of medical care, and who simply cannot afford it. What, if anything, can be done to dispense the largess of modern medical care to these poor and dispossessed sisters and brothers? I do not wish to make a long list of concrete proposals here, but I believe that the analysis which I have offered may provide a hint about where we can begin.

Reflect for a moment on how our deaths often have stunted meaning because we do not believe that our lives have meaning beyond sheer biological extension. With such an outlook, I find it neither strange nor unexpected that our medicine is too often put at the service of cheating our deaths of the meaning they could and should have for those whose deaths they are. Christians, on the other hand, are a people who know that a virtuous life consists of more than mere vitalism or lengthened metabolism; so transforming our collective amnesia, that loss of identity which marks the absence of coherent belief, means facing squarely the most ancient and vexing problems of our species—namely, the meaning and destiny of our lives. Only this will convey meaning and purpose for our deaths.

It is worth remembering that there was a time—it now seems a very long time ago—when there was considerable agreement among men and women about what constituted the common good, even the good life, and how the various parts of society were intended to function in order to serve a meaning and purpose which were shared by the whole society. In those days death was a familiar and constant companion, but beyond this there was a shared and common sense within the community that death was not an unmitigated disaster, and that there was a grander purpose for life than avoiding death at all costs. These were people whose religious and cultural commitments helped them to learn that their service to each other was more important than life itself. As a result, they envisioned forms of care for the sick and the poor that would otherwise have been impossible.

Remember, for example, the great imaginative invention which we now call "hospital," which had its modest origins in the Greco-Roman world, then went through a period of inattention, and was resurrected in the Middle Ages. Such an institution, which we now take so much for granted, could only have been created by a people who, amid the injustice and carelessness of their time, believed that they could take time to care for the dying—that they could care when they could not cure. It is sobering to remember that Western medicine did not derive its moral justification from its power to cure; its reason for being, certainly until very recently, came solely from its commitment not to abandon the sick and dying.

Now, I reckon that the correlations between the phenomena of modern medical care systems and the commitments of baptized Christians might be fairly obvious. If I am right about what is going on in baptism, and if I am right about what is going on in the failure of American medical policies and practices to attend to vast numbers of our dispossessed brothers and sisters, it may be that Christians will begin to ask our medical care system to take some steps which many of us may find it difficult to envision. For example, although trying to get more federal monies to underwrite more research and more exotically equipped tertiary care facilities may be our habit of being, we should have learned by now that this tack tends less to solve our basic health care problems than to exacerbate them, by increasing the range of potential needs to be met by an ever-extending and omnibus biomedical technology. Perceived need is simply an artifact of research and development.

What I am actually thinking about is something much more fundamental: that we will learn to look some technologies squarely in the face and say "no" to them; that we will learn to deny ourselves some of those forms of extraordinary care which biomedical technology currently promises to develop and deliver, because we will have come to some acknowledgments about ourselves and our neighbors which will allow us to accept the notion that service to each other is more important than the life of any one of us. We will have learned, in other words, that the real enemy is not death but all those things which threaten a good and faithful life. It is for this kind of life, for the sake of the well-being of all of us, that the basic kinds of human need must be met. In the measure to which Christians do, in fact, share common commitments about identity and destiny, we will be able to discriminate need from want; and we will further be able to reach agreement about what are believed to be real needs.

Christians have for too long pursued social strategies, such as the delivery of health care, on the assumption that belief in God and the power of the gospel have little or nothing to do with how we think about social justice. We have conveniently compartmentalized justice questions (as we have done many others), arrogantly and stupidly supposing that they have little or nothing to do with the liturgical actions which signify our profoundest beliefs and commitments. So, in the name of charity or perhaps distributive justice, we have sought policies which are more equitable for those who are so often overlooked in our society. This approach has not been entirely futile and fruitless, and I do not mean to disparage these efforts altogether. Nevertheless, it is clear to me that a striving for equity which is driven by the current consumer ethos and by utopian expectations for complete health and total well-being does not and will not suffice. It is further clear to me that efforts like these, in the long run, will function largely to perpetuate the systemic problems which we can presently associate with attempting to deliver finite care in a world of infinite need.

To say it plainly, no account of justice can be intelligible without drawing on the profoundest convictions of ourselves as a community which is gathered and banded together by tradition in a boundaried commons. Baptism generates this kind of identity for us as Christians by initiating us into this kind of community. Baptism thereby denotes the truth about who we are, and who we are destined to become, and what constitutes a good life and a good death. We then understand ourselves to be a people for whom it is better to give than to receive; who save their lives by losing them; who are each other's advocates and not their adversaries; who are God's friends, and not God's enemies.

None of us formulates notions about what is good or bad, or develops ideas about moral agency, apart from a point of view, a somewhat particular way of viewing things. So if we have difficulty with talking about liturgy and ethics in the same breath, this is symptomatic of a point of view which sees liturgy as something other than ethics, or which looks at each of these as relatively independent of the other, or which even sees them as mutually exclusive. This is similarly our typical difficulty with perceiving the Christian life as a life of holiness: we have been acculturated, actually trained, to believe that being a Christian is merely one among several ways of being a good person, a responsible citizen, a decent human being. So plainly, after all, we do require a radical kind of turning, a *metanoia*, if we are to see things differently, if we are to look at ourselves and the world through eyes of faith.

To put this point another way, ritual and liturgy carry meaning prior to our understanding and comprehension (which is as true, incidentally, for secular rituals and "liturgies" as for religious ones). We do not generate this meaning; it is given to us in the measure to which we welcome and embrace and claim what is happening in the liturgy as our own. And this, in turn, helps explain how it is that worship itself is a moral act which displays our deepest convictions about who we understand and intend ourselves to be. Worship is a moral act because it displays both the virtues which characterize the kind of people we are, and the kinds of actions which display the characteristic virtues of such a people.

This is why our convictions are themselves moral and liturgical. The Christian life is not principally a matter of theological beliefs from which liturgical actions flow; it is, instead, a matter of being formed by faithful participation in the liturgy. Liturgy is the source of theology and a life of holiness; or, as we have traditionally put it, *lex orandi, lex credendi*. This has been our inheritance since at least the fourth century, when catechumens regularly *experienced* the "Sacrament of the Lord's table" *before* they were taught about it. Lent was the time for the intensive preparation which was completed by initiation at the great vigil of Easter; and the fifty days of Easter was the time for what was called "mystagogy," for declaring the meaning of the mysteries of baptism and eucharist. Ambrose, Cyril, John Chrysostom, Theodore, and Augustine—all fourth-century Fathers of the church—reinforce the claim that the sacrament of the altar cannot be discerned and comprehended until *after* baptism, that the experience of prayer and liturgy occurs prior to explication of the sacrament. This order and priority sound odd to postmodern ears; but Augustine himself made this point plainly and succinctly in a sermon to the just-baptized:

> I am not unmindful of the promise by which I pledged myself to deliver a sermon to instruct you, who have just been baptized, on the Sacrament of the Lord's table, which you now look upon and of which you partook last night.[31]

This, in part, is why I have wanted to argue that it is both misleading and mistaken to ask, "What is the relation between liturgy and ethics?" (or, more commonly, between theology and ethics). To put the question this way is to suggest that these are autonomous, independent, separable entities which now, by some contrivance, need to be or can be brought into some sort of relation. The Gospel, however, knows nothing of sundering liturgy and the moral life; or, conversely, when the Gospel knows of liturgy and the moral life sundered, it calls this "hypocrisy." So prayer, proclamation, baptism, eucharist, offering, intercession—all of these and more are *moral* acts because they display the kind of people we are.

On these terms, liturgy is everything which the church does in the name of Jesus—services of worship, committee meetings, community service, covered-dish suppers, and ministries of manifold types. *Liturgy is everything the church offers to God in the name of Jesus*. Or, as the encyclical *Mediator Dei* puts it:

> The liturgy is nothing more or less than the exercise of this priestly function {of Christ}. . . . Rightly, then, the liturgy is considered as an exercise of the priestly office of Jesus Christ. In the liturgy, by means of signs perceptible to the senses, human sanctification is signified and brought about in ways proper to each of these signs; in the liturgy the whole public worship is performed by the Mystical Body of Jesus Christ, that is, by the Head and his members."[32]

There can be little doubt that the service and ministry of Christian liturgy have come, in some quarters, to refer to cultic acts; but it is also clear that *leitourgia* has a broader meaning than mere cultic acts in the New Testament. It is principally a mystery in the sense that God is present in the liturgy and that the liturgy is a place where God comes to meet us; it is also, of course, where we come and bring our offering(s) to God.

WORSHIP AS PURPOSELESS AND
PURPOSEFUL BIFOCALITY

On the issue of the purposefulness/purposelessness of worship, a colleague suggested to me a remarkably apt quotation from the distinguished Anglican theological ethicist V. A. Demant. This excerpt is lengthy, but it warrants citing in its entirety. In an essay now more than fifty years old, and commenting on why worship cannot aim directly at social teaching and causes, Demant observed that worship

> *must be in one sense a* purposeless *act, if it is to be true worship. An action has a purpose if it is done for the sake of something else, but worship is for its own sake; or for the sake of God. That is the same thing, because any activity is doing the will of God when it is truly itself. So there is a sense in which Christian worship—liturgical worship—has a meaning but no purpose; means acting for a further result. Worship is the gathering up of all activities before God. In that sense it is purposeless. If we try to give it a moral or social purpose, we are destroying its nature.*
>
> *In the same sense, art or family relationships are also purposeless. No one would think of asking of what use is his mother. The mother is not of use; she is just there. Augustine once said that the essence of evil was to use the things we ought to enjoy and to enjoy the things we ought to use. The things we value for what they lead on to—those we use—are different from those things we value for their own sake—those we enjoy. . . . In worship we have this mode of valuing a thing for its sake, and Christian worship is only of that kind and can only be of that kind if it is truly objective: bringing the whole of our life before God, who is its source."[33]*

Such a claim is bound to sound startling to modern pragmatic and utilitarian ears. Surely worship, of all things, has a purpose—perhaps to motivate us to be moral, or inspire us to do justice, or just make us feel better about ourselves and our neighbors. We think that it simply cannot be without some operational function; that it most assuredly has to serve some human end. But contrary to this conventional wisdom, Demant's claim, which I want to take with utter seriousness, is that worship is of *terminal*, not instrumental, value. This point is bedrock for a project which requires looking at the whole world in general, and at liturgy and ethics in particular, in a different way.

The catechism in the Book of Common Prayer is remarkably explicit and straightforward in this matter:

Q. What is adoration?

A. Adoration is the lifting up of the heart and mind to God, asking nothing but to enjoy God's presence.

Q. Why do we praise God?

A. We praise God, not to obtain anything, but because God's Being draws praise from us.

Q. What is corporate worship?

A. In corporate worship, we unite ourselves with others to acknowledge the holiness of God, to hear God's Word, to offer prayer and to celebrate the sacraments.[34]

The catechism speaks also of prayer, thanksgiving, penitence, oblation, and intercession and petition in order to say that each of these actions, and all of them together, comprise an end which needs no further purpose in order to authenticate or legitimate them. They are, as it were, self-authenticating. One might expect that Episcopalians would unhesitatingly (if not enthusiastically) affirm Demant's point; but my experience as a parish priest suggests that, somewhat like the Bible, the things you are liable to read in the Book of Common Prayer ain't necessarily so, at least not in practice.

There is plainly a sense in which whatever might be associated with, or derived from, acknowledgment of God's holiness, hearing of God's Word, offering of prayers, and celebration of the sacraments, is tangential, peripheral, even accidental. And this reinforces the importance, in the first of it, of understanding that Christian worship is not validated to the extent that it is personally meaningful, or socially useful, or consequential in other ways that are taken to comprise its humanly defined validation. Worship is, as Demant says, "a purposeless act" in the sense that it neither requires nor is predicated upon some utility which it serves, and to which it would therefore be subservient. It is sufficient as its own end, its own *raison d'etre*, and it requires no purpose beyond itself for authentication.

I have labored this point, because nailing it down securely and emphatically is alone what permits us to acknowledge that, *in another and complementary sense*, worship does have purpose and is a purposeful action. That other sense is this: worship is purposeful precisely in the measure to which it is true to itself; and it is true to itself when it acknowledges the holiness of God, hears God's Word, offers prayer, and celebrates the sacraments. It is in the sense of purpose as an answer to the question "Why?" that worship is purposive. Or, to put it differently, it is in the sense of purpose as that for which something is done that worship is purposive. Purposeless and purposeful, in this instance, are antiphonal refrains in a single composition.

So it is in the sense that worship is an action done for God's sake alone, only because God is God and we are who we are, that worship has an end, a goal, an aim, a purpose. One of the brief, traditional formulations of that purpose is the phrase "to glorify God and enjoy him forever." This phrase, taken from the *Shorter Catechism*, does not emerge in the church's teaching as a commentary on worship per se. Rather, it is given in answer to the question "What is the chief end of man?" It does no disservice to this question, and its answer in the *Shorter Catechism*, to understand that the church's teaching is precisely that *worship* is the chief end of humankind, that the goal of human living (and dying) is "to glorify God and enjoy him forever."

In these reciprocating senses, then, worship—and its expression in liturgies, rites, ceremonies, and rituals—is both an end in itself and a means. Indeed, I reckon that, for those of us who are engaged in worship, it is this bifocality of purposelessness/purposefulness which marks it: worship is an end in itself, and this alone permits it, in any authentically derivative sense, to be purposeful or purposive. As Christians comprehend it, only in acknowledging worship to be a purposeless action can we rightly discern it as a purposeful action.

This dialectic serves as an indication, a clue, as to how it is that worship is not monologic but dialogic. It is not merely, or simply, or only, or even primarily our action toward God that worship signifies. It is this, to be sure; but what worship signifies initially is God's action toward us. Worship is therefore our response to God's initiative, and on this point Christians need to be particularly clear. Our worship—prayer, hymnody, psaltery, proclamation, and all the rest—is not *de novo*, self-generated, without antecedent, inaugurated by our own imagination. Whatever else may characterize worship in the traditions of biblical theism, it is plainly human response to divine initiative.

But the corollary is also the priority here: it is only because God initiates, accommodates to our capacity for acknowledgment, graciously communicates to us in creation and deliverance and Decalogue, and in covenant and prophets and preaching, and in a chosen people, and preeminently in Jesus—it is only because God gifts us with epiphanies that there is any possibility at all for our response.

Now, in the last analysis, I suppose that all of this may seem to be much ado about very little. It could be that at the most this is just worrying about getting the "horse before the cart." But I want to suggest that this is not an insignificant worry for Christians at any time, and perhaps especially in a time when pragmatism, relativism, positivism, and personalism (to use the four presuppositions or "working principles" of situation ethics) preside. I believe that it needs to be made as clear as we can make it that we do not worship God in order to use God, that worship is not a way in which we manipulate God to our own purposes. Christians confess that the God we worship is the one, true, living God. And this is why it is right, and a good and joyful thing for us, always and everywhere to acknowledge the holiness of God, to hear God's Word, to offer prayer, and to celebrate the sacraments. This is no more than the bounden duty and service of those people who understand and intend themselves to be disciples of Jesus Christ.

Acknowledgment, hearing, offering, and celebration are the means by which Christian liturgies form us and our stories according to God's holiness, God's story. We Christians are a people who know who we truly are in the measure to which God's story becomes our story; and we know that story by and through the recapitulation, the reenactment, the reappropriation of the epiphany of God in the Prophets, in the Torah, in Israel, and preeminently in Jesus. This is how God's story forms us: it becomes our habit of being; it offers us a different way of seeing ourselves and the world as, we believe, God intends them. It is this recapitulation (which means literally "to repeat in concise form"), done for God's sake alone, which is also the means by which we constantly reappropriate what God calls righteousness and goodness (and, correspondingly, what God calls sin and evil).

Constant recapitulation of the mighty actions of God in worship accounts for how the church means to engender holiness in the lives of the *laos theou*, the people of God. The particular shapes of liturgies, symbols, rituals, and ceremonies become the means to that end, whereby we pray that "we may perfectly love God" and "worthily magnify" God's holy name. I happily defer to St. Augustine to summarize, as he so frequently is able to do for me, these claims:

> *What else, then, but folly or some extraordinary mistake can make a man so belittle himself as to reverence a being whom, in reality, he hates even to resemble? For, how can a man be willing to worship and unwilling to imitate, when the very essence of religion is to imitate the one whom we worship?*[35]

CHAPTER TWO

LITURGY AND THE CHRISTIAN LIFE

Both Christian worship and Christian ethics are marked by a dyadic, or two-sided, complementarity. On the one hand is an attitude of complete submission to and exaltation of God; on the other hand is the act of a whole life faithfully lived and acted out in passionate obedience and fidelity to God. From start to finish, the Bible is rich in metaphors which undertake to make it plain that what God desires is not the sacrifice of "things" but the offering of a broken spirit, a humble and contrite heart, a self out of control and in complete obedience. The true worshiper witnesses to submission to the divine will through a life of holiness, of coinhering acts of righteousness and justice. From the prophets of the Old Testament to the apostles of the New Testament, we are taught that authentic worship consists in the inseparability of these two commitments. Neither alone will suffice; in both Hebrew and Christian piety, each is the indispensable concomitant of the other.

For those of us who cut our liturgical teeth on the 1928 Book of Common Prayer, every time the celebrant recited the Summary of the Law at a celebration of the Holy Communion, there was the not-so-subtle hint that a life of prayer and a life of holiness go together:

> Hear what our Lord Jesus Christ saith: Thou shalt love the Lord thy God with all thy heart, and with all thy soul, and with all thy mind. This is the first and great commandment. And the second is like unto it; Thou shalt love thy neighbour as thyself. On these two commandments hang all the Law and the Prophets."[1]

But recitation of the Summary of the Law did not happen at every celebration of the eucharist, so it turned out over time to be more intimation than persistent formation; and Marion Hatchett's historical note on the place of the Summary of the Law in the American Prayer Book instructively explains how and why the Summary became optional.[2]

Despite this development, the frequency (until recently) with which the liturgy for Morning Prayer served as the principal Sunday service helped to train Episcopalians to acknowledge that liturgy is ethics, that for Christians prayer and holy living are yoked. Probably nowhere is this more elegantly and powerfully conveyed than in the General Thanksgiving of the daily morning office (Book of Common Prayer, 58–59). After giving thanks for "all the blessings of this life; but above all for thine inestimable love in the redemption of the world by our Lord Jesus Christ," we continue to pray:

> *And, we beseech thee, give us that due sense of all thy mercies, that our hearts may be unfeignedly thankful;* and that we show forth thy praise, not only with our lips, but in our lives, by giving up our selves to thy service, and by walking before thee in holiness and righteousness all our days. . .

So I don't imagine that it should sound odd, or come as a bit of novel intelligence, if I make the claim that the evidence is weighty that Christian worship, rightly understood, means to display life in submission to and conformity with God's holiness and righteousness. I also know, of course, that this claim beautifully illustrates another one—that we frequently know better than we do.

THE ACCULTURATION OF
CONTEMPORARY AMERICAN CHURCHES

None of the staple truisms of our time is perhaps better known or more widely acknowledged among observers of contemporary American Christianity than that contemporary American churches are amply and solidly acculturated. The implications of this terse judgment are too numerous to identify here with fine precision; but it is clear that among them is the notion that worship in these churches typically does not make a distinctive statement, and that the virtues to which these churches witness are, for the most part, precisely those secular virtues with which the generality of Americans, churched or unchurched, are fairly comfortable.

The church in America, in other words, is hardly distinguished by its submission and witness to God's holiness and righteousness. A Presbyterian friend of mine says that among the clear evidences of this fact is that "Religion" has made the index page of *Time* magazine, where it is simply one among many topics for well-informed readers to peruse. He declines to speculate on what it means that the "Religion" section typically appears in the later pages of the periodical.

"Worship in air-conditioned comfort" appeared on several church bulletin boards when this engineering novelty became economically feasible for the generality of churches in the 1950s and 1960s. Other congregations advertised their special *geist* with slogans like "The Church with the Warm Heart" or "The Church for Friendly People." Reinhold Niebuhr once argued that churches ought to be places where the afflicted were comforted and the comfortable were afflicted; but phrases like these on church marquees have served to reassure both church members and the general public that American churches are not places where there is cause for any anxiety or discomfort. The corollary judgment is that the failure of American Christianity and its churches is directly proportional to their embrace of sentimentality, whether sacred or secular.

Nowadays one observes that church bulletin boards have taken on a somewhat different mission: if the older aphorisms were meant to be supportive and encouraging, the newer ones appear to be more assertive and abrasive. They frequently carry messages which are meant to indicate the kind of people who attend this church and whose church this is. "People with lots of brass don't need much polish" was the proverb on a church marquee which I saw recently in a blue-collar neighborhood. Nearby, another church's bulletin board was set perpendicular to the street so that motorists could get a message both coming and going. One side declared, "Forbidden fruit makes for a bad jam," and the other side asked, "What if Mary had aborted Jesus?" The first one of these strikes me as not just a bad pun; it means to make the point that God's laws cannot be violated with impunity. And the second apothegm seems to me more than a rhetorical question. Among much else, it implies an entire theology, especially a soteriology, and implies that none of this would be except for Jesus' birth. This different function of church bulletin boards suggests that congregations are more self-conscious about their distinctiveness than they were two or three decades ago. All the same, there may be less to this than meets the eye, and the new look may turn out to be another of those distinctions without a difference.

However much it is to be regretted, I believe that there is considerable evidence for the claim that those of us who venture to understand and intend ourselves as disciples of Jesus do, in fact, inhabit an accommodated church in an accommodated culture, current church bulletin boards not-withstanding. But this claim, in and of itself, is not news. Indeed, it may not even be altogether bad news inasmuch as this circumstance is probably unavoidable as a function of historical contingency and social location. And this suggests that while this condition certainly has its negative aspects, it may also have some positive lineaments which commend it. So I intend to argue that, in addition to—or perhaps alongside—this apparent apostasy, there are also important senses in which close ties with the environing culture are essential if the church is to make faithful and effective witness to the gospel in the world. But close ties are not undifferentiated sameness, and we need to be clear about the apparently contradictory matters which are principally at issue here.

For all their seeming pedantry, words become enormously important as descriptors of the circumstance we mean to delineate; so let me try to say as precisely as I can what I mean here. Ordinarily I prefer to eschew neologisms; but now and then, like herbs in a stew, relatively novel words can produce subtle and nuanced flavorings which might otherwise escape notice. *Enculturation* (sometimes also *inculturation*) is the learning process by which a community transmits, and its children acquire, its culture. *Acculturation* is the learning process by which one adapts to living in a second culture while retaining personal identification with a primary culture.

I first learned these concepts, if not these words, from Will Herberg's seminal study, *Protestant-Catholic-Jew*,[3] which was published my senior year in seminary. Herberg's thesis evolved from his attempt to account for an American paradox which consisted of increasing religiosity amid pervasive secularism. In the period immediately following World War II, church membership was reaching all-time highs and the Bible was achieving record-breaking sales; but there were also disturbing signs, like the polls showing that fewer than fifty percent of Americans could name the four Gospels. Herberg's analysis of this phenomenon was clear and cogent:

immigrants coming to America were expected, and themselves expected, to give up, sooner or later, virtually everything they had brought with them—language, nationality, customs—and adopt the ways of their new home; but whatever else becoming an American entailed, it did not require abandonment of one's old religion and adoption of some native American surrogate.

That last expectation, of course, proved to be entirely fictitious; and Herberg's book is an interpretation of the process which successively relocated the primary context of American self-identification from nationality, to religion (Protestant, Catholic, or Jew), to the "common religion," which is better known as the American Way of Life. The result is what we now call *assimilation*—that is, the learning process by which one community converts another and persons acquire a new culture. "In the end," said Herberg, "the forces of Americanization won out almost everywhere."[4] Protestantism, Catholicism, and Judaism became three equally variant ways of being a good American; they were, and are, the great "religions of democracy." They retain their differences, to be sure, but they are united "in the underlying presuppositions, values, and ideals that together constitute the American Way of Life on its 'spiritual' side. It is The American Way of Life that is the shared possession of all Americans and that defines the American's convictions on those matters that count most."[5]

The secularism which pervades America is fundamentally the kind that thinks and lives in terms of a framework of reality and value which is *remote* from the religious beliefs being simultaneously expressed. The people whom Herberg described are intelligent folk who take religion seriously; so it is not their earnestness, but precisely their *religion*, which is in question. To put it differently, it is the religiousness of our secularist framework, the piety which attends our secularist commitments, which constitutes a very large part of the problem of religion in America. Herberg's thesis is that *both* religiousness and secularism in America derive from much the same sources and, moreover, that they become intelligible only when viewed from that perspective.

For first-, second-, and third-generation immigrants, the new form of identification and self-identification is the product of an *American* reality and an *American* experience, both of which are movements toward homogenization. So ethnic differences begin to disappear as children and grandchildren prefer to be "Americans" rather than something else. To accommodate this preference, the "melting pot mentality" tended to change everything—language, dress, customs, and the rest—*except religion*. And this is why religious affiliation remained for a very long time the primary context of social location and self-identification for third-generation Americans.

But eventually, the more one becomes "American," the more religion is expected to be modified and altered to fit American expectations of tolerance, the American virtues associated with "live and let live," and various American "spiritual" values which turn out to be finally dispensable if they are discongenial with more essential aspects of Americanism. These are among the reasons why the besetting problem of modern American Protestant Christianity is not infidelity or hypocrisy or even blasphemy, but a vapid, insipid sentimentality—that pathetic bathos, sweetness and light, mawkishness, and mushiness which take great care to embrace everything and exclude nothing, to affirm everybody and offend nobody, to hate sin and love the sinner, to let go and let God, etc., etc., etc.

What Herberg described in 1955 is what we recognize today as movement from enculturation to acculturation to assimilation. I suspect that assimilation almost always issues in a kind of *biculturation* or *polyculturation*, processes by which two or more cultures get blended into an amalgam which incorporates and restructures ingredients from its constituents. In fact, the entire process resembles a socialization version of the Hegelian dialectic in which a certain aspect of reality is revealed in the thesis, and a somewhat contrasting aspect appears in the antithesis, and the two are *aufgehoben* in a synthesis. Moreover, the new synthesis can give rise to a new triad; and so on through many permutations.

If a *culture* is a people's learned and shared understandings and ways of life, if it is their communal worldview and ethos and artifacts, the alloy produced by bi- or polyculturation will ordinarily be consistently less cogent and coherent. This, in part, is the claim of a moral philosopher like Alasdair MacIntyre: that modern liberal society has been severed from its roots; that it is a melange of moral traditions and norms which, owing to their remarkable and substantive differences, cannot be reconciled; and that

> *What we possess . . . are the fragments of a conceptual scheme, parts which now lack those contexts from which their significance derived. We possess . . . simulacra of morality.*"[6]

My point in all this is clearly not that either church or culture is *ir*religious. Indeed, the evidence seems irresistible that both church and culture are very religious. The point, instead, is that our religiosity is very largely what is now broadly identified as post-Constantinian religiosity. This generally means that while notions of good and bad, right and wrong, and the like are serious commitments, they are also seriously flawed commitments because they are curiously compounded of strands of social and political and religious philosophies which, as MacIntyre has shown, are incommensurate, incompatible, irreconcilable, and finally unintelligible. "Post-Constantinianism" reflects and symbolizes the identification of the church with the empire, the state, the secular cultus. In the bargain, it turns out that American ecclesial religiosities are frequently only pale reflections, at best, of the gospel which they allege to display.

Sometimes this fact is not thought to be a source of embarrassment, but a badge of honor. Here is how a bishop with whom I share a name has put the matter:

> *The Methodist Church was peculiarly suited to the American scene, whether it was the frontier or the crowded city; it is suited to the American temperament, which it has always expressed and embodied in all its actions and viewpoints. Both preachers and people have been part and parcel of the nation itself. The big Methodist faults—and we have them, let us confess—are the big American faults; and the big Methodist virtues—and, thank God, we have them too—are the big American virtues. . . .*
>
> *When Theodore Roosevelt was President, he once privately remarked to the chaplain of the United States Senate, who was a Methodist, "Your church is the church of America."*[7]

The son of my father's namesake did not write the book from which this paragraph is excerpted for cloistered academics; as he made clear at the beginning of his book, he wrote for people who really want to understand the heart and mind of one of America's great Protestant churches. Truth be known, he has written for lots of us who may be embarrassed by his candor and distressed by his accuracy.

All the same, if accurate diagnosis is the first step toward a treatment which might be beneficial, we probably need to begin by acknowledging the extent to which the church's liturgy and the church's life are discontinuous, divorced, disconnected in the modern world. All of us have engaged in that charade where we "play church" on Sundays, employing strange and bizarre practices and language and the like, which we know to be plainly inadmissible to the "real" weekday world of business, politics, family, and the rest. So the diagnosis may not be mind-boggling in its novelty, but few of us have taken pains to understand its etiology. We suspect that there must have been a time in the church's history when culture and spirituality, piety and holy living, liturgy and ethics, were not divorced but united. If there were such a time, and if these things belong together, how did it come to be otherwise?

Francis Mannion has suggested three reasons why the church's liturgy has lost much of its cultural and social power, why the social and cultural generativity of the liturgy has been conceptually disoriented and, in large measure, destroyed.[8]

First, a spate of books, including Robert Bellah's celebrated *Habits of the Heart*, has shown that it is a widespread assumption in modern American culture that the individual person, rather than any institution or tradition, is the origin and focus of meaning and value and purpose. Bellah calls this "ontological individualism," a notion which carries the conviction that the "individual has a primary reality whereas society is a second-order, derived, or artificial construct."[9] Mannion calls this "the subjectification of reality," a condition which exists when personal experience is believed to be the seat of authority; when personal feeling and will are taken to be the ultimate sources of morality; when the Bible, sacraments, preaching, and indeed all ministry are *instrumental* in the measure to which they serve or confirm prior personal and individual dispositions. The consequence for liturgy and ethics is self-evident.

> *If society and its institutions are regarded as irrelevant to authentic human existence, then the traditional role of the church in transforming society is dismissed as romanticism or imperialism, or . . . collapsed into political action. In turn, because of the tendency to withdraw into individual subjectivity as the foundational source of meaning and value, the liturgy is shorn of its traditional, sacramental formality and reconceived and practiced as therapy."[10]

Mannion's second reason for the weakening of the power of the liturgy has to do with a logical outgrowth of the subjectification of reality which Mannion calls "the intimization of society." He cites Richard Sennett, who has shown how, in the twentieth century, "all social phenomena, no matter how impersonal in structure, are converted into matters of personality in order to have a meaning."[11] Sennett calls this an "ideology of intimacy," and argues that "the reigning aspiration today is to develop individual personality through experiences of closeness and warmth with others [and that] the reigning myth today is that the evils of society can all be understood as evils of impersonality, alienation, and coldness."[12]

This analysis was confirmed for Bellah by religious communities as well. Indeed, his subjects describe the church as a friendly gathering place for individuals who have discovered or experienced the holy in their personal lives and who want and need a community of empathic sharing.[13] So it is not odd that the church should become a preserve for homogeneity in which the "stranger" is unwelcome and the familiar is cultivated and celebrated. But the "stranger," we need to note, is not only the unfamiliar and foreign other; the stranger is also the resident alien in each of us who is similarly forbidden from this association. The "stranger," in fact, is all those selves with whom we cannot achieve intimacy, and who are excluded by this *cordon sanitaire*.

When this happens, it is unsurprising that the primary model for the sacred is not liturgy, but intimacy, and that personality rather than rite becomes the medium for liturgical communication and performance. So it becomes, as I was once told by a rector's wife during a Sunday school class, actually superfluous to "come to church because Jesus and I go apart from everybody else, to be alone, every day." Her meaning was transparently clear to all of us who listened in hushed consternation: our deepest religious experiences are not with a community in ritual, liturgy, worship; they are with those private, individual experiences of intimacy and caring relationship. Such public expression of our deepest religious sensibilities as there is must therefore be "tailored to meet the characteristic needs of the intimate groups. It is deprived of public, social symbolism. Consequently, it no longer stands as a model of redeemed society, and for that reason retains little ability to generate enthusiasm for social and cultural transformation."[14]

Mannion's third reason is the "politicization" of the church. Even though the public, institutional arena is ignored and rejected, it does not cease to exist; nor does it disappear altogether. It is retained, especially in the absence of subjectivity and intimacy, by working out the procedures of "legal and political conventions by which mutual respect for individual freedom, self-determination, and personal autonomy can be created and maintained."[15] This is the principal, and virtually only, public and social issue. Mannion calls it "the politicization of culture," where the rich variety of human processes have been collapsed into the single process of political activity.

As for the church's life, "politicization" means converting the church into an instrument for a political agenda—what earlier I called "assimilation." When this happens, issues of biblical righteousness and social justice issues get collapsed into narrow political schemes in which the stress is on public-policy initiatives, reorganization of systems, revolution, and social reform. In the bargain, liturgy is inevitably manipulated to ideologic ends.

Where, for instance, the eucharist does not directly promote the cause of political liberation, it is prone to being regarded as in captivity to false powers."[16]

So the liturgy, on these terms, is directed by political ideology toward the transformation of politics. Rites and symbols lose their power to generate; generativity comes from politicization; and liturgy gets used—that is, it becomes a means to the ends of ideologic politics.

Mannion's point through all of this is not that subjectivity, intimacy, and politics are evil or altogether wrongheaded or even avoidable. His worry, which many of us share, is that these dispositions claim a priority, that they function as the first principles of a theological system, that they dominate and preside over the ways in which liturgy and the Christian life are understood and acted out. The problem to which his analysis points, in a nutshell, is that this way of comprehending these matters simply gets the cart before the horse.

This, of course, is easy enough to do in churches which have largely abdicated any claim of social significance for the liturgy, and where sacramental life and social action are either estranged or divorced. It is fairly easy in this circumstance, for example, to set "being good" and "being holy" against each other; to suggest that it is not only possible, but perhaps even desirable, to segregate "goodness" from "holiness." And the reason that it is fairly easy to divorce them is the supposition that "being good" is defined by human expectations, whereas "being holy" has something to do with a divine claim on us. Nowadays, on these terms, "goodness" takes its cue from a secular and autonomous liberalism; whereas "holiness" refers to prayer and piety, the church's worship, the Christian community. In sum, "being good" and "being holy," it is widely claimed, ought to be juxtaposed because they refer to being particular, and in fact different, kinds of persons, and to particular and different referents for understanding what kind(s) of persons we ought to be.

Insofar as the Christian life has been profoundly accommodated to its environing culture, and because the church's liturgy has been either separated from "real life" or wholly identified with secularity, an obvious conclusion at this juncture might be that Christian liturgy and Christian ethics cannot, and therefore do not, offer distinctively "good news." Instead they pander to cultic virtues, cultic piety, "goodness" as secular culture wishes to define it; and what it then means to be a "Christian" person becomes virtually indistinguishable from what it means to be, let us say, "a good American"—that is, one who is committed to The American Way of Life.

Now if being "a good American" is roughly commensurate with what Paul termed "being in the world," it becomes clearer how, from the church's perspective, these phrases serve as metaphors for those who exercise their freedom not to believe in God, for those who choose not to acknowledge the truth which the gospel of Christ proclaims, for those who look for the meaning of "goodness" not in an understanding of "holiness" but in a secular and self-generated account of meaning, purpose, and value which Herberg called The American Way of Life. We have to remember, however, that there is an insistent strand in the church's history which claims that a complete identification of church and world is reductionistic and violative of the fundamental character of each.[17]

Alternatively, when the church's liturgy has integrity, there is unavoidable and inevitable tension with the "world." This tension does not need to be and is not meant to be acrimonious or virulent; it is simply strained relations. The church is not the world's enemy; the church harbors no enmity against the world; the church bears the world no ill will or malice.

The church, insofar as it is Christ's body, loves the world and prays for it. Yet the church is also, for all that, in a somewhat nervous, stressed, unrelaxed, upset relationship with its environing culture because of the different account which each offers of "the way things are" and, indeed, of who we are in relation to the different accounts.

This tension is an implicit judgment of the church on all who exercise their freedom to refuse to recognize the truth which the gospel proclaims. To have exercised the freedom to refuse to acknowledge God in Christ is what the metaphor "world" stands for; just as to have exercised the freedom to acknowledge God in Christ is what the metaphor "church" stands for. This, in fact, is the basic distinction between "Christian" and "pagan," between "church" and "world": the church affirms God's freedom and bends itself in obedience to it; the world denies God's freedom and claims freedom for itself, for causes and programs and ideologies of its own genesis and design.

For centuries, the liturgy has been important for Christians because it teaches us who, by God's mercy, we are and are meant to be. Such knowledge is not something we have naturally; we have to learn it; we have to be taught it and trained in it; we have to acknowledge it; it is a gift. Insofar as we receive it, the liturgy shapes us to be the reconstituted family of God, the people of God's new age, the *ecclesia theou*. It forms our lives morally by providing the essential means whereby Jesus' life becomes our life, his story becomes our story, his work becomes our work. It recapitulates the story of God's continuing effort to show the world its true destiny and claim it by God's faithful love. It tells us who we are and who we are meant to be if we purpose to understand and intend ourselves as disciples of Jesus, God's Christ.

A CASE IN POINT: CHRISTIAN MARRIAGE

Like other words which signify specific relationships between persons, "marriage" is freighted with many meanings nowadays. My friends in western Europe and Great Britain tell me that there, as in the United States, two aspects of marriage receive particular attention in popular discussion: one of these is venereal pleasure and satisfaction and the other is the marriage ceremony. The abundance of manuals in print, and counselors in all the media, attest to the former; and the considerable attention to details of law and ritual nicely displays the latter. What is (and ought to be) disturbing to Christians is not that couples and their families think these things important, but that they commit such *inordinate* importance to them.

We are rightly appreciative of the best psychological and biological information about our bodies and psyches which is available to us; and in the measure to which "marriage manuals" provide such information, they ought to be gratefully received. In my reading of it much of this literature does, in fact, show great understanding and sensitivity while discussing some of the most intimate matters which wives and husbands encounter. But a frequent flaw in books of this sort is that the entire marital relationship tends to get reduced to a venereal dimension where the crucial question is whether the partners are sexually compatible and receive genital satisfaction and pleasure. The corollary suggestion is that if this can be achieved, everything else in the marriage will take care of itself.

My own experience as pastor and professor is that the converse is closer to the truth: a man and a woman who love each other, who try to help each other, who communicate their fears and hopes and worries and ambitions, who support each other passionately and intelligently and tenderly—these two are likely to develop a mutually satisfactory sexual relationship. Mutuality, not method, is the key to authentic and happy union.

Similarly with the ceremonial aspects, much popular discussion seems to suppose that if certain legal and ritualistic acts are performed as prescribed by state and church, all questions about whether a marriage is valid are abated. Again, however, a Christian view of marriage has not worried over a theology of the ceremony, and nothing that pertains to the ceremonial aspects of weddings has anything to do with defining Christian marriage.

Strictly speaking, a Christian view of marriage is not concerned with questions of either sexual adjustment and gratification or public ceremonies. What is principally at stake in Christian marriage is whether these persons love each other, pledge their love for and to each other, and ask the church's blessing that their love for and to each other be informed and characterized by God's love for us as we know it in Jesus Christ. In a word, each gives himself or herself away to the other; and it is in this giving, which recapitulates God's gift of himself to us in Jesus, that they become a new unity now distinguished (although not separated) from all other unities of family, race, or nation. They thus become one, as Paul states in

Ephesians 5, in a great mystery which is analogous to the union between Christ and the church.

Of course, husband and wife do not cease to be persons. What is crucial is that in their love for each other, as in Christ's love for the church, a new and profound dimension of existence emerges within this relationship. They are, as Genesis 2:24 puts it, "one flesh"; and coitus not only accomplishes that unity in a biological way but also serves as a symbol of that mysterious oneness between woman and man, the full meaning of which is not wholly divulged by mere bodily coalescence. Their union is organic, not arithmetic, as parenthood confirms.

To state the point differently, in a proposition agreed upon by Catholics and Protestants alike: men and women marry each other. A couple is married when they pledge themselves to each other, consent to be responsible for each other, and reserve to each other those acts which engender, nourish, and establish their unique one-flesh unity. The couple alone is capable of this promise-making between them; and others present at the marriage rite only witness the public declaration that a marriage between these two has taken place and pledge their support.

In a certain sense, this means that the couple is married *before* they make their public vows; and similarly that they are married *before* consummating their vows in all those acts which engender, nourish, and establish their unique unity. On the other hand, it would be a mistake to think of the marriage covenant as a purely private or covert event between these two. As M. Merleau-Ponty has pointed out, we do not know exactly what we are thinking until we say it;[18] and articulation and publication of the marriage vows in a public act both confirm it to the speakers and make it believable to the hearers.

It is in this complementary connection between agreement and action that sound marriage occurs; thus the classical requirements for a valid marriage are *ratum et consummatum* (consent and consummation). We do not need to assign priority to either inasmuch as each depends upon the other for authenticity and trustworthiness.

That the church believes and teaches this ought to be sufficient for Christians; but I find it of more than passing interest that conventional practice tends to confirm the church's discernment. This is, I believe, why the rehearsal never holds the same meaning as the wedding itself: the words are the same, the place is the same, and the participants are the same, but the rehearsal is for practice and the wedding is for real. Or consider whether Christian clergy saying the words of the marriage rite over two bread trucks would cause us then to think these vehicles married to each other. Perhaps the absurdity makes the point: it is appropriate to locate the meaning and reality of these events in the persons themselves. Couples are not married because something is done to them, or for them, or imposed upon them; and we are mistaken to speak of persons as Christianly "married" if this is only or chiefly what we have in mind. It is nothing more or less than their expressed intention and determination to take each other as spouse, sponsored by their love for each other and witnessed to in their vows, which makes them truly married.

In this perspective it is clear that authentic Christian marriage occurs, and is understood, within the context of conjugal love; and that the traditional ends of marriage—*bonum fides, bonum proles, bonum sacramentum,* as Augustine formulated them—come to fruition out of this contextualization.[19] What often gets ignored or neglected is that, for those of us who understand and intend ourselves as disciples of Jesus Christ, how God loves us is paradigmatic for how we are meant to love each other. Indeed we say that the very possibility for our loving is rooted in God's having first loved us. "In this is love," says 1 John 4:10, "not that we loved God but that he loved us and sent his Son to be the expiation for our sins." Or Paul, in Romans 5:8, tells us the extraordinary good news that when there was nothing about us to commend or merit God's love—while we were helpless, estranged, godhaters—we were reconciled to God through the gift of the Savior. As John (3:16) knew, it is only because God loves the world "that he gave his only son." Our obligation as Christians is to love God and neighbor in these same ways.

As there is no rule or law that, by following it assiduously, certifies the authenticity and genuineness of our love to and for God, so there is no rule or law that defines authentic neighbor-loving. Actually, it is the nature of love to transcend every kind of limitation; so the gift of love, God's or ours or another's, becomes real for us and is appropriated to us when we acknowledge and affirm and claim it; and this is as true for *eros* and *philia* as it is for *agape*.

Indeed, in the measure to which we have separated *eros* and *philia* from *agape*, we have denigrated God's incarnation. We do not need to claim that *eros* and *philia* are radically defective, or that they entirely lack the self-giving and self-sacrificing element which distinctively characterizes *agape*. Neither do we have to suppose that erotic and filial relationships must be forsaken if conjugal love is to be pure and holy. The New Testament claim is only that *agape* should preside over our relationships; and this extends to the whole scope of human connectedness. This is how, for example, an authentic instance of human coition might combine all three of these moods: sexual love (*eros*) is complete when it includes a shared and common life (*philia*) and when it desires and establishes a union that is lasting and purposive (*agape*).

Outwardly, of course, Christian lovers are indistinguishable from non-Christian lovers. Objectively, both we and they appear to be engaged in the same act. But there is a difference, and this difference is one of will and intention which embodies the paradigm of God's love for us in Jesus Christ. That difference may have been, at least in part, what Jesus had in mind when he defined adultery as a matter of the heart (Matt. 5:27–28) and invited those "without sin" to stone the adulteress (John 8:3–11). We have long recognized this difference by providing a number of nouns to identify "different" acts of human sexual congress: rape, incest, conjugal lovemaking, adultery, pedophilia, etc. These words acknowledge that the purpose and meaning of an action are not self-evident in a simple observation of the action itself, and that we need interpretive clues from the actors themselves if we are to perceive and target correctly what is going on.

In this way, love and creation are inextricably bound. We cannot perceive God's love for us until God accommodates himself to our circumstance and communicates his love under the conditions of our finitude and temporality. God's love is the presupposition for God's creativity. This paradigm also instructs and shapes Christian marriage, so that conjugal intercourse is the expression of an anterior commitment and promise-making for which pregnancy and birth are the practical results. This means that even the basic species drive to reproduce is not its own explanation for Christians; because Christians know that parenthood is not defined by simple fecundity, and that to be a mother or father or daughter or son signifies more than mere breeding.

I have argued elsewhere[20] that the church ought to say plainly that having children is a vocation for Christians; that we neither choose to have children nor have them because we cannot avoid it; that having children is a duty for Christians because we believe that we are commanded to do so as an expression of our determination to witness faithfully to the God of Abraham and Sarah, Isaac and Rebekah, Jacob and Leah, Joseph and Mary, Jesus, and Paul, and to live in this selfish and sinful world by the power of the world to come. My colleague Stanley Hauerwas has put it this way: "The Christian community is formed by the conviction that the power of this world is not the determining sway of our existence, but rather it is the power we find in the cross of Jesus Christ . . . children witness to our determination to exist as a people formed by the cross even though the world wishes to deny that a people can exist without the power protected and acquired through the sword."[21]

This kind of rhetoric will doubtless prompt some to observe that there is a significant difference between being a fool for Christ's sake and a damned fool, and the force of such a crude observation deserves our serious attention. Others may mistakenly infer that, on these terms, there is no place for celibacy as a Christian vocation, that all Christians *must* have children, or that "having children" may not be accomplished by adoption or some other alternative to "natural" conception, gestation, and parturition, or that virginity (as Luther said) is an evasion of social responsibility. Withal, we know that a pagan and secular environment has eroded many of the traditionally authentic ways of understanding and intending ourselves as disciples of Jesus Christ; and that these developments threaten not only the piety of individual Christians, but the legitimacy of institutionalized Christian communities as well. In this respect, our time may not be fundamentally different from any other time in the opportunity which it offers us for obedient and faithful discipleship.

EUCHARIST AS A TEST CASE

I noted earlier that many Christian rites and rituals have their counterparts in pagan antiquity and modern secular culture; and it can be useful at this juncture to consider the eucharist as a representative of this apparent reciprocity.

The logic of eating together is well known to us as a means of reinforcing the cohesion and sense of belonging to family or clan or wider community. Familiar colloquialisms make the point: the French live to eat, while the English eat to live; *in vino veritas*; mealtime is when youngsters sit down to continue eating. To eat together, to drink from the same cup—these are symbols of solidarity very ancient and very modern. But I have also wanted to show that whatever the apparent correspondence between various secular and Christian rites, Christians understand liturgy to be an activity which is fundamentally shaped, not by its correspondence with "natural" rituals, but by the story of the life, death, resurrection, and ascension of Jesus. What this means for us is that rather than understanding our rites and rituals to be naturally derived from human attempts to make connections between ourselves and God, we understand Christian liturgy as the means by which we are habituated to the heart, and brought into the life, of God.

Natural rites undertake to locate God within our lives; Christian liturgy locates our lives within the life of God, particularly as we have been given to know this in the life of Jesus Christ. So a point which I have emphasized before can be reiterated here: Christian liturgy is recapitulation of the whole life of Jesus; and it is in relation to this recapitulation, this retelling, of that story that we are able to locate our lives within the life of God.

It is therefore a matter of some historical interest that, as anthropologists tell us, common meals are a part of every culture we know anything at all about, from the most ancient and primitive to the most modern and sophisticated. Indeed, it has proven such an obvious connection to some that they have associated (I think mistakenly) eating and drinking in these natural histories with Christian eucharist. It was frequently believed by our ancestors that to eat meat was to ingest the qualities of the animal whose meat it was. So eat gazelle in order to improve footspeed; or eat ox to gain physical strength; or eat lion to acquire courage. And it was similar with drinking: gladiators, as I indicated earlier, are reported to have quaffed the still-warm blood of their victims in order to transfer to themselves the source of the vanquished's strength or courage. I reckon this is why some might "quite naturally" ask: is this not precisely analogous to what Christians understand themselves to be doing when they receive the bread and wine of Holy Communion? The short answer is "no"; but we will need to give a fuller account of why Christians cannot embrace such natural phenomena as cognate with our liturgical and sacramental life.

We know that the early church organized its life—not just its liturgical life, but its *life*—around the Sunday eucharist. There were, of course, weekday liturgies; but those who were unable, for whatever reason, to participate in these worship services were expected to be present without fail on Sundays.[22]

So far as we know, the Sunday eucharist was simple and straightforward. It incorporated the weekday liturgy of the word, which concluded with the peace, and thereafter continued with the *anaphora*. *Anaphora* literally means the deliberate repetition of words or phrases, and signifies that the general form of the eucharistic service was the common repetition of Jesus' institution of this sacrament. The iterated phrases derived from Matthew 26:26–28 and are recapitulated in 1 Corinthians 11:23–26:

> *Now as they were eating, Jesus took bread, and blessed, and broke it, and gave it to the disciples and said, "Take, eat; this is my body." And he took the cup, and when he had given thanks, he gave it to them, saying, "Drink of it, all of you; for this is my blood of the covenant, which is poured out for many for the forgiveness of sins."*

We need not detail here the prayers and practices and canons which came to be incorporated, over the centuries, into the eucharistic liturgy. What we do need to emphasize is that, in the early Christian communities which were the pre-Constantinian church, the centrality of the eucharistic liturgy was clearly acknowledged. But the establishment of Christianity as the official state religion by Constantine brought, as we would now expect, the routinization of the liturgy and its appropriation as a means to ends other than its own. And this, in turn, led to domestication of the sacrament so that increasingly it became, as it were, the church's possession.

Two developments, which turned out to be complementary, appear now to have been occurring somewhat simultaneously over several centuries. On the one hand, and taking seriously 1 Corinthians 11:27–30 (in which Paul admonishes self-examination in order to avoid communicating unworthily, without discernment, and to judgment), clergy undertook to persuade the new Constantinian converts (and their heirs) to take seriously the eucharist. So "eucharistic disciplines," which consisted largely of confession and fasting, were imposed. But the somewhat unexpected result of these requirements was that the laity chose to avoid this dangerous process altogether, believing that it was preferable to do without receiving communion than to risk eating and drinking to one's eternal damnation.

On the other hand, the sacrament became (perhaps understandably) more and more subject to priestcraft; and, in turn, the rite came more and more to be something which the church, through its clergy, did *for* the people rather than an offering which the whole people of God owned and proffered to the Lord. Eventually it developed that mass could be celebrated at times when only a priest and a server were present; and, in later times, it became permitted for priests to say private masses. Meanwhile, the emergence of monasticism encouraged the development of a two-tiered doctrine of piety in which monks and other clergy performed liturgical actions on behalf of the people who, engaged as they were in secular pursuits like farming and commerce, were too busy to perform these actions for themselves.

By the Middle Ages, the people's worship consisted largely in being present at mass as observers. That the liturgy itself was increasingly embellished with ceremonies and actions which exalted the mystery of the mass surely provided an impressive devotional setting for remembering Christ's sacrifice. But processions of the sacrament, inaudible priestly prayers, elevation of the host and chalice at the words of institution, abandonment of lay participation in the chalice, and similar observances tended over time to become more important than participation in the liturgy and reception of the sacrament by the faithful. By the end of the fifteenth century, so many of the laity had virtually stopped receiving communion that legislation was thought necessary in order to get the people to communicate at least once a year.

Robert Cabie, who is professor of liturgy in the faculty of theology at Toulouse, has written:

> At the beginning of the sixteenth century many pastors felt that renewal in the Eucharistic practices of the faithful was a pressing necessity. The Church had to react against popular customs that were often infected by superstition or, in any case, so focused on superficial and secondary aspects of the Eucharist as to make impossible any real participation in the Mass."[23]

The historical circumstances clearly support Fr. Cabie's assessment. For coincident with this pastoral concern among Roman Catholics were the origins of the Protestant Reformation, accounting for why the Council of Trent (1514–63) thereafter found itself trying to cope with both schism and internal reform.

What has been widely described as the reformers' "attack on the mass," however, was neither an attack upon the mass per se nor a repudiation of it. In fact, all the sixteenth-century Protestant reformers—with the conspicuous exception of Zwingli—clearly supported offering the eucharist as the normal and customary Sunday service of the church. What the reformers generally objected to was the developed practice of *noncommunicating attendance* at public masses, which they believed conveyed false teachings about the sacrifice of the mass. Moreover, all of them—this time including Zwingli—taught that the celebration of the eucharist should always be attended with the general communion of all the faithful present. So what is so often mislabeled as the reformers' "attack on the mass" was actually a set of charges directed toward the abuses which had come to be associated with private communions, and the kinds of institutional domestication (as, for example, the sale of indulgences) which were associated with these practices.

This helps to explain why Luther instituted a number of changes that he understood not as providing a new eucharistic rite, but as purifying the medieval Roman rite of mistaken accretions. He omitted all of the private prayers, for example, as well as a large number of variable elements (such as offertory verses, prayers, and collects). Perhaps his most radical liturgical deletion was that portion of the eucharistic prayer which was said inaudibly by the priest. He also instituted a sermon to be part of every eucharist, together with vernacular hymns and (in 1525) a German text for those who did not understand Latin. In Geneva, Calvin had instituted a rite very closely resembling the German one; and both he and Luther directed that the people receive the communion at the chancel or table. So, far from repudiating the eucharist, the Protestant reformers of the sixteenth century—again, excepting Zwingli—affirmed it as the church's central liturgy. The changes they made were believed to rid the sacrament of unsupportable accretions and return it to its primitive simplicity and meaning.[24]

Reforming efforts among Roman Catholics were simultaneously under way at Trent, and doctrinal decisions from the council were accompanied by decrees which were intended to purify and rehabilitate the mass. Thus, according to Cabie,

> the Mass was to be celebrated "with interior cleanness and purity of heart
> and with a devotion that finds outward expression"; superstition was to
> be eliminated, as were undue monetary exactions, secular music, etc.[25]

Preparation and publication of a new missal, which would incorporate critical revisions of the mass in light of these developments, was left, however, to the Pope; and in 1570, Pope Pius V promulgated the revised Roman missal. As with many repatriation endeavors, this one appears to have been less immediately successful than it was in laying the groundwork for future reform. As a matter of fact, various eucharistic reforms have been continuously introduced over the ensuing four hundred-plus years, culminating with Pius X's decree on frequent, and even daily, communion in 1907; Pius XII's encyclical *Mediator Dei* in 1947; John XXIII's convoking of the Second Vatican Council; and Paul VI's *Missale Romanum* of 1970, which implemented certain moves proposed by Vatican II, including the duty of all pastors to deliver a homily on Sundays and the use of the vernacular for certain parts of masses.[26]

I have rehearsed this bit of history because I believe that there is a profound sense in which all of this energy, poured into purifying the eucharist and keeping it unsullied, is the church's effort to reaffirm that eucharist is an essential means which God provides for us to participate in his life. While eucharist always retains some correspondence with "natural rituals," such as eating and drinking, it is not precisely analogous to these rites because, as I have wanted to show, "natural rituals" undertake to locate God within our lives. Eucharist, however, means to locate our lives within the life of God as we have been given to know this in the life of Jesus.[27]

The biblical rubric which commands Jesus' disciples to keep the eucharist is "do this in remembrance of me." "Do this," we are commanded. "Do what?" we ask in response. "Do the sign; but only as a means of the thing signified. The eucharist is a sacrifice; but we do not offer it. Christ offers it; we respond to it." *Anamnesis* is the Greek word which we translate as "remembrance." But *anamnesis* is not a simple memorial or reminiscence; and we do not celebrate the Holy Communion in order now to remember Jesus in the sense that we think of him, reflect on him, or allow our minds to conjure an image of him. In remembering Jesus we do not recall him to our minds through an act of memory; in remembering Jesus we do not recall him through our own effort and determination. To remember Jesus is not something we do, but something that is done to and for us by the one who is remembered.

I have sometimes found it useful to hyphenate the words which are commonly used to express this mystery as reminder of that fact: re-member, re-call, re-capitulate, re-concile, re-constitute, and so on. And, of course, all of these together point to the great penumbra-word re-ligion, which means literally to re-ligate, or re-bind together, what once was sundered, estranged, divorced. The fundamental anomaly is that any two disciples should not be in communion. The grand mystery is that God has re-claimed us.

This is an occasion for thanksgiving, which is what "eucharist" means. In eucharist the church makes an offering; it offers its thanks, its communal sacrifice, its giving itself away, its losing control in order to be faithful and obedient to the God "who so loved the world that he gave his only begotten Son" to the end that all who believe in him should not perish, but have everlasting life. This is how we become one with God, and one with one another; this is how we are re-membered to God, and to one another; this is how the church becomes the body of Christ. And this is why eucharist is the most significant moral act of the church. In the eucharist we have our unity with—and with one another in—God. We have eaten an eschatological meal; a new age, a new history, has really dawned with Jesus' presence among us; and we long for unity and peace and fellowship between and among all of God's creation. Because we have a foretaste of all that in this holy sacrament, we wait expectantly "till we all come to the measure of the stature of the completeness of the Messiah." Somewhere, years ago, I read and thought how right William Temple was to observe that what none but utopians dare hope for ought to be present existential reality for Christians.

To remember is, literally, to be re-minded; it is to have the one remembered come again to our minds and take control, as it were, of our thoughts and passions. Far from something we do to and for ourselves, to remember Jesus is to be out of control to his presence. And I reckon that this is why we do not celebrate Holy Communion in order to memorialize Jesus. We celebrate the Holy Communion to be formed into a people to whom Jesus can come again; we celebrate the Holy Communion to signify that we are such a people to whom he can come again; we celebrate the Holy Communion to acknowledge ourselves as a people who welcome Jesus' coming again.[28]

I find it useful to recall that the church had this sacrament, and celebrated it, before it had the Gospels. This suggests to me (1) that the Gospels (that is, the scriptural accounts of Jesus' birth, life, ministry, death, resurrection, ascension, and so on) are better read through the lens of the eucharist than the other way around, and (2) that worship antedates theologizing, whether primitive or sophisticated. So it is not that form-critical and historical-critical and other interpretive methods are wrong in themselves. The problem with these and other hermeneutics occurs, I believe, when they claim too much, when they suppose that they possess the exclusive means for correct interpretation of the text. This is essentially the same problem which occurs when the church abandons theology to the academy, and theologizing gets separated from worship; it is not an idea of God but God's presence, and the submission of one's whole being to it in worship, that counts.

It may be astonishing, in the last decade of the twentieth century, to appreciate that the practice of noncommunication was common to Protestants and Catholics alike until the reforms of Pius X in the first decade of this century made the practice of weekly communion customary for Roman Catholics. The Book of Common Prayer of 1979 made celebration of the Holy Eucharist normative for the Sunday service of Episcopalians; and there is evidence of this rite's increasing frequency among several Protestant denominations. What appears to be missing from this surge of recovering weekly communion is the accompanying eucharistic discipline, without which the likelihood is great that this sacrament will undergo another period of routinization and trivialization.

Overall, our brief review might show (one more time!) that we often know better than we do. The rehearsal of the Roman Catholic aspect of this story has shown how the centrality of eucharist for the faithful has been recently reaffirmed. In addition, Luther, Calvin, and the sixteenth-century Anglican reformers all considered that the eucharist was the proper Christian service for Sunday, the Feast of the Resurrection. And even Zwingli, who called for observance of the Lord's Supper (only) four times a year, thought that by doing this the necessity of the supper for Christians would be reclaimed, and its proper reinstitution in the life of the church would be reestablished.

One way to describe what all this comes to is to say that the eucharist, along with the disciplines appropriate to it, is not an option or an adjunct but a necessity for Christians. This is so for at least two reasons. The first, although by itself probably not the foremost, is that Jesus commanded it.[29] To say that Jesus commanded it has authority for us because we already acknowledge Jesus to be God's Christ. For it is in that anterior acknowledgment of who Jesus is that what Jesus says to us and does for us acquires its special significance. This is why I say that a "command" of Jesus is alone probably not the preeminent reason that we Christians affirm the eucharist to be a necessity for us. Acknowledging who he is commands our submission, our devotion and obedience, to what he charges and directs us to do. So when he offers bread and the cup, identifies these elements with his body and blood given for the remission of our sins, and instructs us to take these gifts in remembrance of him, thereby proclaiming the benefits of his death until he comes again—this is *sacramentum* and we are obedient; Jesus commands it, and we do it—because we acknowledge him to be the Christ, God's anointed, our Savior, the inaugurator of the new age of the kingdom of God.

The second reason takes a somewhat related, but nevertheless slightly different, tack. Alasdair MacIntyre has argued, as I have noted earlier, that modern society lacks a shared tradition of common values and notions about our nature and our true end. In the absence of such a consensually held set of beliefs, MacIntyre thinks it not strange that we are unable to resolve moral dispute in a rational manner. It is, he says, precisely the presence of such a shared tradition and set of common notions about ourselves, our nature, and our true end which is requisite to any rational resolution of moral dispute. Conversely, if we do not agree on fundamental notions about who we are and who we are intended to be, what shape our destiny and purpose should take, we cannot possibly agree on what is good, right, true, appropriate for us to do. In short, we cannot agree on what to do until we can agree on who we are. Mary Douglas expressed a similar recognition when she wrote, "One of the gravest problems of our day is the lack of commitment to common symbols. . . . But more mysterious is a wide-spread, explicit rejection of rituals as such. Ritual has become a bad word signifying empty conformity."[30]

My suspicion is that, at least since Immanuel Kant and John Stuart Mill, the public necessity of shared traditions and symbols has been progressively eroded because such a requirement conflicts with the concept of autonomous individuals who need to be free from every interference external to themselves in order to pursue their own private interests. We ought to be clear that one of the principal functions of Christian liturgy contradicts that central tenet of liberal individualism. Christian liturgy is directed, as Calvin insisted, *soli Deo gloria*. On account of this, it also means to form people into a particular kind of community, and to offer this community an identity and self-understanding of themselves as the people of God. In Luther's preface to his *Deutsche Messe*, he made a similar point when he argued that orders of service do not exist for themselves but for our sake, in order to make Christians out of us: "the chief and greatest aim of any Service," he wrote, "is to preach and teach God's Word."[31] In and through the liturgy God creates and forms a community of people who, participating in this salvation history, discover themselves and their lives to be situated and located accordingly.

WHERE TO LOOK TO FIND OUT WHO WE ARE

All of us know the importance of identity. Americans know who they are in relation to the rest of the world; southerners know who they are in relation to westerners and easterners, and especially Yankees. Christians similarly need to know who they are. How do we learn these identities? Ordinarily we learn them by participating in rituals and ceremonies and rites which convey to us an inherited set of common values and shared traditions. We learn them by respecting the Stars and Bars, honoring Robert E. Lee, and singing "Dixie"; by eating matzos and gefilte fish, wearing a yarmulke, and observing the Sabbath; by learning the catechism and hearing the Gospel, by being baptized and receiving communion, by praying without ceasing and living a life of holiness.

It is not that, as a society, we have rejected ritual and ceremony and symbol and rite; what is disturbing is that Christians have been accommodated to secularity, that Christians have embraced cultural myths and symbols which are descriptively accurate of who they are. What the gospel offers is, in one sense, merely another way; but "merely another way" denigrates the gospel because, for Christians, there *is* no other way. The gospel, for Christians, is emphatically not one among many alternatives in a game of multiple choice. It claims to be *the* way, *the* truth, *the* precondition of life itself. So the second reason which I offer as to why the eucharist is necessary for Christians is that it trains and forms us to be the people of the new age, the *laos theou*, a community of shared commitment and devotion to God as we have been given to know God in Jesus Christ.

When Thomas Aquinas appropriated the wisdom of Aristotle for Christian theological ethics, he helped us to understand that although human actions are not instinctively and automatically ordered to the good, they can be directed there by well-disposed *habits*. Habits are skills which, learned over time, enable a subject to actualize his or her potential. Athletic metaphors come immediately to mind; but training for the moral life is equally suited to the role of habits. While habits do not guarantee that one will achieve his or her appropriate end, they nevertheless constitute an essential means for perfecting one's various powers and potentials. So it is not surprising that habitual practice is among the prominent ways in which both belief and behavior get engendered and formed. Sometimes students, when confronted by the necessity to preside at a service, or conduct one of their church's rites, have said to me: "What can I tell these people? How can I minister to them? I'm not too sure what I believe. I haven't sorted out all that I believe about marriage, or baptism, or death, or eucharist, or resurrection." My typical response has been, "Just tell them what the gospel says, what the church believes." Then they sometimes say, "But I'm really not sure that I believe all that." Then I give them the same advice my best teachers gave me: "Say it again and again and again and again, until you do believe it." It is the testimony of unnamed millions of our forebears in the faith that regular communication at the eucharist does this, too. It is the habitual practice of receiving the body and blood of Jesus which reconstitutes us in God's image; it is in exposing our hunger for God that we may be filled with the spiritual food of God's presence, so that "we may dwell in him and he in us."

Every philosophical and theological ethics, of course, construes the world in a particular way, and Christian liturgical and moral theology is not exceptional to this general rule. The question for Christians, therefore, becomes: how are the ways in which we construe the world congruent and coherent with the Gospel story, and not with some other? Can we get straight about what "Christian" may mean substantively as a modifier of words like theology, ethics, and liturgy? Where can we look to learn what it means to be a disciple of Jesus Christ? The most serious problem with much, if not most, "Christian ethics" these days tends to be the extent to which the adjective fails to norm the noun. So the first task of Christian ethics is not a matter of learning how to *do* something, how to *act*— although casuistry, as we will see, is an indispensable aspect of a holy life. The first task is learning how to *see*, how to *discern*, how to *penetrate* and *plumb*. Only thereafter is Christian ethics the disciplined effort to train us in the use of those skills which are necessary for us to be the kind of people we are. For similar reasons, the first task of the church is just to be the church, and not something else.

The liturgy trains us to see, to discern ourselves, the church, and the world—indeed all of life and reality—as formed by the Gospel. Because the liturgy is formed by the story of Israel, and the story of the life, ministry, death, resurrection, and ascension of Jesus, its power forms us in its image, after its assumptions, according to its norms. How this happens is easily illustrated by how we attend to the word "God." In the liturgy, "God" is not a theory, or a concept, or a principle, or an idea; in the liturgy, "God" is a *name*, and the only way to learn about that name is by immersion in a tradition which re-tells the story of Abraham, Isaac, Jacob, Jesus, and Paul; of Sarah, Rebekah, Rachel, and Mary; and of countless others who have kept the faith, and by their faithful discipline re-membered the hearers of that story to that name.

Part of the business of construal has to do with choosing what to privilege as real. My bias, as I reckon has become clear by now, is for wholeness rather than fragmentation, for completeness rather than compartmentalization. I believe that what signifies and contributes to wholeness and completeness is what counts as real. So if one of the severe problems with contemporary American Christianity and its churches is a kind of moral and liturgical schizophrenia, in which life-in-the-real-world is divorced from life-in-a-holy-world, the chapters which follow, and which attempt to show how liturgy and ethics are not two but one, might be part of that needed healing.

CHAPTER THREE

GATHERED FOR CONFESSION AND WITNESS

WE GATHER TOGETHER

Historically, Christians have assembled together, in good trinitarian fashion, for three reasons: to worship the Father, to be nourished by the Son, and to be equipped by the Holy Spirit—all for faithful witness to the gospel in the world. Commenting on the postcommunion prayer in the Prayer Book of 1549, Massey H. Shepherd, Jr., wrote that it is both "one of the most remarkable summaries of doctrine to be found in all the formularies of the Prayer Book" and "a felicitous translation of the worshiping congregation from the mysteries of the sanctuary to the 'good works' of Christian service in the world's life." "It relates," he said, "the sacrament of the altar to the tasks of everyday living."[1] This is what worship, whether private or public, means to do in the Christian tradition.

The modern vernacular successor to this prayer concludes the celebration of "The Holy Communion: Rite Two" in the Book of Common Prayer (1979), and expresses the same doxology and supplication:

> *Almighty and everliving God, we thank you for feeding us with the spiritual food of the most precious Body and Blood of your Son our Savior Jesus Christ; and for assuring us in these holy mysteries that we are living members of the Body of your Son, and heirs of your eternal kingdom. And now, Father, send us out to do the work you have given us to do, to love and serve you as faithful witnesses of Christ our Lord. To him, to you, and to the Holy Spirit, be honor and glory, now and for ever. Amen.*[2]

Here, explicitly and deliberately, the gathered community feeds on this "spiritual food" and receives "these holy mysteries," and is sent out to display them in the world as "faithful witnesses" to holy living and holy dying.

The initial provisioning for corporate worship calls for gathering the faithful. In the nature of the case, this is an action both deliberate and necessary inasmuch as we are typically scattered abroad in both our moral commitments and our several residential communities. So it is important, at the outset, simply to acknowledge that coming together for corporate worship is neither accidental nor serendipitous, but resolute and intentional and focused.

To eyes that can see, it will be crystal clear that this assembling of the people *for* worship is neither something we do *before* worship nor something we do which is *different from* worship itself. It is not a preliminary to the main event; it is not a prelude, or a preamble, or a preface, or a warmup for the big game. It is, to extend the athletics metaphor, rather like the opening tip in basketball or the kickoff in football or the faceoff in hockey or the first shot struck in a round of golf: these are actions ingredient to the games themselves.

Just so, gathering is ingredient to worship. Although corporate worship requires and presupposes gathering and convening of the people, the action signified by assembly is itself constituent of corporate worship; it signifies who we are and why we have come together here. Accordingly, gathering is a moral act.

In one way or another, all of the Christian liturgies with which I am familiar take account, either from the very outset or quite soon thereafter, of the fact that we are gathered out of many places into this one place and out of many diverse loyalties to focus singly on the one God who is made known to us in Jesus Christ. In the United Methodist Church's "basic pattern of Sunday worship," the very first liturgical action is called simply "Gathering." In liturgies of the Catholic tradition, following the acclamation which ushers in the service, there is typically a prayer called the "collect." In this instance, name and function coincide inasmuch as this prayer is designed to do precisely what its name implies: it collects the faithful and focuses their attention on the reason(s) for their having come together. In the Episcopal Church, the customary Sunday service offers both a "Collect for Purity" and "The Collect of the Day." One of these establishes an overall orientation toward God,[3] and the other takes account of the particular occasion as this is signified in the church year.

So gathering and collecting the people for worship marks this assembly and this action as distinct and different from day-to-day routine. It names time according to the church's calendar; and this alone is a moral act, for it acknowledges that it is good, appropriate, right, fitting, desirable, to be gathered together *here* rather than being dispersed to other places. But there is more than this to the difference which gathering makes.

After his baptism, and John the Baptist's arrest, Jesus came to Galilee and began to preach. His earliest proclamation, in Mark 1:14–20, announced that the time was fulfilled and that the kingdom of God is at hand. Those who listened to Jesus' preaching were summoned to repent, to believe the gospel, and to follow him. And all of this was marked by a clear and acknowledged urgency to move from one place and circumstance to another.[4] Similarly, when the twelve disciples were summoned, Jesus "called to him those whom he desired; and they came to him" (Mark 3:13). These and similar passages constitute the canonical basis for collecting the people of God. Jesus called his special and particular people together; and we, like the first disciples, leave everything in order to come together, to gather, as his folk.

Of course, it does not happen so dramatically on the customary Sunday morning that we abruptly abandon everything and go to follow Jesus. More likely, we have anticipated the Sunday routine of a later-than-usual rising (unless we are off to early mass), a leisurely breakfast with the Sunday edition of the newspaper, and "getting ready" (i.e., dressing) for church. There is a kind of relaxed and measured resolution about the customary Sunday morning, purposive but not urgent. All the same, I believe that the paradigm of Jesus' call to his first disciples, with its disruption of the usual and customary and its insistent summons and exigency, is important to keep before us because some day just such a preempting call may come to us, and we will need to be alert to hear it. Habituation, for all the virtue which attends it, can also blunt initiative and make it difficult for Jesus' call to get through the protective shield of domesticity. Jesus nevertheless summons us to follow him, to be his disciples, and this command never fails to surprise us, to find us unprepared for it, to catch us off-guard. Domestication deadens the gospel's declaration and call, but the Word cannot be bound and its surprise enlivens us.

What we customarily leave when we gather for worship, both figuratively and literally, is "home," with all of its symbolic attachments of heart and hearth, comfort and security, biological connections and familiar surroundings. Acknowledging this helps us to understand that "church" is a community unlike any other. It is neither defined nor identified by its confirmation of the social, economic, political, familial, or other domestic presuppositions of the presiding secular society. It does not exist in order to underwrite "the way things are." It is not indigenous or congenital in the human condition. Instead, we are taught that the church is an eschatological community whose creation and identity are located in Jesus Christ. It is therefore a people in unity because it is one in Christ. I would reckon that, if not all, then certainly most of us feel that to understand ourselves as this kind of people is strange, and in some ways unnatural. To understand ourselves as this kind of people is plainly not innate or hereditary. All the same, these are the ways that the gospel characterizes this community, which is differentiated not by its diversity and dissimilarity but by its unity in Christ. In order to have this self-understanding, because it is not a natural endowment, we have to learn it, to receive it, to be trained in it.

According to the New Testament, what makes us one people is our unity in Christ. Galatians 3:26–28 describes it in this way:

> *For in Christ Jesus you are all children of God through faith. As many of you as were baptized into Christ have clothed yourselves with Christ. There is no longer Jew or Greek, there is no longer slave or free, there is no longer male or female; for all of you are one in Christ Jesus.*

Now this is plainly peculiar as a "sociology of religion," if not in first-century Palestine, then surely in twentieth-century North America, where the churches are ordinarily and unmistakably homogeneous. Typically, these churches are not places where people go to have their differences dissolved by a common faith. They are instead usually enclaves where people go to have their similarities confirmed. And this accounts for why U.S. churches are among the most, if not the most, segregated establishments in the entire society these days. Not only racially, but politically and economically and socially and educationally as well, these are ordinarily fairly conventional and domesticated places where "birds of a feather flock together."

Gathering the people, collecting the faithful, launches the liturgy as a reminder that we are called out of this kind of world to be, by the mercy of Christ, the baptized sons and daughters of God, among whom there is neither slave nor free, Jew nor Greek, male nor female. This, for Christians, is descriptively accurate of who we are truly meant to be.[5] So entailed in assembling and convening the people of God are the most important sociological assumptions about the church and Christian ethics. Consider, for example, that Christian ethics does not begin in commandments, moral axioms, codes of conduct, or universal principles. Christian ethics begins in (1) the particularity of the gospel, (2) a call to repentance and belief, (3) a new birth/perspective/point of view, and (4) the constitution of the newly baptized as church. This sequencing—or, as I have previously called it, getting the horse before the cart—is crucial in order to make it clear that the sociology of Christian ethics does *not* start with a group of people who, in their natural gregariousness, generate the conditions of their being gathered (and staying) together.

The people who practice Christian ethics are thus a particular people, who have a particular identity and self-understanding. They are a particular people because they acknowledge and affirm a particular story which instructs and forms them into the kind of people they are. It is a particular people with a particular mission and purpose and reason for being. It is the "gathered church."[6]

OUT OF THE WORLD

But being such a particular people has not been without its problems, whether in or out of the church. Can the "gathered church" be "in the world"? Must the church be the world's adversary? Is it necessary that church and world be separated as well as distinguished? Is it the case that the church is basically the same as an assembly of "nice people," people of goodwill, wherever they are found? Is sitting hip-to-haunch, cheek-to-jowl, around a trestle board in a church basement for a potluck supper the same stuff as Holy Communion, only folksier?

I want to maintain, with Karl Barth, that there is no independent, natural Christian ethics. The church is called into existence by the gospel of Jesus Christ; Christian ethics derives from that gospel and from the church which it births. And so in a general sense, the task of Christian ethics is to say, as cogently and clearly and coherently as possible, what this contingency means.

I am aware, of course, that the task of Christian ethics is also to say what bearing the gospel may have upon the contingencies of "the world"; but this is a task which cannot be supposed to have first priority. If there is a problem with Christian ethics, it is indicated, as my colleague Hauerwas has put it, by the extent to which the adjective fails to control the noun. I only add that this is not a novel problem, or one limited to modernity. Measuring the success or failure of the adjective to control the noun is always *the* problem for Christian ethics. I entirely agree with this proposition, and I believe that a way to begin to remedy the typical inversion of priorities is to understand the dependency of Christian ethics upon Christian faith, prayer, worship. If we can get straight about *Christian* ethics, it will be a shorter and more confident step for us toward Christian *ethics*.

So the church is not and need not always be in an adversarial relation with the "world." All the same, when there is cooperation between church and world, that cooperation will be undertaken on the church's terms because it is the church which knows the truth about the world's being and destiny, a truth that the world refuses in its freedom to acknowledge and affirm.

Not all historical typologies have appreciated the importance of this anteriority—but Ernst Troeltsch's monumental study, *The Social Teaching of the Christian Churches*,[7] clearly moves in the desired direction. Troeltsch examined the development of Christian social teaching in order to assess its impact on the social problems of early-twentieth-century Europe. It was his belief that he could show the significance of Christian faith for the pressing problems of his day by describing and analyzing the historical development of Christian doctrine as this had been promulgated by prominent teachers who were influential in their own time. His *bête noire* was the materialist philosophy of Karl Marx, and his project was to show that religion, and specifically Christianity, can be related to social processes without having to be derived from them.[8]

So, emergent from an impressive historical rehearsal of Christian history, Troeltsch proposed three principal types of sociological development of Christian thought: the church type, the sect type, and the mysticism type. Each of these, he believed, transcends historical contingency in its genesis, but each one also embodies particular features which bespeak the relevance of the gospel to everyday social, political, and economic life.

Here is his description of the various types:

The Church is an institution which has been endowed with grace and salvation as the result of the work of Redemption; it is able to receive the masses, and to adjust itself to the world, because, to a certain extent, it can afford to ignore the need for subjective holiness for the sake of the objective treasures of grace and of redemption.

The sect is a voluntary society, composed of strict and definite Christian believers bound to each other by the fact that all have experienced "the new birth." These "believers" live apart from the world, are limited to small groups, emphasize the law instead of grace, and in varying degrees within their own circle set up the Christian order, based on love; all this is done in preparation for an expectation of the coming Kingdom of God.

Mysticism means that the world of ideas which had hardened into formal worship and doctrine is transformed into a purely personal and inward experience; this leads to the formation of groups on a purely personal basis, with no permanent form, which also tend to weaken the significance of forms of worship, doctrine, and the historical element.[9]

Despite the fact that the mysticism type functions, for all intents and purposes, largely as a refuge from social engagement, Troeltsch honors it as a "welcome complement to the Church and the Sects."[10] Nevertheless, as a religious type, its radical individualism forecloses social expression. So Troeltsch's examination and analysis have to be undertaken chiefly with reference to the church and sect types. Thus, for example, while there is no gathering into a terrestrial mystical communion, there is a collecting or belonging to the church and sect types. This happens in interestingly different ways. For example, whereas the church type routinely baptizes infants and thereby imputes membership, the voluntary membership of the sect type enjoins believer's baptism.

Moreover, as regards relations between Christianity and the world, the church type embraces secular institutions under the general rubric of "natural law" while the sect type rejects (or at best only tolerates) secular institutions as part of the sinful order. Or, considering attitudes toward asceticism, Troeltsch claims that whereas the church type regards asceticism as a method of acquiring virtue and heightening piety by repressing the senses, the asceticism of the sect type is the simple principle of detachment from the world and refusal to take part in secular affairs (such as swearing in a court of law or paying taxes or participating in war).

These peculiar marks of church and sect are not always evident in late-twentieth-century expressions of these religious phenomena, particularly when "religion" is a more broadly inclusive term of reference than it is in Troeltsch's vocabulary. For example, North American sects such as Theosophy, Christian Science, Ethical Culture, Spiritism, and Moral Rearmament, together with Seventh-Day Adventism, Pentecostalism, Jehovah's Witnesses, and Latter Day Saints, have grown by leaps and bounds in the second half of the twentieth century while mainline Protestant and Catholic churches have experienced dramatic losses in membership. And in the 1990s it is clear that South American Christianity is experiencing a similar disaffection from traditional Roman Catholicism in favor of sectarian, not mainline, Protestantism.

Indeed, a paradox of the twentieth century is that it has been a time of both the greatest growth of the ecumenical movement and the fastest expansion of sects and cults which further fragment Christians. Not unlike their predecessors in Baptist, Quaker, and Methodist groups, these are the modern culturally, religiously, economically, and politically marginalized and disinherited who find no place for themselves in churches of the respectable and circumspect middle class.

These people are generally suspicious of educated clergy, formal ritual, and printed service leaflets; and they tend rather toward emotional freedom, which frequently suggests a naive supernaturalism. They are, more often than not, biblical fundamentalists who believe in the verbal inspiration and literal inerrancy of scripture. They are frequently advocates of millennialism, perhaps as a compensatory mechanism which rewards poverty in this life with an eternity spent walking on streets of gold; and God is regarded as terrible in wrath to people of "this world" but inexpressibly generous and gracious to the elect. Ethics is reducible to codes of conduct which are legalistic and rigid; vices are chiefly the practices of the opulent and decadent rich, and virtues are simple manners (such as honesty, thrift, abstinence, and simplicity) exalted to the position of moral ideals. The validation of religious experience resides in emotional reactions to direct contact with God, reactions which include speaking in tongues, visions, prophecies, and second and third blessings. Overarching and undergirding all else is an insatiable craving for absolute and certain authority that permits no ambiguity in morality or spirituality.

Whatever the differences between earlier and these later religious organizations and institutions—and they are numerous and impressive— they have their origin in a common source, which Troeltsch identifies as follows:

> The worship of Christ constitutes the centre of the Christian organization, and it creates Christian dogma. . . . All the ideas which have been borrowed from philosophy and mythology are only used as a means of expressing ideas which have grown up out of the inner necessity of this Christian community for worship.[11]

To Troeltsch's three historical types we might have added a modern fourth—namely, the peculiar American phenomenon of "denominations," and undertaken to show how this type has developed its own idiosyncratic responses to the several issues by which Troeltsch distinguishes church and sect from each other. Alternatively, or additionally, we could have rehearsed the familiar typology of H. Richard Niebuhr's *Christ and Culture*;[12] but this would tend, again, to underscore and thereby emphasize centripetal rather than centrifugal forces. With more profit I believe that we could be reminded of the wisdom in Niebuhr's "concluding unscientific postscript," in which he tries valiantly to balance individual responsibility with sociality and cultural kinship.

The issue really is not whether Christ is *against* or *for* culture; this way of putting the matter is too reductionistic, too simplistic. God is clearly for the world; Christians believe that the world is God's world, that God will not abandon the world, and that the destiny of the world is subject to God's sovereignty. And this suggests that the real issue for a gathered church focuses on how we are to make discriminating judgments about the church in the world, and the world in the church.

The fact of the matter, of course, is that the church is *in the world*, and has its life among those who exercise their freedom not to have their lives ordered by God. The real and urgent question for the church from the beginning is how it can be *in* but not *of* that environment. Answering this question depends, in the first of it, on a clear and vivid (and, hopefully, correct) understanding of the kind of people the church is meant to be. So the first question for this people is not what to do but who are we.

Typologies are attempts to show what kinds (or types) of people are displayed by certain kinds of actions and commitments. Gathering the people in worship exhibits a particular kind of folk. Indeed, a close look at gathering reveals that it is a hermeneutical act by which this gathered people learn about themselves. In this process they are enabled (1) to see themselves as God intends them to be—that is, as free to be witnesses to the gospel—and (2) to see the world aright—that is, to see it as God's world and yet be free to be blind and deaf and thereby not to bear witness to the gospel. Far from yielding an adversarial relationship between church and world, this kind of functional analysis suggests instead a church/world dialectic which is both complementary and antagonistic.

The thesis would go something like this: the church (i.e., those who exercise their freedom to believe in God and have their lives ordered by God) is in the world, converting the world to Christianity. And the antithesis would go something like this: the world (i.e., those who exercise their freedom not to believe in God or to have their lives ordered accordingly) is in the church, converting the church to worldliness, to secularism. The synthesis is familiar enough: Christians are a people who live in this world by the power of the world to come.

Owing to sensibilities quickened by two thousand years of Christian history, the thesis may appear to be more readily believable than its counterpart; but there is increasingly ample evidence of the manifold ways in which the world proselytizes the church, persuading it to embrace secular rather than ecclesial values. I think, for example, of how patriotism functions as Christianity in a political mode, of how capitalism acts as Christianity in an economic mode, of how unembarrassed assertions of individualism and autonomy operate as Christianity in a sociological mode.

I confess that I also think of the displacement of ultimate allegiance to God by fanatic loyalties to things like athletic teams. In the university where I teach, it is no secret that for many students everything else in this life is subordinate to the basketball team. Whether the team wins or loses is important, of course, but whether they take the court is the crucial aspect; so the essential thing, to paraphrase Descartes, is *nous jouons, donc sommes* ("we play, therefore we are"). You may therefore not be utterly surprised to learn that sometimes, when asked by visitors to the campus "Where does the university worship?" I have felt diabolically constrained to direct them to the basketball arena. *Mea culpa; mea maxima culpa*! That this question is usually put to me in the shadow of the magnificent gothic chapel which presides over the center of the campus only confirms my sadness and sense of dread at this state of affairs.

Careful examination of Protestant denominations reveals that real differences among them derive from worldly values rather than doctrinal differences. Christian holiness becomes an anemic "I'm okay, you're okay"; and Christian fellowship becomes indigenous congeniality. In important ways, the ecclesial identification of the church with the world is simply the opposite number of another ancient tradition. Historically, and put baldly, the temptation of the church has been to engage in either withdrawal from the world (sectarianism) or identification with the world (ecclesiasticism). But neither of these is quite suitable to the paradox which is suggested by the church's being "in but not of" the world. Hubris and hyprocrisy attend the former, while frank betrayal of the gospel to the cultus attends the latter.

If it just will not work for a church/world dialectic to be "either/or," as Kierkegaard would have preferred, perhaps it can be analogous to Barth's metaphor of theology as a tightrope walker whose endless "yes and no" alternation singularly allows the walker to maintain balance and avoid falling off into either world-without-church or church-without-world fantasies. On some such terms as these, I believe, we will be able to recognize that the church is comprised of both believers and voters, believers and sales clerks, believers and mechanics, believers and unbelievers, and so on.

TO CONFESS OUR SINS

It is clear enough that the church is in the world, converting the world to gospel faith, and it is clear enough that the world is in the church, converting the church to secularism; but it may not yet be clear whether it is possible, or how it may be possible, or even desirable, to acknowledge the ways in which church and world may be coimplicated and complementary. Were we able to achieve this, we might have something less than a synthesis, but more than a paradox. Meanwhile, to talk of gathering and collecting the faithful might provide a clue to comprehending how we can simultaneously acknowledge both church and world.

My experience is that Christians typically ignore or underestimate the sheer moral impact of coming together for worship; but the bare fact of the matter is that assembly, when it is intentional, conveys a powerful and distinct witness. Because convening the people of God signifies the most important sociological assumptions about the church and Christian ethics, Christians would do well to be more self-conscious of the potency and actual leverage which gathering, in and of itself, generates. If we remember that this action is a moral act, that it is a distinguishing act, that it is a hermeneutical act, we will recognize that it is, in a phrase, our first move toward learning to see ourselves and the world aright. Of course, this means to see the world and the church as God intends, as all subject to and belonging to God. The tie that binds all together with God invites us to inquire further into the bonding process; and to do this obliges us to reflect briefly on confession, repentance, penance, reconciliation, forgiveness, pardon, and absolution, because these are the means by which Jews and Christians understand the estranged creation to be re-ligated to its Creator and Sovereign Lord.

All cultures appear to have communal codes, together with various expiatory penalties for those who violate the *corpus juris*. In every society there are certain actions which are believed to be offenses which seriously endanger the common good or disrupt the community-at-large, or which threaten to bring (or actually bring) dishonor and scandal upon it. The penalty for such offenses is typically the separation of the offender from the community, although the meaning of "separation" can range from ostracism to incarceration. So within ancient Judaism, certain offenses brought excommunication or ritual uncleanness; and we know Leviticus as a rich source for apprehending the Mosaic laws, and the penalties for their violation.[13]

Typically, after appropriate penalties, self-examination, testing, and reeducation, the offender might be reincorporated into the community. So, whether secular or religious, here was a repertoire which joined confession, penance, and reconciliation in a series of rites which often included prayers of confession, wearing sackcloth and ashes, fasting and weeping, tearing one's garments, kneeling and prostration, ritual washings, and repeating the seven penitential psalms (6, 32, 38, 51, 102, 130, and 143). The New Testament, similarly, contains evidence of disciplinary measures, including excommunication, for those who scandalized the church or violated its rules. So our earliest documentary record demonstrates that the primitive church both knew that there was considerable precedence in the Hebrew Scriptures for confession, repentance, reconciliation, and even excommunication and reflected that ancestry in its own disciplines. [14]

Now none of this should appear odd, or even the least bit awkward, to Christians, because forgiveness of sins is inseparable from the gospel. In a sense, it *is* the gospel. Christ died for sinners; his sacrifice accomplished our reconciliation; our baptism is for the remission of sins. So much of Jesus' ministry entailed forgiveness of sins—for example, the woman taken in adultery (John 8:1–11), the healing of the paralytic man (Mark 2:1–5), and the parable of the prodigal son (Luke 15:11–32). Indeed, the good news of the gospel is that Jesus did not come to call the righteous to himself, but sinners (Mark 2:17). His preaching, according to the evangelists, essentially consisted of calling his hearers (1) to repent, (2) to believe the gospel, and (3) to follow him (Mark 1:14ff). If we would claim that gospel, we must understand ourselves as the moral equivalents of the woman taken in adultery, the man who was paralyzed, and the son who was a wastrel. The Gospel is unequivocal in asserting that we have to understand that Jesus comes to us when we are severely compromised and incapacitated. In a clear and compelling declaration, the good news of the gospel is that God "proves his love for us in that while we were still sinners Christ died for us . . . while we were enemies, we were reconciled to God through the death of his son" (Rom. 5:8, 10).

The early church appears to have taken the fact of *sin*, together with the particularity of *sins*, very seriously. It invested considerable time and energy in a catechumenate which not only taught what Christians should believe but also provided disciplined training in how Christians should live. It described the forgiveness of sins in language which, had it referred to a matter less urgent or weighty, would have been thought extravagant, exaggerated, excessive. And, following Jesus' example, it signified the metamorphosis from contamination to cleansing in baptism, the sacrament of the new birth. By baptism, former sins are forgiven and a fresh start is offered. By baptism, one becomes a Christian. By baptism, one becomes a new creature. By baptism, one is raised from death in sin to the new life of grace.

Because the primitive church took sins, and the fact of sin, with utmost gravity, postbaptismal sins and the prospect of an imminent end of the world (understandably?) raised sober and portentous questions regarding the reliability of baptismal forgiveness and reconciliation to see one through to the end. Quite reasonably, baptism was thus sometimes postponed until death approached; but in the long run, this experiment proved to be neither practically workable nor theologically tenable.

Tertullian's *De poenitentia* and the *Didascalia*, both produced in the third century, developed rites of excommunication and reinstatement; and these, in turn, presaged the emergence of a liturgy of penance. Over the next few centuries, this liturgy appears to have emerged in three stages: (1) the imposition of penance or excommunication; (2) acts of contrition and penitence, which included the wearing of sackcloth and ashes, prayer and fasting, intercession of the faithful, and dismissal from public services before communion; and (3) absolution or reinstatement, over which the bishop normally presided, consisting of prayer and laying on of hands, together with readmission to the eucharist.

The story of the evolution of the penitential office is fascinating, but altogether too intricate and subtle to be described in any detail here. In sum, public penance had long been related to the Lenten season, and penitents were routinely placed under discipline at the beginning of Lent. By the seventh and eighth centuries, penance was increasingly thought of as a sacrament; and, owing to the gravity of postbaptismal sins, absolution was sought as often as one sinned. By the ninth century, imposition of ashes (thus "Ash Wednesday") and saying the seven penitential psalms were added to the rite of expulsion; and reconciliation, if granted, typically occurred near the end of Lent, on Maundy Thursday or Good Friday. In general, public penance was assigned for sins which scandalized the church, and private penance was imposed for matters of conscience which were confessed privately to a priest. But there was enormous variability in identifying the genre of sin which fitted a particular confession, in assessing its moral seriousness and in prescribing a proper penance. There was also some considerable fluctuation owing to eccentricities of culture, variabilities in priestly education, and the like. What seems to have been missing from all this was a coherent scheme for treating similar sins similarly.

In the main, it appears that Irish monasticism following St. Patrick (389–461 C.E.) was principally responsible for the development, from the sixth to ninth century, of written guides for coping with the increasing need for priests to hear confessions, identify with some precision the sin(s) being confessed, and impose an appropriate penance. These handbooks came to be known as the "penitentials"[15] and served as instructions to priests about how to name sins and prescribe appropriate penance, in order to achieve purity of heart.

By definition, the centerpiece of this process was confession, and this incorporated three aspects: contrition, or a hearty sorrow and thorough detestation for the sin(s) committed, together with a firm resolve to sin no more; penance, consisting of an act commensurate with contrition for the sin(s) confessed; and absolution on behalf of the church, which forgave the sin(s) and bestowed grace in order to help the penitent to bring forth fruits worthy of repentance, to withstand future temptation, and to guard against moral recidivism. In fact, contrition is the presupposition for confession, confession is the presupposition for penance, and penance is the presupposition for absolution.

By the late Middle Ages, priests alone could be confessors, penitents ordinarily were required to confess to their parish priests, confession became a requirement for receiving the Holy Communion, and general (i.e., corporate) confessions and absolutions together with auricular confessions became common with the daily offices and the mass. Luther retained private confession as a sacrament, but rejected penance as acts of satisfaction which were contrary to the doctrine of *sola gratia*. For Luther, acknowledgment and confession of sin(s) were absolutely necessary, but penance suggested that something was lacking in Christ's cross and therefore could not be endorsed. Calvin found no biblical basis for confession, and so he denied the sacramental nature of private confession while allowing absolution as a ceremony to confirm faith in the forgiveness of sins. Within a short time, confession eroded, and disappeared, from Calvinism.

The reformers in England, interestingly, dismantled the penitential system (insisting that grace was fully available to all repentant sinners) while retaining public confession and absolution in every regular Anglican service, both daily offices and celebrations of the Holy Communion. The 1548 Order for the Holy Communion, in an exhortation to worthy preparation for receiving the sacrament, "contained an apologia for noncompulsory private confession for any whose consciences were not quieted by 'their humble confession to God, and the general confession to the church.' " And the Prayer Books of 1549 and 1552 retained this concession to a "private and secret confession to the priest":

If there be any of you which . . . cannot quiet his own conscience, but requireth further comfort or counsel; then let him come to me, or some other discreet and learned minister of God's word and open his grief that he may receive such ghostly counsel, advice, and comfort as his conscience may be relieved and that by the ministry of God's Word he may receive comfort and the benefit of absolution, to the quieting of his conscience, and avoiding of all scruple and doubtfulness.[16]

From earliest times, Christians have recognized that confession acknowledges the discrepancy, the dissonance, the incongruity between what we confess to believe and how we conduct our lives. Confession concedes the contradiction between what Gunnar Myrdal astutely called "creed" and "deed."[17] Myrdal's thesis, put perhaps too succinctly, was that racism is a problem in the United States owing to an unspanned chasm between "the American creed," which consists largely of egalitarian and democratic rhetoric, and "the American deed," which is commonly characterized by behavior that denies equality and citizenship to some Americans solely on the basis of race. In the almost five decades since Myrdal's landmark study, his method for understanding social and political discordance has been widely employed in a variety of settings; and while some have thought the juxtaposition of "creed" and "deed" rather too simplistic, the fact is that it gets quickly to the heart of the matter by assessing whether there is congruity or incongruity between commitments articulated and acted out.

To state this matter another way, we could say that, from earliest times, Christians have believed that the marks of faithfulness and coherence are continuity, congruity, correlation, and connection—in short, a coherent linkage between the *confessio fidei* and actual conduct. On these terms, the opposite number of this kind of steadfast loyalty is hypocrisy, which literally means appearing to be someone or something that one is not. So it is important to understand this relation, or the lack of it, between belief and behavior, or creed and deed, as the warrant for why the generality of us call behavior which is inimical to what is professed, hypocrisy, and why Christians call behavior which is contrary to what the church discerns the gospel to teach, "sin." Conversely, this is also why we call action that coheres with claims of identity, in which what we do is attuned to who we say we are, true morality or holiness.

Confession is therefore a serious challenge to how we think about moral accountability, and Christians believe it not a trivial matter when we act in ways that are incoherent and discontinuous with claims about who we are. In fact, this is exactly how confession of faith (creed) and confession of sin (deed) are tied so closely together: in one we declare who, by God's grace, we are; and in the other we acknowledge how we have denied that identity and preferred some other. At our baptism, the guilt of past sin(s) is washed away; a moral rectitude is conferred on us; and we are accounted as righteous. Baptism is thus a transition from death to life, from old to new, from sin to righteousness. Moreover, baptism is a rite of perfection which restores us to the family of God and reconstitutes us as brothers and sisters together in Christ. So it makes sense that the early church believed itself to be a community of reconciliation and holiness in which this kind of articulated identity ought to get acted out in everyday living.

Our primitive Christian forebears knew that they remained impure and in sin after baptism; but they also believed that they could, by God's grace, overcome sin in general and sins in particular. So fraternal discipline became essential and obligatory in the early Christian communities: now that we are new creatures in Christ, sin violates us both individually and corporately, and it must be treated with the utmost seriousness. Very early on, therefore, the young church accepted responsibility for "binding and loosing" sins,[18] what we continue today in the disciplines of confession, penance, excommunication, absolution, and reconciliation of penitents.

The following excerpts from a beautiful passage by Theodore of Mopsuestia, concerning the sacrament of penance, illustrate the early church's commitment to this responsibility:

> *Let us know that as God gave to our body, which he made passible, medicinal herbs of which the experts make use for our healing, so also He gave penitence, as a medicine for sins, to our soul, which is changeable. . . .*
>
> *This is the medicine for the sins, which was established by God and delivered to the priests of the Church, who in making use of it with diligence, will heal the afflictions of men. The blessed Paul . . . ordered that the sinners should be reproved "with all longsuffering and doctrine," so that they should reveal their sins to {the priests}; and the "rebuke" is administered so that they may receive correction by some*

ordinances, and obtain help therefrom for themselves. He ordered also to "comfort them," in the sense that after they have been seen, through reproofs and rebukes, to be eagerly willing to amend themselves, turn away from evil and be desirous of drawing nigh unto good. . . . Since you are aware of these things, and also of the fact that because God greatly cares for us gave us penitence and showed us the medicine of repentance, and established some men, who are the priests, as physicians of sins, so that if we receive in this world through them, healing and forgiveness of sins, we shall be delivered from the judgment to come—it behooves us to draw nigh unto the priests with great confidence and to reveal our sins to them, and they, with all diligence, pain and love, and according to the rules laid down above, will give healing to sinners. And they will not disclose the things that are not to be disclosed, but they will keep to themselves the things that have happened, as fits true and loving fathers, bound to safeguard the shame of their children while striving to heal their bodies.[19]

Of course, the business of confession, repentance, absolution, and reconciliation depends, first and last, on our ability to identify the discrete ways in which we have violated our commitments and broken our covenants. Indeed, a strong assumption appears to underlie John 20:23 and Matthew 18:18, as well as 1 John 1:8–10,[20] that *sin* is displayed in *sins*, and that we need to learn how to name sins, to identify them, in order to confess them and thereafter gain forgiveness and pardon. Unless with some attention to precision we can designate what we understand sinful behaviors to be, we risk trivializing confession, absolution, and reconciliation.

The task of nominating sins is particularly difficult in a time like ours, when standards of all sorts are able to be challenged by individual sovereignties. As a matter of fact, most of us have cut our moral eyeteeth on the notion that each of us alone is the proper arbiter of what is right and what is wrong for us. Where matters of morality are at stake, that is the modern hermeneutical principle. I believe that Daniel Patrick Moynihan was clearly on target when, some years ago, he accounted (in part) for our contemporary cultural malaise by pointing out that we routinely engage in a process of redefining, reappraising, reconstructing, and relaxing operative notion of sins—downward.

Now and then I ask students in my divinity-school classes whether they believe that there are any inviolable rules, or any actions that one is always wrong to carry out, irrespective of how the individual person might feel about them. After I ask my question, there are usually a few moments of reflection before someone suggests a rule that is normative or an action that is always wrong; but then even fewer moments are required for somebody to point out an exception to the rule, or a set of circumstances which would seem to permit the action. They sound very much like normless situationists and expedient teleologists. At the end of the day, however, it turns out that the students are not altogether what they seem to be, and that there are some candidates (e.g., blasphemy and idolatry) which they can offer in answer to my question. But they have been so deeply conditioned to resist anything that sounds as if it will compromise individual liberty to make determinations of right and wrong for oneself that their initial impulse is to reject out of hand the notion that there are, in fact, sins.

So modern psychological barriers, to say nothing of methodological difficulties, in the matter of naming sins are impressive. Just the same, to fail to discriminate between what is aesthetically unpleasant or prohibited by statutory law, and what is morally opprobrious because it is religiously objectionable, is tantamount to confusing good table manners or legal prohibitions with violations of God's will. So there are both formal and material interests at stake in saying, as clearly as we can, which actions are sins and which ones are not. That large areas of gray ambiguity will doubtless remain despite our best efforts does not excuse us from engaging in this struggle. We are plainly unable to catalog as black or white every imaginable human action, and lexically order them as sinful or virtuous. Nevertheless, if the category "sins" is going to mean something rather than nothing or anything, we will sooner or later simply have to say what actions we are prepared to nominate as sinful behavior, and offer the theological backing necessary to support this naming.

When the Protestant reformers abandoned auricular confession of particular sins and penance, they also lost the sense of specificity with respect to sins, and therewith the ability to name sins—that is, to identify and designate with some precision those behaviors which the church regarded as violative of Christian commitments and covenants. Roman Catholicism has never been a monolithic uniformity; all the same, there was, in the sense of a *corpus Christianum*, considerable accord in naming those actions which, for Roman Catholics, were sins. The radical individualism of Protestantism—if not of all the reformers, then clearly of many who followed them—did not seek such a communitarian consensus; and the consequence is that our Protestant heritage of a general confession freed from penance is a fatal abstraction. Abandoning the confession of particular sins and the imposition of a discriminating penance relieved Protestants of the necessity of identifying particular sins.

I believe that Luther was right to object to penance insofar as it constituted a form of works-righteousness which suggested an incompleteness or insufficiency in Christ's cross; but I believe that he was shortsighted in failing to see penance as a form of fraternal discipline. If we are truly *simul iustus et peccator*, it makes sense that sins remain our constant companions in this life, that we are not actually righteous but only accounted as righteous, and that naming those sins would be important for growing in grace. But this latter notion is precisely what is missing in Lutheran and Calvinist traditions. In the Catholic tradition, justification is the basis for and beginning of the Christian life. As John Wesley claimed, faith opens the way to the "new birth" and fullness of life in Christ, and sanctification in holiness ought to follow: "at the same time that we are justified, yea, in that very moment, sanctification begins," said Wesley.[21] But for Luther and Calvin, both of these movements had been identified in justifying faith, and the whole content of salvation was connoted in and by justification. For Wesley (and the Catholic tradition), salvation is a process of which justification is a primary and basic stage.[22] The Protestant and Catholic differences here help us to understand one of the reasons why inheritors of Protestant traditions are disinclined to name sins, and why the sacrament of penance continues to be a vital part of Catholic piety.

In addition to these matters, the reformer's emphasis on the corporate character of sin, and a public confession but no enumeration of particular sins, have had several important results for those of us who have inherited Protestant traditions. First, we could no longer name specific sins, but could only confess to sin in general. Second, a significant consequence of the inability to name sins is that we have no way to discriminate among different sins in terms of their moral seriousness. Third, being unable to discriminate among sins, we are also unable to determine the gravity of whatever guilt does or ought to attach to sin-in-general, unless it be a corresponding kind of guilt-in-general. And finally, trapped in this generality, we are prevented from saying what may be needed or wanted to make things right, to make amends; in other words, we cannot specify an appropriate penance.

The fateful flaw in this view of sin is apparent when we compare it with the criminal law in Anglo-American jurisprudence. Simply put, the function of the criminal law is to name those actions forbidden by statute, and to indicate appropriate sanctions when one is found guilty of violating the statute. The principal role of juries and lawyers and judges and courts is to ascertain whether the accused is guilty (beyond a reasonable doubt) of having committed an act forbidden by statute. But all of this would be patently impossible if we could not name those actions which the criminal law identifies as proscribed and punishable.

To be sure, statutes do not speak to every circumstance, and "legal loopholes" is the name we give to those behaviors which are ambiguously defined. These occur often enough to remind us that no list of rules can ever be complete enough, or sufficiently sensitive to descriptive nuance, to cover the vast array of concrete situations and contingencies. All the same, the law is not completely muzzled because it cannot speak to every detail of human behavior; and it does what it can do. There is an old moral maxim which expresses the boundary of human obligation and limitation: one can be responsible only for what one can be responsible for. In the measure to which the church persists in displaying its inability and unwillingness to name those behaviors which, as offenses to the gospel, are proscribed and punishable, it appears to be less accountable to what it is responsible for than the criminal justice system.

Of course, what this plainly means is that, since sin and guilt belong equally to everybody, neither of them can be assigned with any particular power to anybody. And this brings us full circle to an understanding of why the church, the community, the corporate body feel obliged therefore to ignore sins. Abandoning confession of specific sins and penances and losing the capacity to name sins and assign their moral seriousness have had important consequences not only for liturgy but also for Christian ethics. With the move toward normlessness, Protestantism largely lost the capacity for doing *Christian* ethics as such, and tended instead to adopt the moral ethos of its secular environment. And when this happened, Protestant individuals and Protestant churches discovered that they were without either the resources or means to challenge the general direction taken by culture on moral matters. The result is a well-known and familiar general disposition by both clergy and laity toward sentimentality and eclecticism. How else could Jerry Falwell have opposed abortion and supported capital punishment?

Our participation in sin, said Barth, is an "ontological impossibility." God created us for a purpose, for a destiny, that sin contradicts. But God is sovereign; so how can this happen? The answer is deceptively simple: we don't know; we cannot explain it; it is a surd. Sin cannot be explained rationally; it confounds rationality, even the rationality of biblical theism. On the other hand, we know beyond the shadow of any doubt that sin is present in our lives, that it permeates our world, that it constitutes (as Rauschenbusch put it) a kingdom of evil in our midst. Now knowing its ubiquitous presence begins to suggest its power, and this in turn is an important clue: we lack the natural, rational means to account for sin. Owing to our impotence, we are forced to rely on someone, or something, beyond ourselves to provide an account of sin and to name sins.[23]

This is why, in the Christian lexicon, christology precedes sin: sin only makes sense for Christians when it is referred to the truth about us which the gospel proclaims. Sins do not exist autonomously or independently of the gospel which identifies and names them. Christians neither know sin, nor know how to name sins, apart from their contrast with God's purpose and destiny for us as we know this in Jesus Christ.[24] The message of the gospel is that we were bought at a great price, and liberated from the power of evil, and reconciled to God. So our fundamental sin is that while we are created for companionship with God, and with each other, we refuse to live out that relationship. Instead of acknowledging the sovereignty of God, we prefer to assert our selves and to proclaim our own autonomy.

To the best of my recollection, it was in the ninth grade that I was obliged to memorize William Ernest Henley's poem "Invictus." My teacher must have thought that this bit of verse would inspire fortitude and self-reliance in young adolescents who had been born during the depression decades of the 1920s and 1930s. I reckon that she was not altogether mistaken in this; and even today I remember fragments of Henley's ode to the sovereign and autonomous self. The entire piece is as follows:

Out of the night that covers me,
  Black as the pit from pole to pole,
I thank whatever gods may be,
  For my unconquerable soul.
In the fell clutch of circumstance
  I have not winced nor cried aloud.
Under the bludgeonings of chance
  My head is bloody but unbowed.
Beyond this place of wrath and tears
  Looms but the horror of the shade,
And yet the menace of the years
  Finds and shall find me unafraid.
It matters not how straight the gate
  How charged with punishment the scroll,
I am the master of my fate,
  I am the captain of my soul.[25]

Of course, I cite Henley's poem now as a wonderfully powerful example of our preference for self-exaltation, human autonomy, and all the rest of our hubris which conspires against acknowledging the sovereignty of God. "Invictus" forcefully conveys those attitudes and actions which will one's own private and selfish good apart from the good of the kingdom of God; and, for good measure, the common good as well. In these respects the poem helps make us aware of what sins to confess. In comparison with dancing on Sundays and playing at cards, these sins go to the core of our being. They get our attention, in somewhat the same way that our bodies react to snow after a few minutes in a sauna.

So it is bound to be a severe shock to the moral equivalent of our cardiovascular system that we are not asked to be sentimental about sin, or to trivialize sin, or even *to feel sinful*. We are told by the church's traditions and scriptures that we are a particular kind of people; that we continue to become that particular kind of people when and insofar as we observe and participate in God's work to establish God's rule over our lives; and that we will understand why we are called to confession of sins and pardon when we acknowledge that we are this, and not some other, kind of people. What this means is that, in the first of it, then, sin is not something we do but someone we refuse to be.

This is why the fundamental character of sin consists in the claims of the self to be a sovereign end in itself. But we know that a self can be a self only in relation to other selves; so this insistence on individual autonomy is thus the self's basic contradiction. Christianly understood, what sin denotes is a fundamental alienation—from God, from neighbors, and in the end from self itself. Or, to put it differently, sin connotes the failure to be the person and the people who, by God's grace in Jesus Christ, we are; and who we are is reconciled daughters and sons in the family of God. On this understanding, we can begin to comprehend the church's claim that the gospel teaches us both *that* we need to confess and *what* we ought to confess.

My strong suspicion is that we continue to resist being taught these things because we recognize that learning them entails judgment. To know both that we need to confess and what we ought to confess means that we are also able to judge; but there is a broad and pervasive tendency among us nowadays not to judge, because we do not want either to judge others or to be judged ourselves. In a pluralist, individualist, secular society such as ours, the principal virtue (of necessity?) is *tolerance*. We are familiar enough with the endless stream of sloganeering which is intended to etch that virtue indelibly into our minds: "we can't legislate morals"; "religion and politics don't mix"; "every person is the best, indeed the only, judge of his or her own interests"; or, as John Stuart Mill so succinctly put it, "Over himself, over his own body and mind, the individual is sovereign."[26]

In addition, many of us find it deeply offensive to suppose that our forgiveness can be bestowed by another, that justification is indeed *sola gratia*. Perhaps no one has expressed this sense of outrage more powerfully than Immanuel Kant, who wrote concerning the Christian doctrine of atonement:

> *It is quite impossible to see how a reasonable man, who knows himself to merit punishment, can in all seriousness believe that he needs only to credit the news of an atonement rendered for him, and to accept this atonement* utiliter *(as the lawyers say), in order to regard his guilt as annihilated. . . . No thoughtful person can bring himself to believe this. . . . Where shall we start, i.e., with a faith in what God has done on our behalf, or with what we are to do to become worthy of*

God's assistance (whatever this may be)? In answering this question, we cannot hesitate in deciding for the second alternative. . . . We can certainly hope to partake in the appropriation of another's atoning merit, and so of salvation, only by qualifying for it through our own efforts to fulfill every human duty—and this obedience must be the effect of our own action and not, once again, of a foreign influence in the presence of which we are passive. . . . {It is necessary that man make it as a maxim that} he shall begin with the improvement of his life as the supreme condition under which alone a saving faith can exist.[27]

For Kant, as for many modern Christians, all that we can do, indeed all that we need to do, is to rely on our own moral stamina to save us from the impotence and disability of sin and guilt.

Our most severe impairment in a secular pluralist society, however, lies in the absence of a *sensus communis*, which—according to Alasdair MacIntyre, Bernard Williams, and others—is preconditional to the capacity for judgment. Lacking a coherent tradition which through time has defined and redefined common and fundamental agreements, we discover we cannot identify or make intelligible the shared commitments which make it possible to discriminate right from wrong, truth from error, good from bad. MacIntyre puts it this way:

What many of us are educated into is, not a coherent way of thinking and judging, but one constructed out of an amalgam of social and cultural fragments inherited both from different traditions from which our culture was originally derived (Puritan, Catholic, Jewish) and from different stages in and aspects of the development of modernity (the French Enlightenment, the Scottish Enlightenment, nineteenth-century economic liberalism, twentieth-century political liberalism).[28]

So we inhabit a culture which is, in the literal sense of the word, confused; and that confusion is reflected in our inability to achieve rational resolution of issues which are morally disputed. To be able to judge presupposes commitments and convictions of a particular sort; these are the fulcrum by which we pry loose particular judgments. They need not be eternal or universal—as a matter of fact, even fundamental agreements tend to change with time and circumstances—but they have to be definite. In the absence of the commitments and convictions of a coherent tradition, we are powerless to adjudicate moral controversies in rationally coherent ways.

I listened recently to a homily an at ordination. The preacher's principal point in that sermon, he said, was to impress upon the ordinand that priesthood consists of compassion and kindness and charity, of doing good for all sorts and conditions of folks in all sorts of strange and uncertain conditions and circumstances. His *bête noire*, he said, was a priesthood characterized by legalism, rigidity, authoritarianism, and sitting in judgment; and he told two autobiographical stories which he claimed to be parallel and illustrative of his point.

In the first story, he told us that prenatal diagnosis had revealed to a young couple that their pregnancy was affected by a genetic trait which prevented development of their baby's lungs. Their baby, they were told by the physician, would die within hours postpartum owing to pulmonary insufficiency. With this information, the couple contacted the preacher and asked whether, in this circumstance, he would attend the birth and immediately thereafter baptize and name their baby. He told us to whom he was preaching that he quickly and enthusiastically agreed to their request; and that following a C-section, he baptized the baby and sealed it with oil. Thereafter the mother asked to hold the baby; and it lay cuddled in her arms until it died two or three hours later.

In the second story, and again to illustrate the preacher's point that "sharing the love of Jesus is all that priesthood is about," we were told about another couple who, like the first one, was ecstatic with a much-desired pregnancy. In this anecdote, however, the fetus was affected by a "sex-linked disorder which promised the child a violent death within minutes of birth." Amniocentesis or some other prenatal diagnostic had revealed this condition; and the couple was very upset because, while they so much wanted a baby, there seemed to be no point in continuing the "obvious futility" of this doomed pregnancy. Like the couple in the first story, they contacted the preacher with a request: were there any canons which would prevent him from baptizing *in utero*; and if not, would he perform a baptism just prior to elective abortion? Again, his response was unhesitating and enthusiastic: of course he would do it, and without (he said) bothering to check the canons or even consult the ordinary of the diocese. So at the appointed time, he went to the hospital, lifted the woman's blouse to expose her distended abdomen, baptized and chrismated "her tender tummy," and named the child. The pregnancy was then terminated.

Now I happen to believe that these stories are not at all parallel, and that they are in fact incommensurate. But they do interestingly complement each other. Let me explain. The first story seems to me quite coherent with the church's understanding of baptism, and simultaneously evocative of many metaphors and images from Gospel narratives. It is pastorally sensitive, canonically proper, sacramentally appropriate; it is, in short, a wonderful story for an ordinand to hear, and be instructed by, on the occasion of the ordinand's priesting.

The second story appears to respond to many of the same claims for compassion and charity and kindness; but there are profound and unanswered questions here—about the meaning of suffering; concerning the bearing of the Gospel on human tragedy; as to whether this case qualifies as an instance of *in utero* baptism, to say nothing of whether *in utero* baptism is proper and permissible; and most of all about the violence, however clinically indicated, of abortion and the clear connections here between baptism and killing.

We have to ask what is really going on here. Does this make sense in the church? Is this another of those times when sacramentality has been displaced by sentimentality? I tend to think so because I am persuaded that our inability to overcome the tragic dimensions of human existence does not license us to make virtue of apparent necessity, nor does contingency authorize us to rename sin as righteousness. Of course, one shares empathetically the pain and sense of loss of a couple trapped in this kind of madness; but the sacraments are not the means of making us feel better about circumstances we would have preferred to avoid in the first of it. What is most evident in this second story is the absence of a critical temperament and sagacious judgment.

It is unsurprising that we have some deep difficulties and serious problems with judging, whether ourselves or others, both because to judge looks and sounds so intolerant and because we are unequipped or ill-equipped to nominate the sins which are worthy of judgment. All the same, there is a judgment upon all of us who suppose that we can escape or avoid assessing and evaluating ourselves and others, and this is that our worst enemy is sentimentality. When trying to name sins gets to be analogous to trying to nail Jello to the wall, the church becomes the therapeutic community where doctrinal issues are decided by phrases like "Well, I don't know; how do you feel about it?" and fraternal discipline gets reduced to a deferential camaraderie which always yields to tolerance. But this is a far cry from the company of penitent and forgiven sinners who are called "saints."

Over years of more or less casual observation, I have formed a number of impressions about adolescents, and among them are two which bear directly on gathering and confessing. The first is merely confirmation of the well-known "herd mentality" phenomenon, in which burgeoning indi-viduation competes with collective appearance and behaviors, and loses. Why else would one insist on being different by wearing the same hair style and torn jeans that everybody else is affecting? But my interest in this state of affairs has more to do with the frank need for getting together, for assembling, for congregating—whether at a party, a sporting event, or a shopping mall. Adolescents are notoriously dependent upon their friends and being with them; and that dependency, together with its corollary need for getting together, strikes me as a pregnant facsimile (of sorts) of the church.

The second impression is reminiscent of Flip Wilson's celebrated apol-ogy, "The devil made me do it!" Actually, this is a trait deriving from all those times I've heard an adolescent deny any fault in a matter. "I didn't do it," or "it wasn't my fault," or some other version of what seems to be an inveterate determination (almost?) never to acknowledge responsibility or accountability for a mistake or mishap is a familiar litany to any parent who has survived a child's adolescence. Of course, this disposition to denial is not unique to adolescents; and they (just conceivably?) might learn it from omniscient and omnicompetent parents. Withal, it is a disposition which displays a tendency that stays with most of us until death or age or circumstance, whichever comes first, renders it immaterial.

To admit to being wrong and/or doing wrong does not come easily to most of us—sometimes because we are unable to name the wrong we are accused of, but usually because we are simply unwilling to acknowledge that we were wrong or did wrong. The old saw goes: "I was wrong only once in my life; and that was once when I thought I was." Being able to confess to wrong-being and wrong-doing, some of us learn, is a grace; but it is a costly grace inasmuch as it obliges us to become vulnerable, liable, pregnable—conditions which most of us, in the euphoria of self-sufficiency and autonomy, prefer not to experience.

So there is an interesting relationship which accounts for the connection among gathering and confessing and witnessing. Congregating, getting together, assembling appears to be a very natural thing for human beings to do. We appear to be endowed, in fact, with a naturally gregarious tendency. Human beings are social beings; and sociality appears to be an observably indispensable fact of our species' existence. But confessing, whether faith or sins, is patently *un*natural to us; and we display a reluctance which borders on refusal in countless ways. So as part of its mission, the congregation called "church" adopts the task of training us, of teaching us both *that* confession is needed and *what* confession needs to be made. In the bargain, we learn that love is forever having to say "I'm sorry," and that testifying to those around us is just an unavoidable consequence of being who we are.

Disciplined and discriminating judgment is part of the sheer moral impact of coming together. Assembling, gathering, collecting the faithful becomes both possible and obligatory for Christians, because we are a people who know that naming sins, with a fair measure of precision and clarity, is requisite to a confession and witness which is not banal but descriptively accurate of the kind of people God intends us to be. The collect for the first day of Lent, Ash Wednesday, puts it well:

Almighty and everlasting God, you hate nothing you have made and forgive the sins of all who are penitent: Create and make in us new and contrite hearts, that we, worthily lamenting our sins and acknowledging our wretchedness, may obtain of you, the God of all mercy, perfect remission and forgiveness; through Jesus Christ our Lord, who lives and reigns with you and the Holy Spirit, one God, for ever and ever. Amen.

CHAPTER FOUR

GREETINGS: PEACE

GREETINGS AND IDENTITY

Basic training is what the Christian life is about. Were Christians a genuinely holy people for whom the paradigm of Jesus' faithful obedience were constantly controlling in their lives, and who regularly made radical promises and gave themselves away to God and one another, they would be such a people because they had been trained to this way. The fact of the matter is that we are not naturally friends of God and people of peace. We have to learn to be the people whom God has destined us to be; we have to learn to be lovers of God; we have to be trained in the ways of friendship. And this, in part, is what a salutation with the peace of Christ intends to express and accomplish.

My experience has been that we have too often forgotten, or perhaps we have just failed to teach, that there are important reasons for a greeting in Christian liturgies. So lots of us wonder what it could mean to include a place in the liturgy for greeting one another with the peace of Christ. Is it more than a courtesy; an ice-breaker; an archaic practice which may have been appropriate in its own time but is very awkward in the modern situation? Is it, can it in fact be, more than the "hello, how are you" that is almost always no more than a social convention? Is this ancient greeting between Christians actually more than a convenient way to mark off the "preliminary" first part of the liturgy from the "main-event" second part? Is it permissible to stare off into space when you say, "The peace of the Lord be always with you," or do you have to look your neighbor squarely in the eye? Does "the peace" connote anything important for theological ethics? Does it suggest anything about moral agency? Does it have any correlation, or even connection, with a life of holiness?

To extend a greeting is a commonplace in human affairs; so there is nothing fundamentally odd about a salutation between friends, or even between complete strangers. Sometimes it is offered in order to welcome another in a friendly or respectful way; sometimes it is nothing more than a form of address; sometimes it presents or introduces oneself to another. Withal, a greeting of some sort is ordinarily neither surprising nor inappropriate; it is, as my Scottish friends say, "just the decent thing."

Reflect for a moment on some more or less familiar greetings. Years ago, before the all-volunteer army, most of the young men in this country received letters from their local draft boards which announced that they had been conscripted for military service. The word that began those letters struck me even then as a bit ironic: "Greetings!" Other letters, like the ones we routinely write, typically begin with what is formally called "the greeting"; and this "greeting" can range from "To Whom It May Concern" to "My Dearest." In the navy, the ship's company is summoned with "Now hear this!"

St. Paul's letters in the New Testament also begin with a greeting, but it is a very different greeting from the ones we are accustomed to give and hear in our ordinary day-to-day congress. "Grace and peace to you from God our Father and the Lord Jesus Christ" is how Paul introduces Romans, 1 and 2 Corinthians, Galatians, Ephesians, Philippians, Colossians, 1 and 2 Thessalonians, 1 and 2 Timothy, and Philemon.

Interestingly, Paul's greeting is also an occasion to identify himself, and to say something about how he is authorized to extend grace and peace from God and from our savior Jesus Christ. So his letters typically begin with phrases like: "Paul, an apostle of Jesus Christ by the will of God" (Colossians, 1 and 2 Corinthians); and "Paul, an apostle of Christ Jesus by command of God" (Timothy); and "Paul, a servant of Jesus Christ, called to be an apostle, set apart for the gospel of God, which he promised beforehand through his prophets in the holy scriptures, the gospel concerning his Son . . . through whom we have received grace and apostleship to bring about obedience to the faith . . . To all God's beloved in Rome, who are called to be saints" (Romans). If Paul's ordering of the way he begins his correspondence is not accidental but intentional, I reckon it important to note that it is only *after* this rehearsal of who he is, which is his authorization for communicating, that Paul extends his greeting: "Grace and peace to you from God our Father and the Lord Jesus Christ."

So the salutation—which, as it turns out, is also functionally an acclamation—serves to make it perfectly clear that we present ourselves to each other in the liturgy as rooted and grounded in a certain identity and self-understanding. In the church's liturgy, this is the presentation of ourselves to each other as the *laos theou*, the friends of God and a people of peace.

We ought to observe here a special and striking feature of Paul's salutation: that it also conveys an eschatological dimension which, in turn, becomes paradigmatic for the greetings exchanged between Christians. What this means is that we surely intend to greet each other in this particular time and place; but a too often forgotten and too much neglected aspect of Christian contextualization, of locating who we understand and represent ourselves to be, is that what is being transacted here and now goes far beyond (both backwards and forwards) what is going on just here and now. In other words, we mean in this action to re-member the past, our Christian origins and inheritance, to this present—to re-call, to re-present, to re-appropriate our origins; as in this present moment we venture also to acknowledge that who we are to be—our destiny as brothers and sisters in the family of God—always stands over against and judges our partial and fitful and erratic expressions to one another of that love wherewith we have been loved. This dialectic, in some form or other, is always part of our self-understanding and identity.

If liturgy be ethics, if this work both of and for the people be authentically expressive of the kind of people we are, the greeting of peace ought to remind both speaker and hearer that God's future for us simultaneously participates in and transcends the here and now. That we both are and are yet to be; that our sanctification into God's holiness is in process, real but yet to be perfected; that we are perpetually (and Augustine and Wesley, together with Paul, would hope progressively) becoming who, by God's mercy in Jesus for us, we already are—these, I would reckon, are among the reasons why Paul so persistently and faithfully introduced himself as he did: as an apostle of Jesus Christ, a servant of the Lord, set apart for the gospel of God.

The temptation is widespread among Christians to read the introductions to Paul's letters in much the same way that scripture is generally attended to in the liturgy: perfunctorily, with respect, but with little substantive attention to what is (or ought to be) going on here. But this, as I have wanted to suggest, is to ignore and otherwise sacrifice a key aspect of

Paul's authorization, together with important clues about why we should credit his writings as authoritative for us. Every action has a presumptive purpose which both transcends and participates in historical contingency.

Consider a common example. In the days when weapons consisted of swords and daggers, it made sense in a society of right-handed dominance to extend the right hand in greeting in order to signify the absence of a threatening weapon and a friendly and hospitable welcome from one person to another. For related reasons, medieval towers were designed with stairway steps going up in left-to-right spirals, so that right-handed defenders could strike from above while right-handed attackers from below were thwarted by masonry on their right-hand side. This also explains why left-handed warriors were much in demand! To this day in Great Britain it is still the custom for road traffic to move forward on the left-hand side, a practice that has its origins in keeping one's fighting right arm ever at the ready.

We very seldom, if ever, reflect nowadays on why we typically shake hands with the right, instead of the left, hand. Indeed, I observe that even the "southpaws" among us extend the right hand in greeting. But there is a reason for this, a purpose, however antiquated and no longer particularly relevant. Shaking hands with the right hand is now merely social convention, nothing more than a custom. If this action is meant to communicate something to another person, however, it is important that we have some idea about the meaning we intend by it and why. In other words, in the measure to which action is purposive and expressive of authentic moral identity, of who we are and mean to be, we need both to understand it ourselves and for it to be appropriate in the situation.

These two marks, in fact, constitute the principal function of a salutation: (1) it communicates one self to an other self, and (2) it does so in a manner that is fitting and proper to both selves.

In the Christian community, we greet each other as the reconciled people of God, as brothers and sisters in the family of Christ. We regard one another no longer as the bastard offspring of a faithless Adam, but as the sons and daughters of God who are reconstituted, redeemed, reconciled, transformed by the power of Jesus' life, ministry, passion, death, resurrection, and ascension. This is the context of our address, our salutation, our presentation of ourselves to one another. We are God's friends; we are a people of peace. Jesus came preaching the good news of the kingdom of

God, and we are the inheritors of his transforming gospel. We are who we are because he is who he is; our lives are shaped by his life, his story becomes our story. "Blessed be God: Father, Son, and Holy Spirit. And blessed be God's kingdom, now and forever. Alleluia. Christ is risen. He is risen indeed. Alleluia."

Now consider further how it is that our liturgical greeting is ethical—that is, that the peace which we speak to one another is an accurate and appropriate communication of who we understand and intend ourselves to be. It is not meant to be a lie, nor do we mean to deceive each other. We present ourselves as among those who have received the "spirit of sonship," as Paul puts it in Romans 8:15ff: "When we cry 'Abba! Father!' it is the Spirit itself bearing witness with our spirit that we are children of God, and if children, then heirs, heirs of God and fellow heirs with Christ." So it is no casual or inconsequential thing that we do when we greet one another with the peace of Christ. Indeed, it is a moral action of significance and great consequence.

MORAL THEOLOGY AS AN ASPECT OF CHRISTOLOGY

Thus far I have argued that liturgy *is* ethics, that ethics *is* liturgy, that worship is a moral act, that indeed liturgy and ethics is everything that the church does which is offered in the name of Jesus. On these terms, it is plain that Christian ethics and moral theology, together with Christian liturgy, is an aspect of christology. That is, it is what we believe about Jesus as God's Christ that certifies ethics as Christian, and moral theology as theology. In order to establish ethics as Christian, and moral theology as theology, we must root them in Jesus Christ himself. So I want to say a bit more now about how that qualifier, "in the name of Jesus," engages and qualifies ethics and moral theology as Christian.[1]

There was a time when professional theologians and pastors were generally criticized for the functional irrelevancy of much of their religious pronouncements; but I believe that time is now past. It was partly to compensate for this deficiency, or to correct this fault, that Karl Barth advised young pastors to carry the Bible in one hand and a daily newspaper in the other—an admonition which was widely, but erroneously, attributed in this country to Reinhold Niebuhr. Barth's priorities were clear: the principal task of the church in the world, he maintained, is criticizing and revising its language about God. For this reason, the "earthen vessels" which communicate the gospel "treasure" must somehow be perpetually changing in order to accommodate human understanding and the changing forms of human need.

Meanwhile, several generations of theological students and seminary faculty, including many who cut their theological teeth on Barth and Niebuhr, have not only reversed the priorities as Barth had conceived them, but have become so successfully preoccupied with dealing directly and "relevantly" with the changing "earthen vessels" as to relegate any thought about an original "treasure" to the limbo of irrelevance.

Who can forget, for example, the general impotency of the church's spokesmen (as they were then) to speak *for the church* and *as the church* as recently as the civil rights struggles of the 1950s or the nation's involvement in Southeast Asia in the 1960s? If theologians and pastors formerly tended to make religious pronouncements which were long on theological rhetoric but short on social and political awareness and application, the situation more recently seems nearer to being the converse. The professional speech of theologians and pastors nowadays tends to be so heavily reliant on scientific and political jargon, so dependent on secular categories, that it often sounds more like newspaper than Bible.

This tendency toward secularism, toward a world in which God is dispensable and therefore denied, is attended by its own camp followers who perceive their task as the development of more or less defensible rationales for emancipating theology from God-talk and embracing fully the secular sphere. The result is that an increasingly prominent point of departure has become culture, or the secular city, or something else, rather than the gospel of Jesus; with the result that the reign of God becomes literally anything we might want it to be in a cosmocentric and anthropocentric theological ethics. How else could we account for the fascination and preoccupation with deciding or not deciding, and for the widespread supposition that decision-making is the *sine qua non* of ethics, Christian or otherwise?

Now I believe that this tendency toward the world has not been altogether misguided or mistaken, because I know that the most powerful symbols eventually grow worn and old. I also believe that the world is God's good creation, that it is therefore not intrinsically or inherently evil, and that Christians appropriately affirm the world and their place in it. To affirm these things is to understand the world as *saeculum*. But there is a significant difference between affirming the world as a good place (indeed the only place) to serve God, and becoming wed to a notion of the world's goodness irrespective of and apart from God. There is similarly a difference between Christian worldliness and worldly Christianity; and it is a difference which is already signified by the relationship between nouns and adjectives. To put it plainly, one perspective is worship, and the other is idolatry.

Of course, the tightrope which stretches between affirming God and appreciating the world is precarious and easy to fall off; and the pole that helps us maintain equilibrium is balanced by several commitments, not the least of which is that we need not (and cannot) make an overly simple identification of beneficent relevance with Christian witness.

Because I teach moral theology in a divinity school my students expect (and I think rightly) that sooner or later I want them to get down to cases, to engage in casuistry, to employ what they have learned about theological ethics to address particular ethical issues or moral problems. Given free rein, their paper topics tend to reflect this expectation, but with an ingenuous twist. My experience with seminary students over three decades now is that these papers almost always demonstrate the student's capacity to do responsible research, and to put together a more or less cogent argument for whatever position the author elects to take in the matter at hand. These are papers that one would expect from people who are, generally speaking, biblically and theologically literate, and who know how to read and digest technical data and information in an area that interests them. If given free rein, however, what these papers generally fail to do is speak directly and self-consciously to the difference it makes or ought to make that one address this matter *as a Christian within the context of Christian tradition, teaching, canon, and the like.*

In the clinical setting of hospital chaplain internships, for example, I observe that the situation has been much the same except that the institutional context is more narrowly prescribed. Consider these excerpts from some old verbatims:

PATIENT: Am I going to die?

CHAPLAIN: That's something you should discuss with your doctor.

DOCTOR: Chaplain, how do you feel about working out "advance directives" with terminally ill patients?

CHAPLAIN: It's really important to talk about that.

PATIENT: Why do you suppose God has abandoned me when I need him so?

CHAPLAIN: Do you feel alone?

PATIENT: Yes, he has always appeared to help me in time of trouble.

CHAPLAIN: Specifically what is troubling you?

PATIENT: Will you pray for me?

CHAPLAIN: What would you like me to include in the prayer?

I appreciate that these excerpts sound like extreme examples of the well-known nondirective approach; but I have to tell you that they are not exceptional in my experience. I have discovered, moreover, that one finds this same phenomenon in the parish. In the late 1960s and early 1970s, when clergy were having to learn a new skill—namely, "problem pregnancy" and preabortion counseling—a group of us conducted a series of statewide workshops for parish ministers. We recorded the workshops on audio tapes, and when I replayed those tapes, I was always impressed by the questions which were prominent, indeed controlling, in the minds of these pastors: What are the medical indications? Does this case qualify for legal abortion under the state statute? What is the woman's family situation? Is she a welfare case? Has she had other "problem" pregnancies? After a lengthy series of such questions as these, I would hear myself asking, "Who speaks about God, or for God, or as a Christian pastor, to a woman who is wanting to talk about a prospective abortion with a pastor?"

At that point the tape would play out an extended silence before somebody said, "We can't impose theological dogma on a woman," or "My job is to help her work through her personal decision, not to preach to her," or "Women have a right to control their own bodies." The opinion widely expressed by these pastors was simply that raising, or even responding to, the "God question" was not their responsibility in this situation. Their job, they believed, was to take care as best they could of the individual, familial, and social factors which impinged on a decision to abort or not to abort a given pregnancy, with humane sensibility and the cultural wisdom which commanded the largest segment of public approbation.

I do not mean to suggest, much less claim, that these brief anecdotal illustrations are conclusive proof that many ecclesial professionals in the 1960s and 1970s adopted a secular style for the exercise of their ministries.

There is, in fact, a large and compelling body of evidence for such a claim which need not be duplicated here. These little examples do show, however, a tendency among clergy to mirror the expectations of others, rather than to define for themselves an articulate identity of their own and to derive their self-understanding from ecclesial traditions. They also suggest how clergy perpetuate and reinforce this alien other-definition by their impotence (or unwillingness) to change it. This seems to me a matter of serious consequence for Christian identity, lay or professional, since in the long run of things we may discover that we are the mediators of virtually everything—sociology, psychology, community organization, brokering of social services, together with a host of other things—except the love of God.

Paul Van Buren once wrote that "the problem now is that the word 'God' is dead."[2] What he meant, I think, was that God-talk is no longer possible and that our only option is to translate "God-statements" into "human-statements." It does often appear in fact that much God-talk is functionally dead, and there is surely evidence of linguistic and conceptual necrosis in a number of settings. But I am not convinced that the "death of God" talk is a sheer necessity in the face of which we are utterly powerless. If our previous heresy was the notion that the church and its ministry is in this life *only* accountable to God, our current heresy is that the church and its ministry is in this life *only* accountable to the human situation (with the implied suspicion that this is all there is). But a richer and thicker understanding of church and ministry would surely acknowledge a bipolar and reciprocating accountability to both God and the human situation.

In recent decades, the most popular—and in some ways the most efficacious—style for many liberal Christians who were seeking meaning and purpose has been transference of one sort or another. They have thus become social workers, pastoral psychologists, urban workers, community organizers, change agents—the list is a very long one indeed. By adopting these functions they have been allowed to identify with the oppressed, the disadvantaged, the marginalized, and the poor in spirit in ways they thought the church indifferent to; and in this identification they have found a meaning and purpose which are personally and existentially satisfying, and enabling as at least a minimal means of their continuing to function at all in ways faithful to their religious commitments. Their evangelical brothers and sisters have managed a similar outcome, but from a posture which is both theoretically and pragmatically more adversarial toward the environing culture and historical human situation.

But the tragic irony is that in this radically secularized identification of service "to the least of these, my brethren," we are in part vicariously participating in an identity the full source and nature of which we seem unwilling, or pathetically unable, to acknowledge. We seem embarrassed to mention anything as irrelevant as the name of Jesus whose brethren both we and they are. I reckon that if we met the need for the cup of cold water and *did not know* Jesus' name, perhaps his blessings could dwell fully within and through this ministry. But if we meet the need for the cup of cold water and, *while knowing Jesus' name*, disregard as irrelevant any "need" of our brother or sister for relationship to him whom the name mediates, we tacitly renounce the identity of Jesus' ministry, and ours.

It is frequently argued—when indeed the issue gets raised at all—that unconcern about a special identity, and the willingness to appropriate other identities and role functions, are proper marks of self-effacing and kenotic humility. Maybe so. But an allegedly Christian identity so amorphous as to renounce any responsibility for a mediating witness to God in the name of Jesus strikes me as altogether another matter. What kind of "humility" is a *God-effacing* humility? Where do we come by the command to be *that* humble? Would we perhaps be more honest simply to acknowledge that our refusal to take responsibility for any direct witness toward God is not self-abnegation but something else cloaking itself under the guise of that misplaced modesty?

On this point there can be no illusions, and nobody ought to disagree with the proposition that the effort to work out an identity which takes responsibility for a distinctively Christian ministry and witness within a largely secularized culture is, under the best circumstances, hard work. It is so much easier, and more immediately and tangibly rewarding, to adopt the kind of "me-too-ism" in which we merely fall back upon the role, status, and palpable prestige which some other identity can provide. Fortunately for us, that temptation gets challenged by an article of faith which seems to be reaffirmed in the unlikeliest situations: God will not be without witnesses. And, fortunately for us, *mirabile visu*, there are signs all about us—among theological students, chaplain interns, parish clergy, seminary faculty, and all sorts and conditions of lay folk—that serious and sustained efforts are being mounted to develop cogent and coherent ways of speaking a Christianly intelligible word in these special settings and circumstances.

That there are times when it is appropriate to be nondirective about God—perhaps sometimes even in response to direct questions—no sensitive person will likely doubt. We may agree at least partially with the words from Ecclesiastes 3:1b that "there is a time for every purpose under heaven," and that this sometimes includes a time to keep silent even about, or especially about, God. The Bible knows full well that God is revealed not only through speech but also through silence.

But the biblical writers do not envision a God who is *only* silent, or any form of witness to God which is *only* silent. If the time to keep silence is indeed seen as "under heaven," there will also be a time to speak. So any Christian ministry worthy of the name will need to include a sensitivity under God to the *kairoi* of when and how to keep silent, but also of when and how to speak (albeit in a human tongue), about the one who can only be invoked because he is, though hidden, always already present.

THE PURPOSE OF GREETING

I suggested earlier that how Christians venture to speak about or for God at all is an aspect of Christology, and now I must say more about how this is so. Although the earliest Christian witnesses certainly made claims about the ontological significance of Jesus as God's eternal Word, their first order of business was to show that what Jesus came to proclaim—which was not himself, but the kingdom of God as a present and future reality—could be grasped only by acknowledging the presence of that kingdom in the life and ministry, passion and death, and resurrection and ascension of Jesus. However our forebears might have done it, our urgent question is how modern folk can appropriate that acknowledgment of Jesus as the Son of God, long awaited but now Immanuel.

For several years now I have begun a lecture which introduces this matter by reading, in Greek, the prologue to St. John's Gospel.

Ἐν ἀρχῇ ἦν ὁ λόγος, καὶ ὁ λόγος ἦν πρὸς τὸν θεόν,
καὶ θεὸς ἦν ὁ λόγος. οὗτος ἦν ἐν ἀρχῇ πρὸς τὸν θεόν.

Although my spoken Greek is barely passable, the students are generally bright enough to grasp the fact that they are listening to unfamiliar utterances. Those few students who have elected to study Greek immediately recognize not only the language but also the passage; happily for my purposes, they are a conspicuous minority. For what I want to ask, after rehearsing John's prologue in *koine* Greek, is whether my hearers have understood what I have read aloud. I want to ask whether any real communication has taken place between us: whether these signs and sounds—in fact, "words"—were an intelligible representation; whether they were proportional to their understanding; whether they were accommodated to their hearing. "Of course you heard," I say to them in English; "but what did you hear?"

I reflected earlier[3] on how the New Testament abounds with the dialectical relationship between seeing and not comprehending, between hearing and not understanding. This juxtaposition is actually characteristic of the entire canon; and so one finds the same notion, in virtually the same language, expressed throughout the Bible. Consider, for example, Psalm 135:15–17:

> *The idols of the nation are silver and gold, the work of human hands.*
> *They have mouths, but they do not speak, they have eyes, but they do*
> *not see, they have ears, but they do not hear.*

In marked contrast to the incapacity of idols and the recalcitrance of humans, God listens, God hears, God answers. So even the deep despair of a Jonah (2:1–2, 10) is not allowed to overtake him, because no tribution can impair the Lord's hearing:

> *Then Jonah prayed to the Lord his God from the belly of the fish, say-*
> *ing, "I called to the Lord, out of my distress, and he answered me; out*
> *of the belly of Sheol I cried, and you did hear my voice. . . ." Then the*
> *Lord spoke to the fish, and it spewed Jonah out upon the dry land.*

From the fifth century, the church subscribed to a theory of the fourfold sense of scripture: (1) the *literal* sense, in which the meaning is self-evident; (2) the *allegorical* sense, which taught about the church and what it should believe; (3) the *tropological* sense, which taught about individuals and what they should do; and (4) the *anagogical* sense, which pointed to the future and awakened expectation.[4] Part of, indeed a large part of, the rationale for this theory of the fourfold sense of scripture is located in the supposition that the language of the Bible opens up a field, rather than some single furrow, of possible meanings. Any interpretation which falls within that field (which is generally defined in the theory by the theological virtues of faith, hope, and love) is therefore valid exegesis of the text, even though that interpretation may not have been intended by the author. So if one asks which sense, which interpretation, of a passage is true, the answer is that they all are true so long as they fall within the field of possible meanings which are created by the story itself.

On these terms, a simple and obvious comment can be made regarding Jesus' teaching about the kingdom of God: communication is occurring here. The etymology of "communication" suggests that it functions "to make common." I take this to mean that "communication" overcomes what separates us as different, and thereby allows us genuinely to share and participate in what is mutual and reciprocal between us. This is precisely what Jesus effects here: by his speech, his word, himself, he creates a commonality, a concurrence, a union of understanding between himself and his listeners. Now let us draw a further, but similarly simple and common-sense, implication from this interpretation—namely, that minimally two persons (a speaker and a hearer) are required for communication, for this kind of being-united-with. And finally, let us make explicit that what unites these two is a word—sometimes written, sometimes spoken, sometimes lived, sometimes even nonverbal—but a word nonetheless which mediates the oneness, the commonality, of these two. An example with which most of us are doubtless familiar is the "consent situation" in medical practice, in which a fiduciary relationship gets established between a patient and a physician, When communication of this sort occurs, we typically say that the result is "community," or being-in-union-with.

I proposed earlier that two conditions must be controlling in a salutation if it means to communicate, and those conditions need to be reiterated here. For such a common understanding to come into being, the speaker must genuinely represent herself or himself to the hearer, and do so in a manner both fitting and proper to both selves. Put differently: (1) the word, in whatever form, must truly represent the person who displays it— that is, the word must be descriptively faithful, honest, true of the one who speaks it; and (2) as our forebears expressed it, the word must be "aptly proportioned"—that is, it must be accommodated to the hearer in a language which the hearer can understand and rightly interpret, and so it must employ symbols and images and concepts and metaphors which are comprehensible and intelligible to the hearer. Reading the prologue to John's Gospel in *koine* Greek to an American audience helps to make this overall point emphatically.

This is a pivotal point, because it is precisely these requirements for creating comm-unity through these controlling conditions which Christians affirm about Jesus. He is, we claim, the authentic Word of God, fully participant in the life of the speaker, who is in the beginning with God, through whom all things were made. He is "consubstantial with the Father" and "true God from true God." The Word which he incarnates and speaks and acts out in his life, ministry, death, resurrection, and ascension is the true representation (re-presentation) of the one true God. It is the claim of the Gospel story that "No one has ever seen God. It is God the only Son, who is close to the Father's heart, who has made him known" (John 1:18).

Jesus is also, we claim, the incarnate Word of God, who was made flesh and dwelt among us, "very man of very man," "full of grace and truth." We believe that under the conditions of our finite existence, and accommodated to our understanding, God in Jesus condescended to our capacity to hear and discern and know God as God. This seems to me a viable exegesis of John 1:14—that in Jesus the Word of God took on human proportion, became humanly present, became palpable, and was thus able to be humanly acknowledged.

The implications which follow from a construal of this sort are far-reaching indeed. The basis for a Christian natural theology and a Christian natural law is laid here, inasmuch as the world is both made by, and is home to, the eternal Word: "He was in the world, and the world came into being through him, yet the world did not know him. He came to his own, and his own people did not accept him. But to all who received him, who believed in his name, he gave power to become children of God" (John 1:10–12). The Word and the world, rightly understood, are neither strangers nor adversaries; they both belong to God. And Karl Barth's insistence (largely lost by his evangelical heirs) that it is a sinful pretension of human autonomy and arrogance to suppose that we can talk about "sin" or know that we are "sinners" apart from Jesus gets reinforced by such a construal as this, because on these terms it is Jesus who exposes and names sin, not vice versa. Conventional Protestant evangelistic formulae notwithstanding, it is not that sin is the necessary requisite for Jesus but precisely the converse. God's Word, whether in the Old Testament or the New Testament, is the presupposition of sin; knowledge of God's will is *ex hypothese* anterior to naming any attitude, action, or condition as sin; otherwise, sin can be (and ordinarily is) a cultural construction defined by the sensibilities of Miss Manners or the wisdom of the Supreme Court. But there is more to say about this when we come to confession.

Meanwhile, the implications which follow from a construal of this sort will also impact epistemology, soteriology, ontology, and the rest of the theological encyclopedia. For example, to appreciate that the controlling conditions of communication entail speaking a true and honest word which is aptly proportioned to a hearer is also to confess that our knowledge of God is not self-generated, but that it is precisely and entirely by acknowledgment. That we know God at all is not, as Karl Barth insisted, our discovery of God, but God disclosing and manifesting himself to us. In the measure to which we have this knowledge, it is something received, a gift. We know who God is, Christians believe, precisely in the proportion to which we acknowledge the Word made flesh, Jesus.

Fides quarens intellectum, or *credo ut intelligam*, as St. Anselm's formulae put it; it is faith seeking understanding, or I believe in order to understand, not the other way around. For it is not that right understanding leads to right faith, but exactly the converse. Right faith leads to right understanding. This does not mean to repudiate, as we have seen, a *ratio naturalis*, a naturally endowed capacity to perceive the workings, and thus the presence, of God in the world. Although the *imago dei* is blurred and blemished by the boundaries of a natural knowledge of God, we do not conclude that it is therefore utterly destroyed in the bargain. What is rather the case is that our natural *cognito* (knowledge) is tempered by an *incognito* (hidden or disguised knowledge) until it is illuminated by *agnitio* (acknowledgment). Blaise Pascal put it this way: "Human things must be known to be loved; but Divine things must be loved to be known."

The analog in the knowledge we have of a human other closely parallels this theological epistemology. And while this is not the place for a lengthy excursus into empiricist "subjectivity" and rationalist "objectivity" as competing epistemologies, we might just observe that to think in terms of "knowledge by acknowledgment" is not only an alternative to Locke and Descartes, but also more faithful to the Biblical insistence on reciprocity and cooperation between speaker and hearer. It is because Christians believe Jesus to be God's self-revelation, that God was incarnate as Jesus, that we conclude that Jesus is God's true and faithful Word to us, both representative of the speaker and proportional to our hearing and understanding. This is to know by way of acknowledging—not by discovering for ourselves, but by having, in other words, this knowledge discovered to us by an other.

I believe that a Christian acclamation and greeting is suitably construed along these lines. If our greeting with the peace of Christ were confined to Sunday worship, if it were limited to the saints in the church, I suppose that there would be no problem in describing God's incarnation as Jesus in such special ways that restricted acknowledgment *only* to the faithful. But I have wanted to argue that the church's liturgy is every action which is done in the name of Jesus; and parts of that action are surely mission and witness and evangelization in and to "the world." Christian theology and ethics is conceived and written especially for Christians, but not for Christians only. And if this be granted, as it seems to me it must be, then we have to ask how the gospel can be communicated to those who do not acknowledge the one whose good news it is. Is there a language for witnessing to Jesus, for greeting the world with the peace of Christ, which is simultaneously the true and faithful word of God and aptly proportioned to those who have ears but do not hear? Putting the question this way is bound to be rhetorical inasmuch as "not acknowledging the one whose good news it is" portrays a state of affairs which surely, at one time or another, is descriptively accurate for all of us. None of us is naturally a Christian; a Christian is someone we become.

To be a Christian is to be in some ways in fundamental contradiction to the world, and to be in some ways in fundamental correspondence with the world. This mysterious dialectic has been formulated in many familiar phrases, among which all of us will doubtless recognize these two: "God's kingdom is not of this world" and "This is my Father's world." If we can get straight about what is distinctive, maybe even unique, about Christian convictions—if we are careful to get the priorities straight, to keep the horse before the cart, the divine initiative preconditional to human response—perhaps we can formulate a viable understanding of a Christian natural theology which, unlike the excessively autonomous formulations of medieval scholasticism, permits us the possibility of communicating the gospel to the world.

So it bears repeating that while it is true that the first audience for Christian theology and ethics is the company of Christians, it is mistaken and graceless to hold that Christians are meant to be the only audience. And therein arises the problem of how we can be simultaneously "in but not of the world"; of how we can faithfully honor the great commission to proclaim the kingdom of God (Luke 9:60b), to "go therefore and make disciples of all nations, baptizing them in the name of the Father, and of the Son, and of the Holy Spirit, teaching them to observe all that I have commanded you; and lo, I am with you always, [even] to the close of the age" (Matthew 28:19–20).

Two hundred miles northeast of Los Angeles lies a foreboding gorge named Death Valley. I'm told that it is an awesome place—the lowest spot in the continental United States, 276 feet below sea level; and also the hottest place on the continent, with an official maximum reading of 134 degrees Fahrenheit. Further despoiling this scene, rivers flow into Death Valley and disappear. One's imagination does not have to work very hard to picture the desolation of Death Valley. But not so many years ago, quite an amazing thing happened: for nineteen straight days, rain fell into this sterile wasteland; and suddenly all kinds of seeds, dormant for years, burst into bloom. In a valley of death, people were surprised by life.

Lent is coming to an end as I write this, and I am acutely reminded that what happened in Death Valley is very like the story of Passion Week and Easter. In a profound sense, this is the story of the entire gospel of Jesus. The passion and crucifixion is the Death Valley of the Bible; it is the lowest spot on the biblical continent. But on Easter the showers of God's mercy fall on the earth; and through the power of the resurrection, suddenly all manner of new life bursts forth from the dead gorge of Jesus' tomb. People expecting death are surprised by life. Mark tells how three women went to the tomb on Easter morning to anoint a dead body—but they were surprised by life. John relates that Mary Magdalene wept uncontrollably at the mouth of the empty grave—until she heard a voice speaking her name. Luke reports that two disciples were traveling to Emmaus and that, as they walked, they unburdened hearts full of sorrow and loss to a stranger; that when evening came the disciples and the stranger had supper together, and "their eyes were opened, and they recognized him [Jesus]" . . . and that immediately they rushed breathlessly to Jerusalem to tell the other disciples, and those who were with them, how with eyes for death they had been surprised by life.

This is an apt summary of the Christian story; and for all of its subtlety and nuance and complexity, the heart and substance of the story is simply that God loves the world and will not abandon it. While the world may reject God, God does not forsake the world; while the world may hate God, God does not become the world's adversary. Despite all of our entitled expectations of ugliness and meanness and death, when we have eyes which see, we are able to perceive that we have been gifted with life rather than the death which we reckon we deserve.

But this is the Christian story not only at its end; it is also the Christian story at its beginning. And while these features are especially prominent in John's Gospel, they are also to be found in the Synoptics.

> In the beginning was the Word, and the Word was with God, and the Word was God. The same was in the beginning with God. All things were made by him, and without him was not any thing made that was made. In him was life, and the life was the light of men. And the light shineth in darkness, and the darkness comprehended it not.
>
> He was in the world, and the world was made by him, and the world knew him not. He came unto his own, and his own received him not. But as many as received him, to them gave he power to become the sons of God, even to them that believe on his name.
>
> And the Word was made flesh, and dwelt among us (and we beheld his glory, the glory as of the only begotten of the Father) full of grace and truth. (John 1:1–5, 10–12, 14)

Timothy O'Connell, in a popular text on contemporary Catholic moral theology,[5] has made the important point that Christian ethics and Christian moral theology are *ex hypothese* an aspect of christology; that is, that these reflections must be rooted in Christ himself, and in our understanding of his person and work if they are to be certified as "Christian."

The prologue to John's Gospel provides a rich reservoir for a prolegomenon of this sort; indeed, the inaugural "In the beginning was the Word" signifies two important and reciprocating truth-claims for

Christians. The first of these is that Christ is the model, the paradigm, according to which the world was created; and the second is that creation is shaped in terms of the Word of God, that everything is created as a ready receptacle for the divine presence. O'Connell identifies four implications from this understanding which, if acknowledged and claimed, describe in fundamental ways the activity of Christian ethics and Christian moral theology:

1. That it follows from this relationship between the Word and Creation that "Christ is the forethought of the Father's creative action, not its afterthought";

2. That the incarnation of God's Word in Jesus Christ makes sense with or without the reality of original sin [Karl Barth had made the similar argument for Protestant theology, when he claimed that sin was unintelligible apart from Jesus Christ; that Jesus is the presupposition for sin, not the other way around];

3. That "the entrance of God's Word into the world is not to be likened to the surreptitious entry of a guerrilla warrior into enemy territory," but of God's Word coming home to his world;

4. That this understanding of Christ and creation "make us appreciate with unparalleled richness the potential of this human world," in view of which Christians will regard this world with utter seriousness because it is a vehicle fecund with God's presence.[6]

The world, on this understanding, becomes truly salvific; it is precisely the place, and the only place, where salvation occurs. God's redemption takes place, in a manner of speaking, on our turf. So we do not look for pie in the sky by and by, or to excuse ourselves from ministering to the least of our brothers and sisters in this place and time and circumstance by engaging ourselves in "spiritual" (translate: dematerial, ethereal, disembodied, unworldly) exercises. This poor and pathetic earth is where God comes to greet us and transform us from enemies to friends, from competitive coalitions into a community of sons and daughters, from belligerent and truculent cliques into a family of sisters and brothers.

Of course, the temporal and mundane do not exhaust the Christian story; this story also affirms God's transcendence, and perhaps nowhere with more beauty and tenderness than in the spatial metaphors of the Psalms:

Praise the Lord! Praise, O servants of the Lord, praise the name of the Lord! Blessed be the name of the Lord from this time forth and for evermore! From the rising of the sun to its setting the name of the Lord is to be praised! The Lord is high above all nations, and his glory above the heavens! Who is like the Lord our God, who is seated on high, who looks far down upon the heavens and the earth?" *(Ps. 113:1–6)*

To be sure, the psalmist knows that God, being "high above all nations," is not thereby disaffiliated and unassociated with the earth below. The psalmist, indeed Biblical theism as a whole, does not confirm Barth's borrowed-from-Kierkegaard claim that God is *totaliter aliter*—wholly, entirely, altogether other—and separated from us and the rest of creation by an "infinite qualitative distinction." Consider how the remainder of Psalm 113 (vv. 7–9) suggests that the exalted God is very much in touch with earthly things:

He raises the poor from the dust, and lifts the needy from the ash heap, to make them sit with princes, with the princes of his people. He gives the barren woman a home, making her the joyous mother of children. Praise the Lord!

Psalm 103 is probably more generally familiar, and conveys the same point more powerfully.

The Lord is merciful and gracious, slow to anger and abounding in steadfast love. He will not always chide, nor will he keep his anger for ever. He does not deal with us according to our sins, nor requite us according to our iniquities. For as the heavens are high above the earth, so great is his steadfast love toward those who fear him; as far as the east is from the west, so far does he remove our transgressions from us.

As a father pities his children, so the Lord pities those who fear him. For he knows our frame; he remembers that we are dust. As for man, his days are like grass; he flourishes like a flower of the field; for the wind passes over it, and it is gone, and its place knows it no more. But the steadfast love of the Lord is from everlasting to everlasting upon those who fear him, and his righteousness to children's children, to those who keep his covenant and remember to do his commandments. (Ps. 103:8–18)

Although Christian faith is closely allied to and deeply dependent upon biblical religion, these two are neither synonymous nor coequal; and, in fact, it is confusing (as well as incorrect) to speak of a "Judeo-Christian faith." Of this I will need to say more later. But just now, and especially as regards the matter of transcendence and immanence, it is important that we acknowledge a very close correspondence between the greater weight of the biblical corpus and the mainstream of Christian theology. In this connection, I should refer to the finest treatment of this matter with which I am familiar—namely, the two chapters on "The Transcendence of the Immanent" and "The Immanence of the Transcendent" in William Temple's *Nature, Man, and God.*[7] In sum, Temple notes that God is active in the world, and that its process is God's activity; yet God is also the world's creator, and therefore transcendent of it. Transcendence and immanence are not to be sharply contrasted terms: "It is the Transcendent who is immanent, and it is the Immanent who transcends."[8]

The Christian story embraces this dialectic by testifying to "the most high God" and also by exhibiting itself as the most materialistic of religions. Among all the world's religions, Christianity is the only one to venture the audacious claim that its God has become human, incarnate under the conditions of our worldly existence, and that all of creation has been hallowed to be a receptacle planned and prepared for its God's presence. This is why we ought not apologize, or experience the least embarrassment, for the apparent outrage of saying that we encounter God, experience God, come to know God most profoundly, in materiality, in the water of Holy Baptism, in the bread and wine of Holy Eucharist, in the communion and fellowship of the body of Christ the church. These, like Christ's incarnation, are accommodations to the contingencies of human knowing, discerning, understanding. And the crucial matter is that *in and through these things* we are gifted with our true identity, with the knowledge of who we truly and authentically are: we learn through materiality that we are the reconciled people of God, sheep of Christ's own fold, lambs of his own flock, sinners of his own redeeming.

With this knowledge, which we have by acknowledgment, the fundamental ethical command is simply to be what, by God's mercy, we already are. Paul put it this way:

> *If anyone is in Christ, he is a new creation; the old has passed away, behold, the new has come. All this is from God, who through Christ reconciled us to himself and gave us the ministry of reconciliation; that is, God was in Christ reconciling the world to himself, not counting their trespasses against them, and entrusting to us the message of reconciliation. So we are ambassadors for Christ, God making his appeal through us. We beseech you on behalf of Christ, be reconciled to God. For our sake he made him to be sin who knew no sin, that in him we might become the righteousness of God." (2 Corinthians 5:17–21)*

This is why Christian ethics cannot be reduced to a system of codes, or rules, or formal principles; Christian ethics, instead, is a faithful and dynamic articulation, amid the chaotic and manifold contingencies of human existence, of the meaning of Jesus' command that we should *be* the person and people whom he has made us to be.

THE PEACE OF CHRIST AND THE THREAT OF VIOLENCE

The challenge of Christian ethics is that the "knowledge of God which is sufficient unto salvation" does not always (does it ever?) translate facilely into public policy or pliantly into judicious behavior. Not only do we not know the good beforehand, but there are occasions, as Paul well knew, when we are prevented from doing the good which we think we know. An example of how divisive this challenge can be for the community which understands itself to be God's friend and a peaceable people, is the troubling set of existential questions which are posed by the threat—and sometimes the reality—of violence, and particularly of war.

Roland Bainton, in his classic *Christian Attitudes Toward War and Peace*, has shown that, "broadly speaking," Christians have offered three responses to the violence of war. All of them recognize human depravity and each of them signifies a certain relationship between the church and the world:

> *Pacifism has commonly despaired of the world and dissociated itself either from society altogether, or from political life, and especially from*

war. The advocates of just war theory have taken the position that evil can be restrained by the coercive power of the state . . . The crusade belongs to the theocratic view that the Church, even though it be a minority, should impose its will upon a recalcitrant world. Pacifism is thus often associated with withdrawal, the just war with qualified participation, and the crusade with dominance of the Church over the world."[9]

That there are devout and articulate advocates for each of these attitudes toward war only confirms that there is no single, normative, imperative reading or hearing of the Gospel. I sincerely regret that this is so, if only because it represents a serious affirmation of our fractiousness, our obstinacy, our muleheadedness, our inclination to sin. All the same it is true, and in much the same way that the many schisms in Christianity also bear witness that there is no single, monolithic, normative reading of the Gospel. My beloved teacher, H. Shelton Smith, used to say that the scandal of Christianity is that there are more sects than insects. As regrettable as this observation is, it seems unarguably clear that this circumstance is part and parcel of the human condition. Maybe we would do otherwise if we could, but our situation is actually the condition of sin, *non posse non peccare.* So a certain irony attends all this inasmuch as the theological genesis of schism in the Christian tradition appears to have deep roots in an irrepressible piety which simply will not be suppressed by the superordinate authority of a parent church.

The conclusion seems therefore self-evident to me that not all of us read the Gospel, or hear the Christian story, in the same way. I am embarrassed by this fact because it shows our sinful determination—yours and mine—to invert priorities and make God in our image and our story God's story. I could wish that we believed the same things in the same ways, and that we exhibited those beliefs in behaviorally recognizable ways. But the fact of the matter is that we don't.

This explains in part why there is no such thing as Christian ethics in the sense that there is a set of notions, universally subscribed to, about the content of God's good for us which we unmistakably and faithfully incarnate in our own lives. Instead there are only Christians who, in their work and indeed their whole lives, exhibit, as they are given light to see it, God's good for us. This is their liturgy, and ours. Emil Brunner put it succinctly when he observed that God's command does not vary in its intention, but that it does vary in content according to circumstance.[10] The Great Commandment, the "summary of the Law," is that we should love God with all our heart, soul, mind, and strength, and love our neighbor as ourself. The divine command in the New Testament requires only one thing, and that is the service of God. This, in fact, is what distinguishes and differentiates the Law, which either interdicts or requires certain prescribed behaviors, from the Gospel.

Yet another way to stake this claim is to say that we do not know the good beforehand in any material way. We can only know the good beforehand in a formal way, and that way is to love God with all our heart, mind, soul, and strength, and our neighbor as ourself. We do not and cannot know how to incarnate that command apart from the circumstance in which we are asked to exhibit God's good for us. Nor can we be confident that a simple observation of behavior will permit us unambiguously to discern its purpose, that it is "the right thing done for the right reason." It is a well-worn moral maxim, but perhaps it bears repeating here, that the meaning of an action is not self-evident in a simple observation of the action itself. So I want to invite you to consider in very practical terms, that the behavior of a parent toward a child, or of a wife toward a husband, or of a professor toward a student, or of a pastor toward a congregation—and vice versa, of course—may vary in its specific mode(s) of conduct according to different circumstances, and yet remain stable and constant in its intention.

By Christian standards, the Rabbinic formulation of the "Golden Rule" inverted the axiom: "do not do to another what you would not like done to yourself." In my own experience, I confess that naming what I would not like done to me tends to be a considerably easier (and clearer) task than saying with precision what I would like done to me, and what I therefore ought to do toward my neighbor. In this regard, the Decalogue continues to be a perennial challenge to my moral imagination. "Do not kill." Right; I accept this commandment as a moral maxim which rightly governs my relationships with my neighbors. But what about this particular neighbor in this particular circumstance? "Do not steal." Right; I accept that as a rule it is wrong to take what belongs to another. But my family is starving, and you have a bakery full of bread which you will sell only at exorbitant prices;

does your greed and selfishness plus my family's need equal the unqualified sanctity of property rights? "Do not lie." Right; I believe this is a useful, perhaps even an imperative, claim which we have toward one another. But even if we could say with surety what constitutes truth, are we always and in every circumstance obliged to tell it? Even to this small child? Even to this sociopath who means to make truth the means to harm? "Love God!" Of course. No Christian can dispute this imperative. But the imperative does not resolve the agonizing interrogatory: How? Well, by loving your neighbor. Right; but how do I do that?

To fail to take account of indicative circumstance as the condition which makes it possible to connect specific behavior to the Gospel imperative(s) carries with it three dubious consequences: (1) One of these is to impose more or less arbitrarily a historically conditioned judgment of the circumstances without taking account of the subtlety and range of possible intention. (2) Another tendency is to suppose that one is immune to or emancipated from being in a particular place and time (and circumstance) and thereby to deny finitude and creatureliness, what some call "social location" and what I have just associated with historical conditioning. (3) The third possible consequence is the risk of discounting the need(s) of the other in favor of the need(s) of the self, because the only thing that counts is supposed to be the self's fervent intention undisciplined by the neighbor's need.

We have for a long time played elegant games with words like power, force, and violence; games in which we develop a spectrum of meaning(s) so that, for example, the psychological power expressed by persuasion is reputed to be licit while other kinds of power, which may express themselves forcefully or even violently, are ruled out of court. My own judgment is that treating and understanding language of this sort in this way is too facile, too neat, too simplistic a set of distinctions.

I take the presence of students in class to be a kind of tacit consent; I do not take their pulse at every class meeting, or even give them a preview of things to come and seek their approbation for it. I take the responsibility for deciding whether these materials, books, lectures, and the rest are what students need to hear and learn; and in these senses I suppose that one could say that these students are violated—maybe in relatively benign ways, but violated all the same. Sometimes there is a question interjected into a lecture, or even a modest disagreement with what is being said; and then I am obliged to give an account of why I say what I do. Far from diminishing at all, much less denying, the ways in which there has been a kind of force field between the student(s) and me, these circumstances demonstrate again for me how there are no human relationships which are void of power. Similar kinds of things happen between spouses, pastors and congregations, parents and children, and so on. And so it is just too facile and neat to claim that the licitness of power relationships between and among persons is arbitrarily defined by resorting to these kinds of word games and without referencing judgment to both principle and circumstance.

World War II, the Korean War, the civil rights movements of the 1950s and 1960s, and the Vietnam War have vividly and harshly confronted us with questions of power and violence. I remember particularly the period between *Brown v. Board of Education* and the civil rights acts of the mid-1960s. Of course segregation and racism are wrong; of course the doctrine of separate but equal is untenable; of course Jim Crow justice is barbaric and xenophobic. But what is a person who understands and intends himself or herself to be a disciple of Jesus Christ to do about it? Many people said, "Well, I really don't know what to do about it." And a number of us thought that if this were the truth, these folks really didn't believe these things were wrong, because if these things were wrong they were morally intolerable and something had to be done to correct them. So some others of us said that these things really were wrong, and that we had to set about changing and correcting them. "That's fine," we were told, "but what are you going to do about them?"

One answer was, "I'm going to work for the passage of civil rights legislation which will require those people who don't share our vision and belief about racial justice to affirm (however grudgingly) the rights of oppressed minorities to eat in public restaurants, attend neighborhood schools, live where they please, and experience nondiscrimination in the workplace. I cannot be conditioned by what racists think is right and good; there is a higher law, a better notion about what is just and true and good, and my loyalty is to that law." And even though so-called nonviolent methods were employed to concretize this vision of racial justice and harmony, it was clear to me that my racist friends were being violated. Is there a way to imagine how any witness to reform which is grounded in the Gospel can avoid this kind of violation? I rather doubt it, if only because we are not naturally friends of God and a people of peace; we have to be trained to be the kind of people God wants us to be, and that training involves *metamorphosis*, the kind of profound alteration that transforms a caterpillar into a butterfly.

We have too long thought, because this kind of violence is relatively benign, that it is inconsequential, or otherwise does not belong in the spectrum which includes violence. And I confess that this kind of moral calculus is attractive and appealing. All the same, it is naive to suppose that even persuasion occurs in the absence of a power field; and this means that if we refuse to acknowledge certain actions as violent, it is only because we give them another, more compatible, name.

So yet another reason for believing that thoroughgoing pacifism is morally mistaken is that love is preferential in this life. Love is not an oblong blur, without definition, reduced entirely to dimensions of feeling and sentiment. It is emphatically not impossible to get a grip on love; love in this life is not the relational equivalent of trying to take firm hold of a greased pig. It is simply preferential; it makes difficult choices; it suffers no illusions about its obligations and its limitations. This is why we have some people as friends and not others, why we hug some people and shake hands with others, why we eat with some and not with others, why we sleep with one and not with others, and so on.

That love is preferential in these ways is, I believe, a function of our finitude and creatureliness; preferential love demonstrates how it is that we cannot imagine ways to transcend those boundaries and limitations. What we hope, of course, is that God will increase our capacity to love with that love wherewith we have been loved. While Catholic Christians affirm a doctrine of sanctification, we are chary of any suggestion that we achieve perfection in this life. We are not as bad as Calvin believed, or as good as Pelagius thought. It turns out that we are a kind of living contradiction, at once justified and sinful, *simul iustus et peccator*. Being justified doesn't mean that we are good; it means that God accounts us as good, doesn't hold our sins against us, forgives us when our preferential neighbor-love violates the command to love neighbor as self. This, of course, is precisely why casuistry must always be attended by penance.

It is true, I think, that there are times when we ought to heed the maxim "Don't do anything, just stand there." The urgent question, again, is which times are those? My experience is that they are likely to be those times when one has the perception that nothing is seriously gained or lost by inactivity. This is only to say that there seem to be times when one's action or inaction does not seriously make a material difference. There are surely other times when one discerns that the gain of activity outweighs any loss that might be attached to inactivity. I have wondered now and then whether some such notion might have sponsored Martin Luther King's commitment to nonviolent resistance. I have also suggested earlier that this phrase is a euphemism which cannot bear the scrutiny of careful grammatical analysis if it means that "we won't do anything because the gain of nonviolent power clearly outweighs the loss which would be associated with another form of power more nearly akin to violence." My experience was that sitting-in in restaurants and shops was a violent action; it surely provoked violent responses. I sat-in and got arrested for it, and that was a violent act—both my action and the reaction it generated. Of course, it is not the same violent act as firing a sawed-off shotgun point-blank into someone's face, but in its own way it is violent all the same.

Perhaps it is helpful to remember that there is a bifocality in all this. One clear focus is that God is sovereign; that everything, even the tragic dimension of human existence, is under God's care and keeping; and that therefore it really doesn't matter whether we do something or nothing at all. God is sovereign, and our pathetic and piddling little stuff is not going to change that. One of James Weldon Johnson's sermons was wonderfully titled, "Young Man, Your Arm's Too Short to Box with God"; and his point was simply that God, not us, is in control. The other side of this dialectic is that covenant fidelity requires us to cooperate as best we can with whatever we discern to be God's will and purpose. So we are faithful, as best we can be, to the rigorous requirements of the Gospel.

The urgent question is emphatically not whether Christians ought to be a peaceable people and eschew violence. The question rather locates in the recognition that the peace of Christians is God's peace, and that we are powerless to bring that peace about. It is "the peace of God," not our own peace, which we offer one another; and because it is not our peace but God's, we likely contaminate it with our sin. Only God can achieve God's peace, and that may be different from the kind of conventional equilibrium between and among people that we typically have in mind when we use the word "peace." I prefer to think that our best efforts are not committed toward peace as we perceive it, but toward God; and I suggest that the considerable difference between these two is worth our attention. One is likely to be ideologic advocacy; the other more nearly resembles worship.

From initial considerations of greeting with the peace of Christ as authorized self-presentation which authentically communicates the self in a fitting way, we moved further to argue that, for that kind of community to be birthed, two conditions need to be controlling: (1) the word (in whatever form) must be truly representative of the one who speaks it, and (2) that word must be aptly proportioned and appropriate to the one who hears it. We proceeded then to claim that this account rehearses precisely those controlling conditions for community which Christians confess about Jesus: that he is the authentic Word of God, fully participant in the life of the speaker, and thus a true representation of the one true God; and that he is also accommodated to our understanding, incarnate under the conditions of our existence, "like as we are in all things save without sin."

The role and function of greeting with the peace of Christ serve to confirm how it is that our knowledge of God (and of one another) is not self-generated or self-originated, but reciprocally dependent upon acknowledgment of the other whose self-knowledge we are privileged to have disclosed to us. If we believe with John that "no one has ever seen God," that God is made known through "the only Son, who is in the bosom of the Father," it follows that the knowledge of God "sufficient for salvation" is ours in the measure to which we acknowledge Jesus as God's true and authentic representation and recapitulation. Knowledge of this sort is a gift.

GREETINGS AND PROMISES

This should make it easier to appreciate an organic unity between liturgy and ethics, between a life of prayer and a life of holiness, and how these two are actually one in both concept and practice. Consider, for example, the connections we can make between "greeting with the peace of Christ" and "promise-making." If we extend a greeting with an outstretched right hand, the implied promise is that we intend the other no harm; indeed, the implied understanding is that this is a friendly gesture. So it would be surprising if, simultaneously with the outstretched right hand, the left hand attacked with a switchblade knife. Understandably, the one receiving this version of the "glad hand" would feel deceived, tricked, lied to. Or if, in verbal exchanges, what is said to one is contradicted by what is said to another, we perceive that the speaker is untrustworthy, undependable, and that the speaker's word is not a true word. Thus we experience gossip, or malicious rumor, or hypocrisy. The speaker is dishonest, we say.

A greeting, we think, ought truthfully to convey what is meant to be conveyed and not something else which is, in fact, false. "Say what you mean, and mean what you say," we say. A greeting is a promise that I am truly, in this or that way, as I represent myself to you to be. You can count on it; my word is my bond; you can depend on me: these and like phrases call to mind the wonderful definition of a neurotic as a person who, when you ask how he or she is, tells you. What endows a promise with power is that it generates confident expectations; and when those expectations are not lived up to, we conclude that the promise is not true (or has not come true), that the promisor has violated our trust. And in the measure to which this is so, community between us is fractured, even ruptured. But this, we should remember, is precisely the opposite outcome from what is intended by a friendly salutation.

Of course, not everyone agrees that lying is wrong, and some even argue that certain kinds of lies are licit.[11] But a mischievous and malicious greeting of the sort described above is not the sort of venial mendacity which many of us would regard as "excusable lying," as letters of recommendation sometimes turn out to be. It is, instead, a form of deliberate and harmful deception which St. Thomas would have labeled a mortal sin. Augustine argued this point with elegance and sagacity in response to a request for a summary of his thought on the essential teachings of the Christian faith. In *The Enchiridion*, literally the "handbook" or "manual," he illustrates how *who we are* translates into *what we do*. Following a brief passage in which he argues that error, though not always a sin, is always an evil, Augustine writes about lying:

> But every lie must be called a sin, because not only when a man knows the truth, but even when, as a man may be, he is mistaken and deceived, it is his duty to say what he thinks in his heart, whether it be true, or whether he only think it to be true. But every liar says the opposite of what he thinks in his heart, with purpose to deceive. Now it is evident that speech was given to man, not that men might therewith deceive one another, but that one man might make known his thoughts

to another. To use speech, then, for the purpose of deception, and not for its appointed end, is a sin. Nor are we to suppose that there is any lie that is not a sin, because it is sometimes possible, by telling a lie, to do service to another. For it is possible to do this by theft also, as when we steal from a rich man who never feels the loss, to give to a poor man who is sensibly benefited by what he gets. And the same can be said of adultery also, when, for instance, some woman appears likely to die of love unless we consent to her wishes, while if she lived she might purify herself by repentance; but yet no one will assert that on this account such an adultery is not a sin. And if we justly place so high a value upon chastity, what offense have we taken at truth, that, while no prospect of advantage to another will lead us to violate the former by adultery, we should be ready to violate the latter by lying? It cannot be denied that they have attained a very high standard of goodness who never lie except to save a man from injury; but in the case of men who have reached this standard, it is not the deceit, but their good intention, that is justly praised, and sometimes even rewarded. It is quite enough that the deception should be pardoned, without it being made an object of laudation, especially among the heirs of the new covenant, to whom it is said: "Let your communication be, Yea, yea; Nay, nay: for whatsoever is more than these cometh of evil." And it is on account of this evil, which never ceases to creep in while we retain this mortal vesture, that the co-heirs of Christ themselves say, "Forgive us our debts."[12]

Because our customary greetings frequently include touching of some sort—a handshake, a hug, a slap on the shoulder, or some other bodily contact—we can further illustrate how a salutation correlates with a promise by considering this tactile dimension in which all of us, at one time or another, have participated.

Among the first things to observe in this connection is that all of the means by which we communicate with each other are incarnate, embodied, material means. Our thoughts are transmitted by electrical and biochemical impulses in the brain, our sounds by the larynx and tongue and lungs, our movements by the limbs and joints and muscle, and so on. *We express who we are through the agency of our bodies.* Indeed, in Western culture, the measure of community between persons tends to be calibrated by the extent of physical intimacy which they desire and permit. So we do not touch those who are estranged from us, except perhaps to harm them (e.g., by assaults of various sorts, or sometimes by capital punishment); but we do touch perfunctorily, and within definite boundaries of established social convention and personal protocol, casual acquaintances (e.g., by shaking hands); or we may touch completely and without inhibition our lover, our beloved (e.g., by engaging in coitus). Touching is proportional to intimacy, and intimacy is a function of shared promise-making. Touching, in other words, has everything to do with clear, however contingent, self-understandings, both of the one touching and of the one being touched.

Thus, to repeat a point made earlier, Christians need not apologize for saying that we encounter God most profoundly in touching and engaging materiality: in water, and bread, and wine, and other persons. Nor are Christians scandalized to say that God was in Christ, incarnate, enfleshed, embodied; to claim that God is manifest fully and perfectly and completely to us in the materiality of this one, Jesus, who was like us in all things except that he was without sin. Christians are a people who know that materiality is the vehicle for human communication; that the body is the agent of the mind (as well, we might just acknowledge, of whatever it is we mean to point to when we say "spirit"); and that body is the means by which we extend ourselves in the world. Body and mind (spirit) work together to express the self, which incorporates but transcends both of them.

To be sure, there are some who have difficulty with this kind of talk. Indeed, it probably sounds quite nonsensical in a time when so much recent philosophy and theology and psychology—to say nothing of popular self-realization hucksters and their glib psychobabble—have ventured to annul psychosomatic wholeness. There is a lot of Manichaeism still loose in the modern world. Yet, with the possible exception of some schizophrenics I know—not all of whom are institutionalized—*I do not know any disembodied selves*. The only selves I know are bodied-forth.

The eucharist has been for Christians one of the principal battlegrounds in this matter, examples of which are the two questions which currently preoccupy ecumenical conversation in the World Council of Churches. One of these is, how can we understand the *sacrifice* of Christ in the eucharist? The other is, how can we understand the *presence* of Christ in the eucharist? Both questions are related to our interests here, but the question of presence is particularly apposite to reflections on greeting-as-promise-making through the agency of materiality. We will give further attention to eucharist; but it may be useful in this context just to point out that modern scholarship has rediscovered some biblical and patristic meanings of *anamnesis*[13] which might go a long way toward ameliorating those famous conflicts between Luther and Zwingli, in which Luther insisted on "real presence" while Zwingli maintained that the event of the Lord's Supper was nothing more than a rehearsal of the Last Supper.

The account in the Lima text,[14] for example, takes its cue from understanding *anamnesis* in a threefold way: (1) this rite, the Holy Communion, is not a human construct but a God-given rite; (2) *anamnesis* does not affirm absence but is the means by which one is made present; and (3) the *epiklesis*[15] is offered in order to make real the sign, to remember God to the faithful through the elements of bread, water, and wine.

These are the key concepts that the aforementioned document employs for understanding the presence of Christ in the eucharist. Jesus does not come to us disembodied, dematerialized—which is unhappily and mistakenly the too-often supposed meaning of "spiritual" nowadays—but in and through Holy Spirit indwelling matter. This is how Jesus is made present to us: God has promised it; Jesus has commanded (*sacramentum*) it; and here in this action, in this materiality, we are re-collected and re-membered by God. It cannot be too strongly emphasized that for Christians this is not something of our own doing. We are not remembering ourselves to God by some exercise of devout piety, much less by a sentimental reminiscence; we are not accommodating God to our lives. God re-members us, God incorporates us, thereby training us to be his people. We are God's witnesses in this world.

This seems to me properly descriptive of what goes on between us in greeting-cum-promisemaking-cum-touching. We are being re-membered in discrete ways to an other who is other; and what is wanted is that this touching be both true and proportional, honest and appropriate. Among many circumstances in which touching occurs—following a touchdown, visiting a physician's office, making love with one's spouse—there is ordinarily a near-perfect congruence between the controlling conditions and authentic touching *when the action promises no more than it can truly represent, when the action delivers no more than it can promise.*

This is also why the meaning of an action is not self-evident in a simple observation of the action itself. If the meaning of an action is to be evident, it must first of all be defined by the true meaning of which the agent is capable; and then the action must be accommodated, fitted, to the other to whom it is addressed. Consider that what appears to be a simple action, like touching, can be helpful or harmful, loving or hateful, affirming or exploiting. This, in part, is why the church's teaching about intimacies between woman and man has affirmed that coitus is appropriate only within marriage. Outwardly, in the realm of appearance, married lovers may be indistinguishable from unmarried lovers; simple observation leads us to suppose that they are both engaged in the same action: they touch, they fondle, they kiss, they "make love" as we say. But Paul knew, as we ought to know, that there is a difference within sameness here; and this difference may well have been what Jesus had in mind when he defined adultery as a matter of the heart (Matt. 5:27–28).

It is also a difference which, however much we have tried to suppress it, remains recognizable in our language. We still have a number of nouns which identify different acts of human sexual congress: rape, incest, conjugal love, adultery, pedophilia, etc. Each of these words signifies a boundary which suggests whether a true or mistaken representation of self is present here, whether promises are signified which can or cannot be kept, whether this action is a "word" faithful and proportional to the speaker and the hearer in ways which are conducive to community between them.

I am frequently reminded of Woody Allen's acerbic commentary on the fact that, now and then, a situation offers us less than meets the eye. "For sure," he said, "the lion and the lamb shall lie down together; but the lamb won't get much sleep." The "greeting with the peace of Christ" in the liturgy is rooted and grounded in a certain self-understanding and a certain self-presentation; and it occurs early on, so that our identity to each other is clear at the outset. If it is true, as I have claimed, that liturgy is ethics and vice versa, and that every work of Christians done in the name of Jesus is liturgy, then promise-making as presence to another describes the limits as well as the possibilities for our community together. This is another way in which a life of prayer and holy living are dimensions of the same reality.

CHAPTER FIVE

OFFERING AND INTERCESSION

Every pastor who has ever declined to feature "Mother's Day" or "Earth Day" or "Boy Scout Sunday," or some other equally compelling but banal secular cause or crusade as the principal focus of a Sunday service, has also been asked, "Why not?" And while I have learned that most (if not all) things are simple and uncomplicated to fools and children, I have also come to believe that there is a plain and straightforward answer to this serious and genuine query from well-meaning layfolk. The streamlined short answer is that Christian liturgies are not properly devoted to celebrations of these kinds of things; but this answer, in my experience, just gives rise to further questions "why?"

Throughout the preceding chapters, I have wanted to emphasize—and it bears repeating now, as we consider the place of offering and intercession in the liturgy—that Christian worship is for God's sake alone. It is not a means to any other end; it is an action solely directed to God and for God. If only because of the manifold uses to which worship gets put nowadays, and the increasing number of campaigns which it gets called upon to serve, I reckon that it needs to be said as plainly and unequivocally and forcefully as we can say it that worship is not instrumental to any end other than the glory of God. It is, as the old formula puts it, *soli Deo gloria*.

Nailing this point down emphatically permits us to affirm that, in another sense, Christian worship plainly ought to be, and can be, a *purposeful* action. And it *is* purposeful when it is true and faithful to itself, when it acknowledges the holiness of God, when it hears God's word, offers prayer, and celebrates the sacraments.[1] A consideration of offering and intercession illustrates this point well, because these features of the liturgy are precisely what liturgy and ethics are about from beginning to end. To be sure, there is a certain redundancy in treating offering and intercession as relatively discrete aspects of the liturgy; nevertheless, it is instructive to reflect on why the church's liturgy has provided particular places in its services and offices for oblations and supplications.

ORIGINS, TYPES, AND PURPOSES OF OFFERINGS

The origins of sacrificial offerings are many and diverse, and no mono-genic theory suffices to account for the rich variety of these rites in antiquity. Even the Christian canon is not exceptional to this general rule, and there we discover offerings of several sorts. A rough typology, with examples from both the Old Testament and the New Testament, would include the following species of offering:

- *Propitiary* offerings, which are made in order to secure favor. For example: (1) "Pul the king of Assyria came against the land; and Menahem gave Pul a thousand talents of silver, that he might help him confirm his hold of the royal power" (2 Kings 15:19); (2) "But if any one sins, we have an advocate with the Father, Jesus Christ the righteous, who is the perfect offering for our sins, and not for ours only but for the sins of the whole world" (1 John 2:2).

- *Tributary* offerings, which represent the deity's share of human pro-ductivity. For example: (1) "All the tithe of the land, whether of the seed of the land or of the fruit of the trees, is the Lord's; it is holy to the Lord . . . and all the tithe of the herds and flocks, every tenth animal of all that pass under the herdsman's staff, shall be holy to the Lord" (Lev. 27:30–32); (2) "Then he [Jesus] said to them, 'Render therefore to Caesar the things that are Caesar's, and to God the things that are God's' " (Matt. 22:21, Mark 12:17, Rom. 13:7).

- *Votive* offerings, which are made in order to fulfill a vow or promise. For example: (1) "I will go into thy house with burnt offerings; I will pay thee my vows which my lips have uttered, and my mouth has spoken when I was in trouble" (Ps. 66:13–14); (2) "After this Paul stayed many days longer, and then took leave of the brethren and sailed for Syria, and with him Priscilla and Aquila. At Cenchreae he cut his hair, for he had a vow" (Acts 18:18).

- *Thank* offerings, which acknowledge favors or blessings received. For example: (1) "[When Manasseh] was in distress he entreated the favor of the Lord his God . . . he prayed to him, and God received his entreaty and heard his supplication and brought him again to Jerusalem into his kingdom . . . and he [Manasseh] took away the foreign gods and the idol from the house of the Lord . . . and he restored the altar of the Lord and offered upon it sacrifices of peace offerings and of thanksgiving" (2 Chron. 33:12–16); (2) "And Jesus said to them, 'How many loaves have you?' They said, 'Seven, and a few small fish.' And commanding the crowd to sit down on the ground, he took the seven loaves and the fish, and having given thanks he broke them and gave them to the disciples, and the disciples gave them to the crowds. And they all ate and were satisfied." (Matt. 15:34–37a).

- *Voluntary* (sometimes called "free will") offerings, which appear to be prompted solely by the giver's impulse. For example: (1) "All the men and women, the people of Israel, whose heart moved them to bring anything for the work which the Lord had commanded by Moses to be done, brought it as their freewill offering to the Lord" (Exod. 35:29); (2) "Walk in love, as Christ loved us and gave himself for us, an offering and sacrifice to God" (Eph. 5:2).

- *Expiatory* offerings, which are made in order to purge sinfulness, to cancel the pollution of sin, and gain thereby purification and regeneration. For example: (1) "The flesh of the bull, and its skin, and its dung, you shall burn with fire outside the camp; it is a sin offering" (Exod. 29:14); (2) "This is my blood of the new testament, which is shed for many for the remission of sins" (Matt. 26:28).

- *Guilt* offerings, which typically constitute fines paid for trespassing the law or for material damage to another. For example: (1) "He shall also make restitution for what he has done amiss . . . and the priest shall make atonement for him with the ram of the guilt offering, and he shall be forgiven" (Lev. 5:16); (2) "As one man's trespass led to condemnation for all men, so one man's act of righteousness leads to acquittal and life for all men. For as by one man's disobedience many were made sinners, so by one man's obedience many will be made righteous" (Rom. 5:18–19).

The earliest biblical record of offering is the story of Cain and Abel in Genesis 4, in which "Cain brought to the Lord an offering of the fruit of the ground, and Abel brought of the firstlings of his flock" (vv. 3–4). These actions by Cain and Abel are correctly interpreted, I think, in the context of ancient worship as it was typically practiced (so far as we are able to determine) among all religions and nations contemporary with the ancient Israelites.[2]

Almost certainly, before 750 B.C.E. (a date usually associated with the prophet Amos), ancient worship meant providing whatever domestic services were needed by the gods—food, shelter, or whatever else made life pleasant and happy. Indeed, from both the Bible and extracanonical sources[3] it is clear that in antiquity proper and correct worship embraced two requirements. One of these was positive: do whatever is pleasing to the deity, such as providing offerings of food or drink or firstfruits. The other was negative: avoid whatever annoys or displeases the deity, such as uncleanness or impurity. Over time, the positive demands came to be associated with offerings, and the negative requirements evolved into purification rites of one sort or another.

Interestingly, these ancient requirements which extend into prehistory are still honored in Jewish and Christian worship. If in ancient times Uzzah was killed for touching the Ark (2 Sam. 6:7) and seventy men of Beth-shemesh were killed for looking into the Ark (1 Sam. 6:19), it made sense that the best defense against the dangers associated with holy places was keeping distance from them. But sometimes one was obliged to come into the immediate vicinity of the deity; and when this happened, certain precautions were to be taken, like covering the face (Exod. 3:6; 1 Kings 19:13). We preserve that sensibility today when Jewish men wear their hats in orthodox and conservative synagogues and when Christian women cover their heads in Catholic churches.

Moreover, because cleanliness is pleasing to God, worshipers are expected to wear clean garments and to be clean themselves. Dirtiness defiles the deity (Exod. 28:41, 30:29; Josh. 7:13; Job 1:5); so a ritual bath (a *mikvah*) was sometimes required, and usually garments had to be freshly washed (Lev. 14:9, 15:11, 17:15; 2 Sam. 11:2, 12:20). Holy Baptism is, of course, the instance par excellence in Christian liturgy which indicates the persistence of this ancient sensibility. But Christians also retain the forms of these purifications in other continuing practices as apparently disparate as blessing oneself from a holy water font, wearing "Sunday-go-to-meeting clothes," and using a lavabo at Holy Communion.

In sum, the basic notion of worship in antiquity is _service_, a notion which we retain when we speak of "worship service" or "religious service." It is a meaning that makes sense when we remember that the original meaning of the words for worship in Hebrew and Greek is precisely "service": to honor, to bow down, to serve, to prostrate onself, to revere, to wait on, to venerate, to do obeisance. As servants of God, we ought therefore be presentable (clean) and serviceable (supplying what God desires).

At this juncture I want to prescind from consideration of the requirement for purity in God's presence (in part because we have noted this already in the discussions of confession and baptism) in order to focus attention on supplying what God desires—that is, on offering. And the first biblically recorded instance of offering, to which we referred earlier, is an instructive place to begin.

Why there is no mention of offering in earlier narratives about Adam and Eve, we simply do not know. Nor are we told why the first instance of offering is also the context for the first homicide recorded in the Bible. But the coincidence is remarkable and should strike us as both interesting and anomalous. It has to be odd, if not a strange contradiction by our lights, that the first recorded act of God-ordered generosity in scripture is also the occasion for the first murder. The Genesis explanation is plain and straightforward enough: "The Lord had regard for"—that is, God approved and accepted—Abel's offering; "but for Cain and his offering God had no regard"—which appears to mean that Cain's offering was not accepted (4:4–5). Cain then became very angry and killed his brother. Considered alone, that Cain killed Abel because of Abel's favor with God seems hardly a complete or compelling explanation of an account such as this. We want to know more. Verse 7 suggests that Cain was victimized by sin; but scholars also think that this verse is likely a later addition to, and a corruption of, the text.

Maybe this is one of those points about which nobody can pretend to know or understand the intention of the author of Genesis. It seems fairly clear that jealously prompted Cain to kill Abel; and we know that envy eventually got included among the "seven deadly sins." Even so, traditional wisdom teaches that envy has an appetite that can never be satisfied; nothing can gratify it, nothing can ever bring it joy. So Augustine's wonderful aphorism, _peccatum poena peccati_ ("sin is the punishment of sin"), is perfectly apposite here. Envy must always try to do away with what it cannot have. Envy is deadly to the person it possesses, says Henry Fairlie, "less because it destroys him, than because it will not let him live."[4]

On the other hand, what we can do with this little story is try to make some sense of the apparent contradiction; and one way to do this is to read Genesis 4 through the lenses of the later prophets of the Old Testament and the New Testament apostles.

Consider, for example, Amos (750 B.C.E.), who was the first of the reforming prophets to denounce lavish sacrifices in the sanctuaries of Yahweh, and to demand in their stead a morality of righteousness and compassion and justice:

> *I hate, I despise your feasts, and I take no delight in your solemn assemblies. Even though you offer me your burnt offerings and cereal offerings, I will not accept them, and the peace offerings of your fatted beasts I will not look upon. Take away from me the noise of your songs; to the melody of your harps I will not listen. But let justice roll down like waters, and righteousness like an everflowing stream. (Amos 5:21–24)*

This is a relatively new teaching, but one that is to be consistently repeated in the Old Testament and later considerably refined in the New Testament. Consider these examples from the Old Testament:

> *And Saul said to Samuel, "I have obeyed the voice of the Lord, I have gone on the mission on which the Lord sent me, I have brought Agag the king of Amelek, and I have utterly destroyed the Amelekites. But the people took of the spoil, sheep and oxen, the best of the things devoted to destruction, to sacrifice to the Lord your God in Gilgal." And Samuel said, "Has the Lord as great delight in burnt offerings and sacrifices, as in obeying the voice of the Lord? Behold, to obey is better than sacrifice, and to hearken than the fat of rams." (2 Samuel 15:20–22)*

Or, again, because the old ways continued to be practiced, a prophet like Jeremiah (750–600 B.C.E.) conveys God's desire for righteousness:

> *To what purpose does frankincense come to me from Sheba, or sweet cane from a distant land? Your burnt offerings are not acceptable, nor your sacrifices pleasing to me . . . if you truly amend your ways and your doings, if you truly execute justice one with another, if you do not*

oppress the alien, the fatherless or the widow, or shed innocent blood in
this place, and if you do not go after other gods to your own hurt, then
I will let you dwell in this place, in the land that I gave of old to your
fathers for ever." (Jer. 6:20, 7:5–7)

Or Isaiah:

Bring no more vain offerings; incense is an abomination to me . . . I
cannot endure iniquity and solemn assembly. Your new moons and your
appointed feasts my soul hates; they have become a burden to me, I am
weary of bearing them. . . . Wash yourselves; make yourselves clean;
remove the evil of your doings from before my eyes; cease to do evil, learn
to do good; seek justice, correct oppression; defend the fatherless, plead
for the widow." (Isa. 1:13–14, 16–17)

Or Hosea:

For I desire steadfast love and not sacrifice, the knowledge of God,
rather than burnt offerings." (Hos. 6:6)

Of course, none of these passages helps us to understand why Abel's
offering should have found favor with God, or why God had no regard for
Cain's offering. They do, however, show an important transition in Israelite
theology: what pleases God is not offerings of appeasement, but upright
and holy living. And on these terms, Cain might have dimly understood
that his relationship with Yahweh depended on the offering of himself
rather than "the fruit of the ground"; but this is a sensibility which is
probably later, and more attuned with the New Testament than with the
Old Testament.

Perhaps nowhere is this distinction between pacification by oblations
and peacemaking through holy living more familiarly expressed than in the
invitatory which introduces the psalmody for morning prayer. In the
Western church, conventional practice is to say only verse 15 as a versicle, except at the Ash Wednesday liturgy, when it is said in its entirety; but in the Eastern church today, the whole of Psalm 51 is often
sung at the beginning of the morning office. The familiar versicle, together
with the following two verses, instance again the reform initiated by
Amos.

O Lord, open thou my lips, and my mouth shall show forth thy praise.
For thou hast no delight in sacrifice; were I to give a burnt offering,
thou wouldst not be pleased. The sacrifice acceptable to God is a broken
spirit; a broken and contrite heart, O God, thou wilt not despise." (Ps.
51:15–17)

It would be a mistake, I believe, to conclude from these and similar passages that the prophets intended to abolish all ritual and ceremonial, and to institute instead an unadorned "spiritual" (in the sense of a *dematerialized*) worship. Neither Amos nor the other great prophets repudiated sacrifice and other rituals, as is frequently but mistakenly believed; but they did protest their abuse and, in the name of God, called for their proper religious location. In fact, sacrifice retained a central position in the Second Temple at Jerusalem, from its inauguration in 516 B.C.E. until its destruction by Titus in 70 C.E.

It seems reasonable to conclude that what the prophets opposed was the mishandling and misappropriation of ceremonial and ritual and sacrifice, a misuse which employed these things with the supposition that God could be manipulated (or perhaps even bribed) by them. And while it is true that offerings and sacrifices continued during the period of the Second Temple, there is some evidence that this occurred with a twist which honored the prophetic injunction: these gifts were no longer intended to appease God or otherwise influence the deity's relationship with Israel; instead, they were offered as expressions of gratitude for God's great mercy and as symbols of a devout intention to lead a holy and upright life before the searing righteousness of the sovereign God.

Against this background, it may become clearer how a service of worship, conveying as it does strong emphasis on offering and intercession, glorifies God by purifying us in his presence. That purification, through the liturgy, is the foundation for living a holy and upright life.

Meanwhile, the troubled marriage of Enlightenment rationalism with Protestant pietism has too often (if not virtually always) produced a disadvantaged liturgical offspring. Simplicity to the point of barrenness has robbed us of so many rich ceremonials and rituals that we have had no recourse, in a church building void of color and symbol, but to turn in upon ourselves for sustenance. And the long-term result of this is that we have cannibalized ourselves. Depending upon ourselves for nourishment is the essence of narcissism; so it is little wonder that so much of Protestant spirituality has grown anemic on such a diet.

But what some branches of Protestantism appear to be recovering is the recognition that the sum of who we are and how we respond to the *mysterium tremendum* is more than *fascinans*, more than a mere aesthetic satisfaction which is exhausted by intellectualizing the full range of human responsivity to mystery. This, of course, is why the rehearsal for marriage is never the same as saying the vows "for real"; the words and actions simply do not engage us powerfully, as the marriage rite itself does. Similarly this is why "bending the body" to the yoke of the Gospel is a metaphor of perhaps trivial consequence unless and until it gets acted out on one's knees at prayer. Or again, this is also why all of the showers and baths we ever take will pale by comparison with the cleansing and purification which the waters of Baptism connote. In sum, the point was made compellingly clear by Maurice Merleau-Ponty: we do not know what we think until we say it; speaking concretizes and places, in unmistakably thick and solid ways, our thoughts.[5]

So the things of the liturgy are not ends in themselves. We deliberately use these things—postures, paraments, vestments, wine, water, bread, crosses, candles, books, symbols of all sorts—because they assist in conveying God to us and us to God. And some of us have discovered that "spiritual worship," if this means dematerialized devotion, invariably becomes the *homo incurvatus in se*, ourselves turning back in upon ourselves, neither needing nor willing to be summoned out of this impossible isolation and concentration upon ourselves, and thus being either unable or unwilling to be encountered by God when he offers himself to us.

This, it strikes me, is a particularly cruel irony: that things which were removed from the liturgy as obstacles to God get discovered, in their absence, to produce precisely the unwanted result, namely, God's absence. But the ancient Hebrew prophets knew better: they knew that the gifts we offer are themselves material expressions of ourselves, offered in gratitude for God's great mercy, that they are oblations of intercession which express our devout intention to lead a holy and upright life.

The invitation to Holy Communion in the Book of Common Prayer, which dates from 1548, puts it well:

*You who do truly and earnestly repent you of your sins, and are in love
and charity with your neighbors, and intend to lead a new life, following the commandments of God, and walking from henceforth in his holy
ways: Draw near with faith." (p. 330)*

And Paul, never to have been upstaged by Cranmer, put it this way, in what
is probably one of the most familiar passages from his writings:

*I appeal to you therefore, brethren, by the mercies of God, to present
your bodies as a living sacrifice, holy and acceptable unto God, which is
your spiritual worship." (Rom. 12:1)*

PARADIGMS FOR OFFERING:
ABRAHAM AND ISAAC, JESUS

At various points in the preceding pages I have wanted to emphasize that
the faith of Israel is an important and vital part of the faith of the church,
and that the Christian canon comprises both the Old Testament and the
New Testament. Indeed, the examination of offering in the Old Testament
helps to show yet again that, for Christians, the Old Testament is both
essential to and yet unintelligible apart from the New Testament.

For all that they share in common, Judaism and Christianity are two very
different religions precisely because the Old Testament functions within
them in very different ways. For Jews, who yet look forward to the coming
of the Messiah, the Torah (the "teaching" or "instruction") consists principally of the Pentateuch: this is the law of God, of which the Talmud is its
exposition. The Talmud actually fulfills the Torah by making the Law
applicable to the changing situations of Jewish life. So the Torah, interpreted by the Talmud, provides the guide for how life should be lived by
Jews in the interval before the new messianic age.

Christians, however, are a people who believe that the new messianic age
has dawned in the advent of Jesus, that all the purposes and promises of
God in the Old Testament are fulfilled in him, and that the entire direction
of the Old Testament and its chief hope have been accomplished in Jesus'
inauguration of the kingdom of God. So when I visited Jerusalem and was
shown the Messiah Gate, which is bolted shut until the Messiah comes to
enter the Holy City through it, I suggested to my Israeli guide that some of

those in his tour party believed that the gate should be open. He was not amused; but this, symbolically, is precisely the difference between Christianity and Judaism (together with other religions as well).

It is not that we do not share prophets; it is, specifically, that Christianity is the only religion to claim that God has come to us incarnate as Jesus Christ. Christians believe that the juridical and forensic purposes of the Torah have been superseded by the New Covenant of grace offered us in Jesus, and that we are now to be obedient to the Law, not in order to merit God's approval but in order to witness to the plenitude of God's grace. Paul put it succinctly:

> Are we to sin because we are not under law but under grace? By no means! Do you not know that if you yield yourselves to anyone as obedient slaves, you are slaves of the one whom you obey, either of sin which leads to death, or of obedience which leads to righteousness? But thanks be to God, that you who were once slaves of sin have become obedient from the heart to the standard of teaching to which you were committed, and having been set free from sin, have become slaves of righteousness." (Rom. 6:15–18)

Indeed, Paul—more than any other Christian evangelist—emphasized throughout his writings that the Gospel both presupposes the Hebrew Scriptures and goes beyond them to correct and fulfill them; and that Jesus is the new creation of the new Israel, no longer defined by Torah or ethnicity but deeply rooted in Abraham all the same, except that Jesus' progeny are now not biologic successors according to the flesh, *kata sarx*, but by adoption through the miracle of faith, *kata pneuma*.

Among all the accounts of offering in the Old Testament, none is more poignant or profoundly disturbing than God's temptation of Abraham to sacrifice his son, Isaac:

> And it came to pass after these days (i.e., after Abraham had made a covenant with Abimelech at Beer-Sheba) that God did tempt Abraham, and said unto him, Abraham: and he said, Behold, here I am. And he said, Take now thy son, thine only son Isaac, whom thou lovest, and get thee into the land of Moriah; and offer him there for a burnt offering upon one of the mountains which I will tell thee of. (Gen. 22:1–2)

The rest of the story is the familiar account of how Abraham took Isaac to the place of which God had told him, and gathered wood and built an altar, and bound Isaac and placed him on the wood on the altar, and "stretched forth his hand and took the knife to slay his son," when an angel of the Lord interceded and acknowledged that Abraham was indeed fearful of God and prepared to be obedient even to the extent of killing his own son; and how Abraham then sacrificed a ram "in the stead of his son," and how God was so pleased with Abraham that he blessed him and all his progeny: "And in thy seed shall all the nations of the earth be blessed; because thou hast obeyed my voice" (Gen. 22:3–18).

I have learned, over the years, the standard interpretation of this story, which goes something like this: Abraham lived in a very primitive time and place, a time and place in which human sacrifice was not at all uncommon or unknown among the worshipers of pagan deities. The "sacrifice of Isaac" story is intended to show that Abraham was as fully committed to his religion as the pagans around him were committed to theirs, that he was as fully prepared to demonstrate his obedience to his god as his pagan neighbors were to their deities. Abraham, in a word, was prepared to go as far as they were; Abraham's devotion to Yahweh was no more boundaried than was theirs. He saw these people offering up their children to show their faith and obedience to false gods; he could do no less as a worshiper of the one true God. But at the climax of the story, Jehovah turns out to be quite different from the pagan deities: this is a god of love and compassion who, if we will but trust him to the farthest depths of our devotion, will finally not require us to do things which are distasteful or unpleasant, but bless us in ways we cannot otherwise imagine.

I believe that Christians ought to have serious problems with an interpretation of this sort. To make murder, or even the willingness to commit murder, the means to God's grace and favor is offensive and repugnant by Christian standards. And I reckon that there is also just a bit of latent Pelagianism and works righteousness in conceiving one's relationship with God to be a function of something we can do, an action we can perform, such as making a sacrifice. Moreover, as coarse and crude as it may sound to say, and as indecorous as it may be to modern secularized sensibilities to hear, the threatened sacrifice of Isaac is actually not the centerpiece of this story. So it violates our cherished notions, inherited from the Enlightenment, about the inestimable value of every individual to suggest that

Isaac's role in this story is instrumental; because to talk this way profanes Kant's third universal moral maxim, which states that persons are always to be treated as ends only and never as means.

All the same, Abraham is the principal character here. Isaac is important as a son whom Abraham loves, and he is the means which Abraham is prepared to employ in order to demonstrate his obedience. Remember that Isaac is the miracle which comes to Abraham and Sarah in their very old age; that despairing of having children, Abraham had, at Sarah's initiative, sired Ishmael by Sarah's maid, Hagar; but that Hagar's contempt for her mistress had prompted Sarah to send her and her son away; and that later, after the birth of Isaac, again at the behest of Sarah, Abraham had banished Hagar and Ishmael to the wilderness of Beer-sheba. So now, very old and with his son Ishmael gone from his sight, and not knowing whether Ishmael was living or dead, Abraham's only remaining son was Isaac. Little wonder that he should have loved and cherished him. This seems a perfectly natural thing for Abraham.

But Christians, who are this people of the new age, who through baptism are ushered into death in order to be born again into newness of life, can know that the question being put to Abraham was not whether he was willing to murder his own (and now, perhaps, only) son, but whether he himself was willing to die to all earthly affections. Christian liturgies remind us, in several places, of the centrality of this requirement. Candidates for Holy Baptism are asked, "Do you renounce all sinful desires that draw you from the love of God?" The Great Litany prays for deliverance "from all inordinate and sinful affections; and from all the deceits of the world, the flesh, and the devil," and "that it may please thee to give us a heart to love and fear thee." And the Collect for Proper 20 puts it this way: "Grant us, Lord, not to be anxious about earthly things, but to love things heavenly; and even now, while we are placed among things that are passing away, to hold fast to those that shall endure."

In the early church, this story about the threatened sacrifice of Isaac provided Christians with one of its types for describing the death of Jesus. Indeed, this story could well underlie Paul's comment in Romans 8, which begins:

> *There is therefore no condemnation for those who are in Christ Jesus.*
> *For the law of the Spirit of life in Christ Jesus has set me free from the*

law of sin and death. For God has done what the law . . . could not do; sending his own Son in the likeness of sinful flesh and for sin, he condemned sin in the flesh, in order that the just requirement of the law might be fulfilled in us, who walk not according to the flesh but according to the Spirit. (Rom. 8:1–4)

What may be a particular reference to the Isaac typology comes toward the end of the chapter:

What then shall we say to this? If God is for us, who is against us? He who did not spare his own Son but gave him up for us all, will he not also give us all things with him? Who shall bring any charge against God's elect? It is God who justifies; who is to condemn? Is it Christ Jesus, who died, yes, who was raised from the dead, who is at the right hand of God, who indeed intercedes for us? Who shall separate us from the love of God? Shall tribulation, or distress, or persecution, or famine, or nakedness, or peril, or sword? . . . No, in all these things, we are more than conquerors through him who loved us. (Rom. 8:31–37)

Jesus, like Isaac in some ways, but acting out the complete scenario in ways which Isaac did not and could not, is also the only son; but God, unlike Abraham, "did not spare his own Son but gave him up for us all"; and this Jesus, who died and was raised from the dead, accomplishes the vicarious sacrifice. He has done for us what we could not do for ourselves; and, as appropriate to an offering, a sacrifice, he now intercedes for us "at the right hand of God."

Of course, this sounds strange (maybe especially) to modern ears because we have been enculturated since Bacon to understand, as Addison put it, that "nothing is more gratifying to the mind of man than power or dominion." We have, virtually all of us, cut our moral eyeteeth on the Yankee ethic whose virtues are perseverance, industry, prudence, thrift, and common sense. So it makes perfectly good sense, on these terms, to regard Paul's rhetoric as odd, bizarre, even illusory to the hard-nosed and autonomous rationality of modern men and women.

None of our intellectual forebears probably did more to shape this perception than Immanuel Kant, whose accomplishment it was to emancipate us from dependency, servanthood, and mystery, and in their place establish autonomy, mastery, and universal reasonableness. I cited the following passage by Kant earlier in another context; but it is so clear and plainspoken in its claims, and so exemplary of the Enlightenment commitments which Western Christianity has, in large part, embraced, that I venture to quote it again:

> It is quite impossible to see how a reasonable man, who knows himself to merit punishment, can in all seriousness believe that he needs only to credit the news of an atonement rendered for him, and to accept this atonement utiliter (as the lawyers say), in order to regard his guilt as annihilated. . . . No thoughtful person can bring himself to believe this. . . . Where shall we start, i.e., with a faith in what God has done on our behalf, or with what we are to do to become worthy of God's assistance . . . ?
>
> In answering this question, we cannot hesitate in deciding for the second alternative. . . . We can certainly hope to partake in the appropriation of another's atoning merit, and so of salvation, only by qualifying for it through our own efforts to fulfil every human duty— and this obedience must be the effect of our own action and not, once again, of a foreign influence in the presence of which we are passive."[6]

Eschewing any understanding of ourselves as creatures who are out of control, who give ourselves away to the dominion and control of another, who find life by losing it, Kant's whole program is designed to sacralize autonomous moral agency. And the sum of it is that no action is moral unless it is freely legislated by the untrammeled "good will" of an individual. In the measure to which we are unfree or boundaried in our liberty to control and shape our own reasonable ideas about the "good will," in that same measure we are immoral.

Even if we somehow managed to do the right thing but for the wrong reason, Kant's stringent judgment would remain. For Kant, and his modern disciples, the essence of human beings is their autonomous freedom; there is nothing good except and apart from a "good will"; the highest purpose of human life is to will autonomously. So the thoughtful person will readily recognize that, insofar as Jesus' offering of himself, and his intercession "at the right hand of God," accomplishes on our behalf what it is not within our own power to do for ourselves, we have forfeited our autonomy, our self-determination, the power to control our own destiny. For Kant and his disciples, however, if there is anything vicarious about Jesus' atoning merit, it is vicarious only because we have achieved—through effort and obedience which are the products of our own actions—the moral standing requisite to participating (or, more accurately, sharing) in that merit.

Kant, of course, completely misread the human condition, because, as anyone over thirty ought to know, autonomy is either a grand illusion or a wonderful fantasy (maybe in some ways it's a bit of both). In any case, autonomy is not descriptively accurate of the human situation. Our navels are a primitive evidence of our ineradicable connectedness and dependency. And most of us understand that *Robinson Crusoe* is a believable fiction in ways that *Tarzan of the Apes* is not, precisely because Crusoe was socialized by other human beings. It takes more than imagination to accept that Tarzan acquired (or achieved) human virtues either from apes or on his own. The fact is that, while lots of people talk about autonomy, I have yet to meet anybody who has it. Luther knew better than Kant that the will is always ridden, controlled, by something else. Even more to the point, William Temple knew that moral freedom (which is, after all, what autonomy talk is all about) does not consist in indeterminacy but in the ability to choose who (or what) will determine the self.

The Isaac story is appointed in the lectionary of the Episcopal Church for Lent 2 (B). Interestingly, the Epistle appointed for that same Sunday is Romans 8:31–39. And to complete the lections, the Gospel is read from Mark 9:2–10, which is Mark's account of the transfiguration of Jesus. In this pericope, the evangelist emphasizes the difficulty which the disciples have in understanding Jesus, because at this point Jesus is presented not as an epiphany of the divine power but as the suffering Son of man. Beyond this emphasis, Mark reiterates here the familiar "messianic secret" which is so characteristic of his Gospel: don't tell anybody about Jesus' transfiguration. Unlike some other places in Mark, where the disciples are urged to keep silent, the reason is fairly clear here that they should not tell about the transfiguration because to disclose it would express the wrong Christology—namely, that there is glory without the cross. Mark's message, however, is clear: no cross, no crown. This surely can be made to sound like

Kant; but to do this would require, I believe, a willful and determined eisegesis.

Bonhoeffer's distinction between "cheap" and "costly" grace seems to me to summarize these points about offering, sacrifice, intercession, and autonomy quite well:

> Cheap grace is the deadly enemy of our church. We are fighting today for costly grace. Cheap grace means grace sold on the market like cheapjack's wares. The sacraments, the forgiveness of sin, and the consolations of religion are thrown away at cut prices. . . . Cheap grace means grace as a doctrine, a principle, a system. It means forgiveness of sins proclaimed as a general truth, the love of God taught as the Christian "conception" of God. An intellectual assent to that idea is held to be of itself sufficient to secure remission of sins. . . .
>
> Cheap grace means the justification of the sin without the justification of the sinner. . . . Cheap grace is not the kind of forgiveness of sin which frees us from the toils of sin. Cheap grace is the grace we bestow upon ourselves.
>
> Cheap grace is the preaching of forgiveness without requiring repentance, baptism without church discipline, communion without confession, absolution without personal confession. Cheap grace is grace without discipleship, grace without the cross, grace without Jesus Christ, living and incarnate. . . .
>
> Costly grace is the gospel which must be sought again and again, the gift which must be asked for, the door at which a man must knock.
>
> Such grace is costly because it calls us to follow, and it is grace because it calls us to follow Jesus Christ. It is costly because it costs a man his life, and it is grace because it gives a man the only true life. . . . Above all, it is costly because it cost God the life of his Son . . . and what has cost God much cannot be cheap for us. Above all, it is grace because God did not reckon his Son too dear a price to pay for our life, but delivered him up for us. Costly grace is the Incarnation of God. . . .

Grace is costly because it compels a man to submit to the yoke of
Christ and follow him; it is grace because Jesus says "My yoke is easy
and my burden is light."[7]

When this grace lays hold, it shatters one's whole existence; and it does this by requiring the abandonment of a compartmentalized and domesticated life. It does this by obliging us to live out of control by giving ourselves away. All the saints and martyrs—from Paul to Augustine, to mystics like Blessed Henry Suso, to Luther and Wesley, to Martin Luther King, Jr.—learned, and most of them at considerable sacrifice and pain, that faith finally drives us from the relative comfort and security of our own religiosity to life in the world. They learned that the only way to follow Jesus was by living in the world by a power and a grace which is not of this world.

The post-Constantinian blunder has been to suppose that Christian discipleship could be readily, and sometimes rather easily, accommodated to the world. The sectarian mistake has been to believe that a good and holy life is possible in direct proportion to withdrawal from the world's sin and torpor. The Enlightenment error has been to suppose that holiness is directly proportional to a generalized reasonableness and individually generated goodness. But if grace is the datum of the Christian life, nothing less is required of us than that we learn both to think through and to live out our discipleship in the world. This was Bonhoeffer's achievement, warts and all.

The critical issue here has to do with accounting for the meaning of discipleship. It is clearly not any lifestyle which grace makes possible; nor is it some form of reasonable secular wisdom that can be baptized as discipleship. The Christian life is a life shaped and formed by a particular, however scandalous, understanding of ourselves as imitators of Christ, as a people who have abandoned autonomy and submitted outselves to the yoke of Christ. We are, and ought to be, a people who are dying daily to worldly affections. I believe this is what we ordinarily mean by sanctification.

"If with Christ you died to the elemental spirits of the universe, why do you live as though you still belonged to the world? . . . If then you have been raised with Christ, seek the things that are above, where Christ is. . . . Set your minds on things that are above, not on things that are on earth. For you have died, and your life is hid with Christ in God. . . . Put to death therefore what is earthly in you. . . . And whatever you do, in word or deed, do everything in the name of the Lord Jesus, giving thanks to God the Father through him" (Col. 2:20; 3:1–3, 5, 17).

The New Testament, no less than the Old Testament is very much concerned with offering and intercession—and nowhere more urgently than with the work of Christ, and especially as this bears on the doctrine of atonement. Jesus' atonement is his intercession for us. Here again, however, it is clear that there is disagreement among the New Testament authors, and that they do not share a univocal view.[8] So it should come as no surprise that the later controversies in the church over this matter have their roots deeply embedded in different New Testament teachings. The word "atonement," for example, does not occur at all in the New Testament. But the meaning of the word—that Christ overcomes the estrangement and alienation between God and us, and in that action intercedes for us and makes us "at-one" with God—is clearly present throughout the New Testament. The word itself, however, enters the theological vocabulary of Christians in later doctrinal controversies.

Why is "atonement," the word, not present in the New Testament, especially since it has engendered so much debate and controversy in the church's history? Answers can be speculative at best; but one of the appealing hunches is that the need for atonement was so pervasively assumed by the New Testament authors that they thought it unnecessary to be more explicit. What makes this surmise appealing is that it runs like a connecting thread throughout the fabric of the New Testament. Consider Paul's letters:

> And you, who once were estranged and hostile in mind, doing evil deeds, he has now reconciled in his body of flesh by his death, in order to present you holy and blameless and irreproachable before him." (Col. 1:21–22)
>
> Remember that you were at that time separated from Christ, alienated from the commonwealth of Israel, and strangers to the covenant of promise, having no hope and without God in the world." (Eph. 2:12)
>
> While we were yet helpless, at the right time Christ died for the ungodly. . . . God shows his love for us in that while we were yet sinners Christ died for us. (Rom. 5:6, 8)
>
> Since all have sinned and fall short of the glory of God, they are justified by his grace as a gift. (Rom. 3:23–24)

So the need for atonement appears to be simply assumed; and it seems, further, that the cause of this need is sin, persistent disobedience, and faithlessness to the holy will of God. The New Testament knows that the wages of sin is death (Rom. 6:23); indeed, it knows that sinners are already dead through their trespasses (Eph. 2:1). This is no romantic Enlightenment anthropology; the human condition is a sinful condition which is equivalent to death.

For a human condition so profoundly and radically disordered and eccentric, only a comparably radical remedy will suffice. If we have problems with the extravagance of New Testament claims about the miracle and mystery of Jesus' passion and death, and his salvific work, it is probably because we do not share the New Testament's basic assumptions about the severe helplessness and the profound hopelessness of the human condition without Christ.

Withal, it is on these predicates that Christ's salvific work is the effective means of our at-one-ment with God,[9] an action which is associated preeminently with the cross of Jesus,[10] by which a new relationship between us and God is inaugurated and made existentially real in the cross,[11] and through which alone we have access to God[12] by faith.[13] In a word, Jesus is the new way to God,[14] in consequence of which we have peace with God[15] and are delivered from sin.[16]

Luther was on the right track, I believe, to insist that *Christian* theology, as distinct from every other kind of theology—and particularly from those theologies which only seem to be Christian—stands or falls as a *theologia crucis*. This does not claim that *theologia crucis* is the sole desideratum, but only that it is a central and essential one. There is, in fact, much to support the notion that whatever is distinctive about *Christian* theology as such hinges on, depends on, derives from, the cross. Over and above everything else in Christian faith and practice looms the cross. Such a notion as this was clearly appreciated by the New Testament authors as they rehearsed the principal atonement motifs which subsequently gave rise to controversy in the church. Moreover, such a claim also comports well with the notion that the New Testament authors interpreted backwards, from cross and resurrection to God's story in both the Old Testament and Jesus' birth and ministry. Against this background, a brief look at the foremost atonement motifs in the New Testament is instructive.

Mark 10:42–45[17] records that Jesus himself spoke of giving his life "a ransom for many." And while exegetes have differed widely, and still do, in their interpretations of this passage, nobody denies that the motif of these verses is clearly associated with Jesus' intercession for our redemption.

> *And Jesus . . . said to them, "You know that those who are supposed to rule over the Gentiles lord it over them, and their great men exercise authority over them. But it shall not be so among you; but whoever would be great among you must be your servant, and whoever would be first among you must be slave of all. For the Son of Man came not to be served, but to serve, and to give his life as a ransom for many.*

This notion of Jesus as ransom, of Jesus' death as payment for a stipulated price of which our release from the bondage of sin and death is the benefit, is also conveyed in the words of institution of the Holy Eucharist in Matthew's Gospel: having blessed and broken the bread, and given thanks over the cup, Jesus says, "This is my blood of the covenant, which is poured out for many for the forgiveness of sins" (Matt. 26:28).

Part of the difficulty with New Testament interpretation, particularly as it bears upon atonement, is that the same verse or passage may lend itself to more than one theory of the atonement. So Paul's claim, in 1 Corinthians 15:3, that he received from the apostles the teaching that "Christ died for our sins in accordance with the scriptures," can be variously interpreted as supporting a *ransom* theory, or a *substitution* theory, or a *vicarious sacrifice* theory, or even a *propitiation* theory.

In this regard, the problem the early church faced was actually twofold: (1) how to show that Christ's ignominious death was not, as the Jews claimed, demonstrable proof that he was not the Messiah but that the cross is, in fact, coherent with the Messiah's mission; and (2) how to interpret aright for the fledgling Christian community—that is, for internal purposes—a theology of the cross. Paul had actually put the task succinctly in 1 Corinthians 1:18, 21–24:

> *For the word of the cross is folly to those who are perishing, but to us who are being saved it is the power of God. . . . For since, in the wisdom of God, the world did not know God through wisdom, it pleased God through the folly of what we preach to save those who believe. For Jews demand a sign and Greeks seek wisdom, but we preach Christ crucified, a stumbling-block to Jews and folly to Gentiles, but to those who*

*are called, both Jews and Greeks, Christ the power of God and the
wisdom of God.*

Even readers with only a superficial knowledge of the Pauline corpus
know that Paul has been (and can be) enlisted in both enterprises. But with
respect to the latter one—that is, with respect to articulating a certain
understanding of atonement for the Christian community—the greater
weight of Paul's letters seems to endorse a theory of substitutionary
atonement. Jesus became "a curse for us" (Gal. 3:13). Christ is a sinless
sufferer who voluntarily and in our behalf (since we are powerless to
accomplish it for ourselves) pays the penalty for sin and thereby effects
reconciliation between us and God: "God was in Christ reconciling the
world to himself, not counting their trespasses against them, and entrust-
ing to us the message of reconciliation" (2 Cor. 5:19). "For God has not
destined us for wrath, but to obtain salvation through our Lord Jesus
Christ, who died for us so that whether we wake or sleep we might live with
him" (1 Thess. 5:9–10).

Or again: "Grace to you and peace from God the Father and our Lord
Jesus Christ, who gave himself for our sins to deliver us from the present
evil age, according to the will of our God and Father" (Gal. 1:3–4). "It
[i.e., righteousness] will be reckoned to us who believe in him . . . who was
put to death for our trespasses and raised for our justification" (Rom. 4:24–
25). "What then shall we say to this? If God is for us who is against us? He
who did not spare his own Son but gave him up for us all, will he not also
give us all things with him?" (Rom. 8:31–32). "While we were yet
helpless, at the right time Christ died for the ungodly. . . . God shows his
love for us in that while we were yet sinners Christ died for us . . . we are
now justified by his blood . . . while we were enemies we were reconciled to
God by the death of his son" (Rom. 5:6–10).

But these and similar passages, it turns out, are not solely supportive of a
substitutionary theory; they can also be read as vicarious sacrifice, as moral
cleansing rather than legal satisfaction, and hence acquittal from guilt. 1
Peter 1:18–19a conveys the classical vicarious character of Christ's sacrifice:
"You know that you were ransomed from the futile ways inherited from
your fathers, not with perishable things such as silver and gold, but with
the precious blood of Christ." Or again in 1 Peter 3:18: "For Christ also
died for sins once and for all, the righteous for the unrighteous, that he

might bring us to God, being put to death in the flesh but made alive in the spirit."

To complicate (or maybe enrich?) matters further, the writer of the Epistle to the Hebrews states that Jesus is the figure of a new priesthood whose sacrifice once and for all atones for sin (9:26–28; 10:12) and confers this benefit (10:10, 14), the long-standing Levitical priesthood having been unable to attain the abolition of the old order and the inauguration of the new (7:11). This metaphor is reinforced in the Revelation to John, where the prominent image is of Jesus as the Lamb whose blood and vicarious suffering and death are the means of our purification from sin.

We could mention finally, in this cursory review, the emphasis in 1 John, which falls not only upon deliverance from sin but also upon Jesus' role as mediator and intercessor: "if any one sins, we have an advocate with the Father, Jesus Christ the righteous; and he is the expiation for our sins, and not for ours only but also for the sins of the whole world" (2:1–2). So "if we walk in the light, as he is in the light, we have fellowship with one another, and the blood of Jesus his Son cleanses us from all sin" (1:7). Jesus' sacrifice in 1 John is clearly propitiation, appeasement: "In this is love, not that we loved God, but that he loved us and sent his own Son to be the expiation for our sins" (4:10).

Now all of this variety and nuanced difference in the New Testament is the stuff of which great doctrinal controversy is made; and from the early Fathers to the present, the church has seen its share of advocacies for one or another theory of the atonement. But one thing is constant in all the debate, and this is that the crucified Jesus is the savior victorious over sin and death. The cross was scandalous in the first century C.E.; it remains scandalous today: "Behold the Lamb of God, which taketh away the sin of the world." However the several New Testament authors express themselves on this point, they are all congenial with the characteristic witness of Paul, the first Christian with whom we have direct access: "I delivered to you as of first importance what I also received, that Christ died for our sins according to the scriptures" (1 Cor. 15:3). *How* this was accomplished has been and remains a matter on which devout Christians disagree; *that* we are reconciled to God by Christ's sacrifice is for Christians a fundamental and essential article of faith.

Without presuming to know precisely how atonement works, without supposing that we fully understand this mystery, there are nevertheless some aspects of atonement which I believe to be consensually held by virtually all sorts and conditions of Christians, and which therefore shape and form the kind of people we understand ourselves to be. I can identity four of these: (1) The New Testament clearly affirms that the cross somehow fulfills God's purpose; that, however apparently tragic, it is also God's action which manifests grace. (2) The New Testament also makes it clear that Jesus' sacrifice is representative for the sins of the whole world, that it alone and by itself embraces us all, and that he who knew no sin "was made" sin for us. (3) The New Testament further makes the claim that Jesus' representative action is efficacious, that it is effective *pro nobis*, that Jesus' intercession accomplishes what we ourselves are helpless even to ask for, much less to do. (4) And, finally, through his dying and rising again, we are united with Christ; we are *in Christo.*

Having said this, however, it is important to reiterate that the church has not officially sponsored any one of the atonement theories which later emerged from these New Testament claims. That the church clearly affirms atonement is not to be doubted; but the church is, and has been, more interested in witnessing to the claim *that* Jesus has interceded for us and accomplished our reconciliation with God than with explaining *how* he did it. The simple and unembellished affirmation is that God in Christ has effected our at-one-ment:

> *But now in Christ Jesus you who once were far off have been brought near in the blood of Christ. For he is our peace, who has made us both one, and has broken down the dividing wall if hostility, by abolishing in his flesh the law of commandments and ordinances, that he might create in himself one new man in place of the two, so making peace, and might reconcile us both to God in one body through the cross, thereby bringing the hostility to an end." (Eph. 2:13–16)*

CAPITAL PUNISHMENT AS A TEST CASE

To consider capital punishment in the context of offering and intercession helps to concretize and solidify the claim that liturgy is ethics, that ethics is liturgy. This juridical penalty, as it is exercised in our society, employs so many of the figures and metaphors associated with the liturgical underpinnings of sacrifice, forgiveness, and reconciliation that an organic connection between them is difficult to ignore. Indeed, if the rhetoric of capital punishment advocates is to be believed, the death of a condemned criminal serves to achieve ends which are very similar to Christian notions about the efficacy of Jesus' cross.

Of course, the condemned criminal does not accomplish these things directly, as Jesus is said to do; but they are nevertheless part of the cultural mythology about the worthwhileness and appropriateness of continuing to execute our worst criminal offenders. We say, "He [and, rarely, "she"] has paid his debt to society"; or "All of us can rest easier now, knowing that justice has been done." Translated, these colloquial formulas mean that we're satisfied that the criminal has atoned for past sins, and that an affront to just sensibilities has been righted by forfeiting this life. So we use the conceptual apparatus, if not always the precise language, of retribution, satisfaction, ransom, vicarious expiation, substitution, vengeance, and sacrifice to characterize the virtue which we associate with the execution of criminals.

Now none of this comes easily, nor should it. Joe Freeman Britt, now a Superior Court judge in North Carolina but at one time a two-county district attorney who was proudly responsible for four percent of the death-row inmates in the United States, once mixed his metaphors in observing that "there's a little kernel in all of us that says we must preserve human life. It's the prosecutor's job to extinguish that flame."[18]

All the same, I believe that the arguments both for and against capital punishment fail, and that they do so for two distinguishable but related reasons: (1) they develop from different assumptions and premises in order to support very different conclusions; and (2) they do not share common convictions about the kind of people for whom these assumptions and premises would be reasonable and compelling. So it is futile, in both the first and the last of it, to argue for or against capital punishment because the arguments themselves are predicated on adversarial, not communitarian, postulates.

Arguments for the inestimable worth of every human life, and counterarguments for retribution and retaliation and vengeance in the face of egregious trespass of life against life, might sound as if they were predicated on a common regard for the sanctity of life; but these arguments are incommensurate in their starting points. One argues against the taking of human life, and the other argues for extracting the punishment of death for one who violates the prohibition against the taking of human life. Both arguments claim that they cherish the inviolability of human life, but one adds the codicil that those who do violate human life are exempt from the protections associated with inviolability. They are literally outside the law: "outlaw." Everything else—deterrence, unfairness, irreversibility, barbarity, financial costs, and all the other ingredients in this mix—is rationalized icing on the basic cake.

But more important, as I have argued earlier, Christian ethics is not ethics for everybody. While Christian ethics is not stipulated for Christians only, it is nevertheless undertaken for Christians particularly and specifically. And as this bears upon capital punishment or other advocacies for justifying the killing of human beings, it ought to be clear that the Gospel prohibits our killing one another. So far as I am aware, there are no New Testament exceptions to this general rule. I know, of course, that there are twenty-three offenses nominated in the Old Testament for which the death penalty was exacted. But this may only help us to see, in yet another way, how it is that biblical ethics is not Christian ethics.

The only explicit reference to capital punishment in the New Testament is John's account (8:3–11) of Jesus' response to the charge against the woman who was taken in adultery. To the accusers he said, "You who are without sin cast the first stone"; and to the woman he said, "You are forgiven, go and sin no more." Within the past two or three decades and following this example, all of the major Christian churches, together with Jewish bodies and other groups, have adopted or reaffirmed official positions opposing the death penalty.

The condition may be preexistent; but in the era of the post-Constantinian church, it is widely agreed that the distinctiveness of Christian ethics as such is contaminated. The history of the church's rapprochement with capital punishment is less articulate than its warranting of just war; but the Inquisition and similar atrocities, together with the articulated criteria for just war, help make it believable that the church conspired with the state to exempt some instances of human killing from the general prohibition on the grounds of expedience or utility, which were then rationalized as defense of the faith. Christians conveniently forgot that God had chosen not to exercise dominion by carnage but by the cross.

We continue this tradition at the end of the twentieth century. In those states (of which mine is one) which retain "the supreme penalty," the reasons given for retention are a familiar litany: (1) It is a merited punishment, and neither sufficiently cruel nor unusual as to violate the Eighth and Fourteenth Amendments to the Constitution. (2) It is retributory, following the logic of the *lex talionis*, as the only penalty appropriate as repayment, and it helps (as in a ransom theory) to make a wrong right. (3) It is vicarious in the measure to which it serves as a deterrent. (4) It is satisfaction for society's sense of moral outrage at the criminal violation for which this is the penalty. (5) Although seldom acknowledged, capital punishment also functions in a remarkably subtle way as substitution, to cleanse a profound sense of guilt which derives from this society's failure to train us not to be a violent people. (6) In a similar way, the death penalty serves as an expiatory sacrifice to the violence which is deeply embedded in each one of us. The death penalty is, however, in all these things highly stylized and ritualized according to the canons of secular society. And if one of the purposes of stylized ritual is to surround with mystery, the execution of a criminal in this society succeeds admirably in this regard.

That some who call themselves Christian continue to support the death penalty is a witness not so much to the Gospel's lack of clarity on this matter as to Enlightenment Protestantism's scholasticism and individualism, and its commitment to a cultural ideology in relation to which we are plainly determined to control the kind of people we are and are destined to be. But we have seen already that the function of scripture and tradition is to train us to live as a people who are clearly out of control. We have seen that it is from this material that the Christian community has heard the Word of God, and from which it expects to hear it again. And we have seen that it is this Word of God which governs and norms authentic Christian witness. People killing people, in whatever form the homicide may take, is a contradiction of that story.

What that story says to us in the case of capital punishment, or war, or self-defense, is that Jesus was nailed to the cross for the sins of the world; that his execution alone exhausts the thoughts of Christians about expiation, sacrifice, satisfaction, ransom, and the rest. If expiation is required for human transgression, Christians believe that this has been accomplished by the death of Jesus. If retribution in the form of judicial homicide is willed by the state, Christians know that this action defies and denies the claim that Jesus is the sinless sufferer who pays the penalty for our sins, "who was put to death for our trespasses." And if such judgments sound impractical and unrealistic, I plead again that what is at stake is a matter of perspective and commitment. A Christian vision of these matters is only that: a Christian vision. Two anecdotes may illuminate what is at issue.

I had taken services one morning in a small parish some distance away; and I was idly listening to the radio as I drove home, when one of those ubiquitous Sunday afternoon religious programs caught my attention with a fragment from its opening announcement. But I did not entirely understand what I thought I heard, so I stayed with the program in the hope that the announcement would be repeated. And at the end, I was not disappointed. The radio evangelist repeated his offer: "We need your support," he said, "in order to continue this ministry; and if you will just send us a donation to help us stay on the air, we will send you a beautiful plastic tablecloth with Leonardo da Vinci's immortal painting of 'The Last Supper' printed in four colors in the center. This is a tablecloth you'll be proud to have on your dinner table for both family and friends. Just send us a donation, and we will send you this gift." Then the evangelist concluded with the comment I had gotten only a piece of almost thirty minutes earlier: "This is not a cheap imitation that we want to send you," he said. "It is a genuine simulated replica of the real thing." Now carry this thought along to the second anecdote.

In the early hours of All Souls' Day, at 2 A.M. on 2 November 1984, Velma Barfield became the first woman to be executed in North Carolina in forty years (and the first in the United States in twenty-two years). She was fifty-two years old, a grandmother, and the confessed poisoner of her boyfriend, her mother, and two others. At 2 A.M., two doses of sodium thiopental began flowing into her arms, and she went into a deep sleep; moments later, two doses of procuronium bromide, a muscle relaxer, were injected and her breathing stopped; her heart stopped beating several minutes later, and a doctor waited five minutes more before entering the death chamber to pronounce her dead at 2:15 A.M. The next day, newspapers reported that at precisely the same time, in a small town south and east of Raleigh, family and friends of the victims were celebrating at a party.

Vengeance and retribution are surely present here; but how they can be tolerated while so prominently and unapologetically present probably has to do with very subtle things, such as the air-tightness of our corporate alibi when executions take place. Three people pushed plungers connected to Velma Barfield's IVs; but not all of them pushed lethal drugs. With firing squads, not all of the weapons are loaded with live ammunition; with eletrocution or cyanide gassing, only one lever among several releases the current or discharges the cyanide pellet into the acid. The genius of this deception, of course, is that nobody is supposed to know whether his or her action is the one which is the cause of the killing. As a radio newscaster explained prior to Velma's execution, this way nobody will have to bear the guilt of killing Velma. But, of course, what this exercise in bad faith produces, as Peter Berger has poignantly demonstrated, is the cherished social fiction that nobody did any killing at all.[19] It was the law that killed, or justice that killed, or the state that killed. But law and justice and state are abstractions, and abstractions cannot execute condemned criminals: only people can do that.

For a while, at the vigil on the capitol square in Raleigh, I carried a sign which read: "Not in my name"; but I soon abandoned that sign because I knew that so long as men and women are tortured and killed anywhere, none of us can be insulated from that violence or immunized against that barbarity. From Jim Crow justice onward, I have learned that courts can and do perpetrate lawful crimes against human beings. So we must be painfully clear with ourselves on this point: people who kill people are responsible for their actions, and the people of a society which underwrites killing are morally contaminated, however reluctantly, by that action. "My personal convictions about the death penalty," we say—from governors to wardens to executioners to ordinary citizens—"have to be suspended while I discharge the duties of my office." And in this fiction of playing out a social role, we suppose that we have succeeded in deceiving ourselves beyond any personal accountability. At best, however, we are likely to have become only genuine simulated replicas of the real thing.

We have argued, conversely, that Christians are accountable for more than playing mere social roles, and that what it means to be a "good judge" or a "good jury" or a "good" anybody obliges Christians to ask where to turn to find out what is "good." Where can we look to learn the meaning of "good"? The short answer is that we do not reason rightly about the good we ought to do until we reflect morally on the kind of people we ought to be. The puzzles of practical reason have to do with contingent matters of fact, and these matters typically get worked out and resolved only within a tradition, a socially embodied set of notions about who we are and who we are meant to be. So when Christians use "good" as a descriptor of themselves or their actions, they know that its meaning is not autonomous or generated from some extraecclesial source, but that it is derived from a church's consensual self-understanding rooted in the long and rich and complex story of God's pilgrim people. People killing people is a contradiction of that story.

The puzzles of practical reason are not exhausted by ordinary and customary situations, however, so it warrants asking whether the reasons given in support of capital punishment could ever be compelling in unusual or extraordinary circumstances. Perhaps the answer, in an exceptional situation, would be different. Could it ever be permissible for people to kill people? Barth's reflections on this matter are among the cogent reasons which could be given for developing a casuistry for the death penalty under circumstances of this sort. He acknowledges the truism that "circumstances alter situations" and argues that, in response to this fact, special agents will have to undertake special responsibilities on behalf of and in the special service of the entire community. Thereafter, he lays down three conditions for allowing an action under extraordinary circumstances which, in normal situations, would be forbidden:

> (1) a recognition, which is not immediately apparent, that it is better for one person to die . . . than that the whole nation should perish; (2) a recognition, which is basically possible only from the depths of the Christian faith, that it is the will of the gracious God in relation to this man that he should be made a companion of the thieves who were crucified with Jesus, they as a just reward for their sins, but He having done nothing amiss and in expiation for their sin; and (3) a dreadful recognition that causing him to die is the only mercy which can be shown to this man.[20]

These requirements cannot be exegeted in the absence of an extraordinary circumstance; but one may intuitively appreciate their bearing on the uncommon situation to which these requirements are addressed. They are, I think, Barth's way of acknowledging the tragedy which sometimes accompanies the human condition. Sometimes we are confronted by circumstances which offer us no desirable or acceptable alternative. Naming the tragedy for what it is, we understand that "we're damned if we do, and damned if we don't."

My experience is that what I am here calling the "tragic dimension of the human condition" is exceptional but not uncommon. All of us have encountered sets of circumstances which are simply beyond our best efforts to make them right. They are pernicious in their culpability; they present themselves to us as genuine moral paradoxes; they exhaust the limits of our moral imagination and resolve; they test the very intelligibility of our moral assumptions; they threaten our usual principles and guidelines and self-understandings; and doing all this, they threaten to undo our moral vision of the kind of people we believe ourselves to be. Tragedy of this sort is not a failure of reason, because it occurs where moral sensibility stretches beyond where reason can go. Tragedies of this sort are not irrational, but nonrational.

So I have learned, for example, not without a little pain and sorrow, that there are some persons with whom I appear destined, despite my best efforts and theirs, never to be reconciled in this life. It is possible, of course, to say that our "best efforts" simply are not good enough; and this may well be true. But if this is so, it is precisely the truth of that judgment which confirms the conclusion that this is a tragic situation, one in which we are, to the best of our knowledge and ability, powerless to engineer to a different and happier result.

By pointing to this dimension of the human condition, I do not intend to romanticize it, or to make it easier for us to abandon the moral struggle in the presence of what appears to be intractable conflict. I do mean, however, to acknowledge its positive as well as its negative aspect. The tragic dimension sometimes overcomes us, I am persuaded, because of our failure to have a sufficiently modest sense of the moral limits which are involved in every attempt to be for and with one another in this life as we know God means for us to be. It happens in marriages; it happens in families; it happens in classrooms; it happens in courtrooms; it happens in churches. It is the powerful and possible dark underside in every human relationship. Only with a profound and tender sense of this tragic dimension can we have the courage to be decisive in these moments without the pretentious arrogance of supposing that we are also, in these moments, definitive for all time and circumstance.

So as important as any requirement which might be laid down is the indispensable awareness that the situation for which the requirement is laid down is truly exceptional. Only on that condition can the requirement(s) become creditable and protected from application in normal or routine situations. The substantive mistake of purveyors of consequentialist and situation ethics was to suppose that desiderata which gained their moral credibility, and thus were in some sense obligatory, in exceptional circumstances could be appropriately and habitually employed in ordinary situations. There is, therefore, more than a hint of irony in the fact that application of the requirements designed for exceptional cases becomes a moral imperative in situationism and consequentialism.

Just so, in following what Barth seems to propose, it must be transparently clear that the extraordinary action is only permitted; it is not mandated. That it is only permitted and not mandated reflects the awareness that moral agency here is deeply embedded in a tragic human condition. Thus a proposition which is more or less faithful to the practical reasoning proposed here would go something like this: the killing of human beings is for Christians always wrong, irrespective of circumstances; but sometimes killing human beings may be preferable to the circumstances which, as best we can foresee them, would prevail in the absence of it.

To talk this way is to embrace and employ a modified version of the ancient principle of double effect, and I am aware that some will regard this as moral doublespeak. But I do not mean for it to be nonsensical or internally contradictory; nor do I believe that it is. We sometimes speak this way about an abortion; we sometimes speak this way about a war; we frequently go to great lengths in our lexical ordering of various homicides to discriminate between what we believe to have been, and not to have been, avoidable killing. I think rather that some such proposition is yet another way of acknowledging that, Christianly understood, grace conveys the capacity to live without some of the choices we would have preferred to have. It affirms an absolute prohibition and acknowledges the contingency of human moral agency. Whether Jesus would have sanctioned it is relevant to the absolute prohibition; whether I can avoid or must engage it is relevant to the contingency of my human moral agency.

GIVING YOURSELF AWAY

To talk of offering and intercession, as I have wanted to suggest throughout, is to embrace the church's liturgy from beginning to end, since all that we understanding ourselves to be *doing* in any of the church's rites and offices is offering. To paraphrase the Book of Common Prayer in regard to consecration of the eucharistic elements: here we offer and present ourselves, our souls and bodies, to be a reasonable, holy, and living sacrifice to God. In doing this, we humbly petition that God will accept this offering of ourselves and thereby fill us with his grace and blessing, and make us at-one with him so that he may dwell in us and we in him. Before that, we have offered intercessions for all sorts and conditions of our sisters and brothers, for the congregation present and absent, for government, for the sick and needy, for the sorrowful and troubled, for all people everywhere that their eyes may be opened to acknowledge and thereafter honor and worship God.

For most all of us, I reckon this to be a sincere, but qualified, offering; because all the things which we offer—money and bread and wine—are meant to symbolize what is most precious to us and therefore most difficult to give away. I mean, of course, ourselves.

If the rhetoric of modern liberalism is to be believed, the autonomous individual self is what has to be held onto at all costs. As in most heresies, there is a certain self-evident truth in this claim; but it is not the whole truth. Several years ago, a former student gave me a poster which I still dislay on my office wall. It consists of a quotation attributed to Janice Joplin: "You better not compromise yourself—it's all you got." The truth in that claim seems to me to be the same one the church has always taught in respect of conscience: *conscientia est semper consequentia*. Do not disobey conscience, even an erroneous conscience; if you are not faithful to your fundamental commitments, you are a hypocrite; disobedience to conscience is dishonesty.

But this, of course, is not the whole story; and the church has never taught that conscience is the self-generated intuition of an autonomous individual about what is right and wrong, good and bad. Conscience is the character which is shaped and formed by a community of moral discourse; it has to be learned. So while Christians have "claimed" and "owned" their commitments, they have not created them; and what Christians mean by conscience is not merely a religious way of asserting that one's morality is and can be *only* what one's will creates.

Just as navels are the perpetual physiological reminder of our biological connectedness, in the matter of moral judgment conscience has performed a similar function by reminding us of our connectedness to the moral community of our ancestors and forebears in the faith. So it probably makes little or no sense to talk about "giving the self away" in a culture where it is supposed that the atomic individual is the fundamental and irreducible reality; but it can and does make sense, in a community formed by a different moral tradition—one which understands the self as "not valid if detached"—to appreciate the possibility of giving ourselves away. This, I believe, is at least in part what Jesus meant when he said that if we undertake to hold onto and control our lives we will surely lose them, but that those who are prepared to lose their lives for his sake will find them.

Before anything else, Christian ethics is the abandonment of the self to God; an abandonment which, as Jesus promises, issues in fulfillment and realization as a holy life, formed by God's story and acquired through sanctification to become our story as well. Only on these terms can we talk intelligently about *doing* the will of God, because it is only on the terms of giving the self away, of being out of control, that we are opened to God's possibility for us. Augustine knew the costs and benefits of thinking about ourselves in this way when he said that God always wants to give us something, but cannot so long as our hands are full.

An offering is a giving-away. In the church's liturgy, we are forever giving away fragments of ourselves in time, money, talents, prayers, bread, wine, and water. What is hoped for, and devoutly wanted, through this training is that we will learn also how to offer God "our selves, our souls and bodies, to be a reasonable, holy, and living sacrifice."

CHAPTER SIX

SCRIPTURE AND PROCLAMATION

THE BIBLE AS CANON

Every Christian church that I know has a Bible prominently on display; and some even make a considerable ceremonial out of carrying it into the sanctuary as part of an entrance rite, frequently alongside flags and banners and whatever else is thought appropriate to signal this as a very special event. Among my clearest recollections of services in the Church of Scotland are of the verger, processing down the center aisle with a massive Bible held aloft, while leading the minister to the pulpit. So it may appear redundant, or otherwise out of place, that we should consider the place of Scripture and proclamation in the liturgy, since in every Christian tradition the Bible occupies a focal point. But lest this distinction be misconstrued or distorted, we need to remind ourselves now and then why Scripture claims such pride of place in this religion.

We should note at the outset that the Sunday liturgy is compounded of two parts: the liturgy of the Word and the liturgy of the sacrament. In themselves, and quite apart from various ceremonials associated with the Bible, these components would appear to ensure the permanence, if not the primacy, of Scripture in the liturgy. Beyond this, however, there is a rich heritage of prayer and praise which underwrites both literally and metaphorically the prominence of the Bible in both parts of the Sunday service.

These two parts have different (some say even separate) origins. (1) The first part is an amplified and Christianized version of the pattern of synagogue worship, which we call the *proanaphora* (literally, "preceding the offering"). This part consists principally of a salutation in God's name, praise through psalms, opening prayers, reading and hearing of the Scripture, all interspersed with more psalms, teaching and proclamation, affirmation, and corporate prayers. (2) The second part reenacts and recapitulates the supper of Jesus with his disciples in the context of Passover, with an eye fixed on Jesus' postresurrection meal with the disciples[1] and on the apostolic witness of gathering together for teaching and fellowship and prayers and "the breaking of bread."[2]

Despite the different origins of these two parts of the liturgy, they were, early on, incorporated in Christian worship into one unified liturgy.[3] So virtually from the beginnings of Christian devotions, and certainly from the second century onwards, the basic shape of the liturgy has been developed around (1) reading, reflecting on, teaching, and proclaiming the Scriptures, together with (2) obediently following Jesus' command to share the sacramental meal of his most blessed body and blood.

All the same, familiarity has a way of breeding contempt; routinization has a way of domesticating mystery; and ceremonial has a way of separating piety from ordinary day-to-day living. So if the Word is not to be bound (in this instance by merely perfunctory attention to it), it may be that Christians ought to reaffirm periodically why the Scriptures, together with the other treasures of the tradition, are important—indeed, indispensable—for acknowledging and understanding who we are when we celebrate and participate in the liturgy as the new people of God's kingdom, the *laos theou*.

Among the first reasons to give for the special place of Scripture in the church is that it is the church's account of God's continuing communication with his people. Or, to say it in a different way, it is the church's story of the journey through time of those people who believe and understand themselves to be created and called to be the people of God. Putting the matter this way is useful because it obliges us to acknowledge quite explicitly some very important claims about Scripture which might otherwise be obscure.

This account of the place of Scripture suggests, first of all, that *Scripture is the church's account of God's self-disclosing Word.* The canon of the Hebrew Scriptures was effectively closed with Daniel in the second century B.C.E.; and it was officially closed (some say owing to common usage) at the Council of Jamnia (ca. 90 C.E.) when the Hebrew Bible was limited to twenty-four books: five in the Law of Moses, eight in the Prophets, and eleven in the Writings.[4]

Meanwhile, the earliest New Testament writings were beginning to be circulated within Christian communities. It appears that these letters and other writings which were read in the churches and Christian assemblies almost immediately attracted attention, gradually earned obedience, and soon inspired reverence in these communities. A larger number of writings than now comprise the New Testament were read in the primitive church, and varying attributions of authority to these writings were made. Over time, both the number and the authority of these writings grew.

Historical scholarship indicates that in the period leading up to about 220 C.E., the thirteen Epistles of Paul and the four Gospels were read in the churches, and that these writings—together with Acts, 1 Peter, and 1 John—were gradually received as sacred texts. All these writings appear to have had their authority recognized by 220 C.E. In the same period, some other writings—among them the *Didache*, the *Shepherd of Hermas*, the *Epistle of Clement*, the *Epistle of Barnabas,* the *Apocalypse of Peter*, the *Acts of Paul*, and a second *Epistle of Clement*—were candidates for admission to authority by Christians, which is to say that these books were read by some Christians but that they failed, in the end, to gain the kind of general recognition and acceptance which was achieved by the first group.

This experimental pattern largely continued over the next hundred years or so; and eventually it seemed a propitious time—for many reasons, including the use of documents in churches, the import of apostolic authority, and appeals to the teachings of these books against certain heresies of the day—to agree upon the New Testament canon. This agreement was reached at the Council of Carthage in 397 C.E.; and from that time forward, the church recognized, approved, and confirmed as its canon the same twenty-seven books that we in the Western church have today as the New Testament.[5]

Now all of this is just to say that the Bible, as we have it, is *the church's book*. We will never know precisely and certainly all of the considerations which led the Council of Carthage to confirm these books, and not some others, as the Christian canon. The tradition claims that Holy Spirit informed this selection, and this seems as plausible for Carthage as for other councils of the church. However canonization may in fact have happened, two things are clear: one is that the New Testament canon was confirmed at Carthage; and the other is that, since that time, the church has claimed these two collections of writings—the canons of the Old Testament and the New Testament—to be its Bible, its Scripture, its story, its account of God's dealing with his people.

That the Bible is the church's book is important and essential to acknowledge when we go on to ask about the place, role, and function of Scripture in the liturgy, because it is from this material that the Christian community hears God's self-disclosing Word. This, indeed, is a second reason why the Scripture is accorded such a special and prominent place both in and by the church. We believe that it is *from and through and in* this material that God speaks; that the Bible points *beyond* itself and witnesses to the one who is its subject. Christians, together with Jews and Muslims, have consistently emphasized that God initiates revelation, that God speaks and we hear. Biblical theism claims that God discloses—we do not discover—what we know of God. The principal reason for this way of setting the priorities is to acknowledge God's sovereignty and initiative, God's transcendence and power; but it also teaches us incidentally that this is precisely how we learn about anything other than and beyond ourselves. Human perception of everything, including God's speech, tends to be varied; and applied to revelation, this means that, while all of us may participate in it, none of us fully comprehends God's self-disclosing.

Sometimes the question gets asked this way: Is the Bible revelation, or the record of revelation? Is revelation in the book, or is revelation in the events which the book records? William Temple's plain and direct answer was that revelation could not be in the book unless it was first in the events, because it is to the events that the book bears witness. So the Bible, properly speaking, is not itself revelation, but it *witnesses* to the revelation.[6] Karl Barth made a similar point, but formulated it differently. The Bible itself is not God's past revelation, said Barth; it *attests* to the past revelation. On this account the Bible claims no authority for itself, but points beyond itself to the singular Word of God spoken.

Is revelation God's speech or our hearing? The answer is that it is both, and not one or the other. Revealing occurs, whether from God to us or from us to each other, as the coincidence of speech and hearing, as the correspondence of presentation and acknowledgment. So what we have in divine revelation, we can modestly claim, is knowledge of a transcendent other which is filtered through human sensibility and appreciation. The doctrine of the "inspiration" of the Bible is therefore not an explanation of how the Bible came to be, and it has nothing whatever to do with a dogmatic assertion about the method (usually thought to be verbal dictation) by which God's Word gets conveyed to us in the biblical text. What the doctrine of "biblical inspiration" means consists basically of two claims. One of these claims is that this Holy Scripture contains all we need to know to be in right relationship with God, our neighbors, and ourselves—that is, it contains all that we need for salvation. The other claim is that our faithful and devout attention to this Scripture will invite Holy Spirit to be present in our lives and make us ever anew to be the holy people whom God created us to be—that is, it elicits holy living.

The Bible is thus the church's canon, its control and *regula fidei* ("rule of faith"), because revelation engendered the Bible which attests to it. And it is in this way, says Barth, that *both* proclamation and Bible are Word of God.[7]

THE FUNCTION OF CANON

How to be faithful to the sense of the canon as a whole, in the absence of direct and explicit scriptural address, clearly offers a serious challenge to our moral imagination. Of course, we do not always succeed as we might like; and the search goes on for assistance in faithfully connecting the canon with issues not specifically addressed by it. How this task can be forwarded has been helpfully defined and wonderfully illuminated, I think, in an essay by Walker Percy, called "The Message in the Bottle."[8]

The story, very briefly, asks us to imagine a man castaway on an island. He is shipwrecked, and has no recollection of who he is or where he came from. All he knows is that one day he discovers himself cast up on the beach. He soon discovers that the island is inhabited, and that the islanders have a remarkable culture with highly developed social institutions, a good university, first-class science, and flourishing industry and art. The castaway is warmly received by the natives; and being a resourceful fellow, he makes the best of the situation—he gets a job, builds a house, takes a wife, raises a family, goes to night school. He becomes, as the phrase goes, a useful member of the community.

So far this sounds like a story which (with perhaps adaptations) could happen almost anywhere; but there is more. The castaway forms the habit of regularly exercising with a walk on the beach in the early morning; and in the course of these walks, he regularly comes upon bottles which have been washed up by the waves. The bottles are tightly corked, and each one contains a single piece of paper with a single sentence written on it. Some of the messages are trivial or nonsensical, some of them state facts and draw conclusions, and some of them are false. Here are some of the messages:

Lead melts at 330 degrees Fahrenheit.

At 2 P.M., January 4, 1902, at the residence of Manuel Gomez in Matanzas, Cuba, a leaf fell from a banyan tree.

2 + 2 = 4.

Tears, idle tears, I know not what they mean.

Chicago, a city, is on Lake Michigan.

A war party is approaching from Bora Bora.

The pressure of gas is a function of heat and volume.

Being comprises essence and existence.

In 1943 the Russians murdered ten thousand Polish officers in the Katyn Forest.

There is fresh water in the next cove.

As the castaway sets out to sort these messages, they appear to him to fall naturally into two quite different groups, which Percy distinguishes as "pieces of knowledge" and "pieces of news." A piece of knowledge is what anybody, anywhere, at any time can arrive at; it is knowledge *sub specie aeternitatis*. One may be glad to get this knowledge, but it is not indispensable. Pieces of knowledge are messages like "lead melts at 330 degrees Fahrenheit" and "Chicago, a city, is on Lake Michigan." Knowledge of this sort is not to be disparaged, but it is just knowledge that can be arrived at by anyone on any island at any time.

Each of the other group of messages, however, expresses what Percy calls a "contingent or nonrecurring event or state of affairs which . . . is peculiarly relevant to the concrete predicament of the hearer." This is a piece of news, and consists of messages like "there is fresh water in the next cove" and "a war party is approaching from Bora Bora."

The distinction which Percy draws between "knowledge" and "news" is straightforward and direct: "The scale of significance by which the castaway evaluates news is its relevance for his own predicament."

Now there is much more to this story (e.g., there is an instructive discussion about what happens when one mistakes a piece of knowledge for a piece of news, and vice versa); but I have found this basic distinction to be helpful and illuminating in accounting for how it is that the scriptural canon controls our Christian sense about what is dispensable knowledge and what is indispensable news. The claim of Christian faith is that the Gospel is emphatically not *sub specie aeternitatis*—objective, discoverable at any time by anybody, anywhere. We say, instead, that faith is not a form of knowledge but the *euanggelion*, the glad tidings, the good news of the Gospel. And we say that it is this precisely because it tells us about ourselves in our own predicament. It instructs us as to who we are; it does what a compass does for a marine navigator: it gives the position from which any future course gets plotted; it tells us that we are the reconstituted family of God, the people of the new age, a people called to holiness and perfection *in our predicament*.

I become more and more persuaded that understanding the canon as authoritative for Christian witness in these ways, as a control which both allows and requires that we be out of control, is very difficult for us modern, autonomous, secularized folk. The reason that fundamentalism, a literal reading of Scripture, sloganeering,[9] one-to-one correlation of Bible prophecy with history, and the like will not work is precisely because Scripture does not function in these settings and circumstances as canon, as norm and control. Instead, we are fully in control when Scripture is used in these ways. We are forever imagining and discovering and inventing ways to authorize Scripture, rather than be authorized by it.

This is yet another way of falling prey to the notion that the Gospel consists of "objective goods" which are "out there," impressing themselves upon us in ways similar to imprinting on a Lockean *tabula rasa*, and defining what we are to do in the face of moral quandaries.[10] But I have wanted to argue that authentic Christian ethics cannot be confused with either idealism or pragmatism, with a rationalist ethics or an ethics of calculation. What the Gospel offers is not a self-validating rational standard, but a community of loyalty. Christian ethics has to do with the *ethos* of Christians,[11] with a style of life which reflects the character of a new people who are shaped by living now in the new age. It is a community ethics, because it is the story of a people's journey; it is a religious ethics, because it is the story of a people's journey with their God. Blaise Pascal once observed that human things must be known to be loved, but that divine things must be loved to be known. This is precisely the point. In the last analysis, this way of ethics calls for wisdom rather than rules or extempore predilection; and wisdom, as Socrates ascertained, has to be learned but cannot be taught.

These are among the compelling reasons, I believe, why the entire first part of the liturgy continues to focus on and derive from Scripture. These are also among the reasons why the second part, the liturgy of the sacrament, is clearly recognizable as also heavily dependent upon the language of Scripture in sursum corda, sanctus, consecration, Lord's Prayer, and postcommunion thanksgiving.

As the church's book, as the church's account of God's self-disclosing revelation to this people, the Bible has a variety of functions within Christian life and witness, within Christian ethics and Christian worship. Charles Wood has summarized these functions and pointed out that the Bible is:

> *our principal means of access to the communities of faith whose product it is; our primary, and occasionally our only, source of data—such as it is—concerning various historical figures, including Jesus; a collection of texts for meditation; the source of innumerable images and metaphors, ideas and modes of expression which have found incorporation into the church's thought, speech, and life. Scripture is, in short, the primary source for Christian witness: the main, though certainly not the only, source of the data, the concepts, and the language out of which Christian witness is formed and nourished.*[12]

Beyond this, of course—that is, beyond its function in the church's liturgy and the Christian life—the Bible has been widely appropriated in colleges and universities for what is nowadays called the "academic study of religion." In this mode, the Bible is regarded as a repository of history, poetry, myth, narrative, cultic ceremonial, pious devotion and meditation. The "academic study of religion" posits that the Bible can be studied in exactly the same way as any other interesting literary text, employing the same methodologies of critical and comparative investigation, analysis, and assessment.

It is important to take note of the "academic study of religion," because this intellectual outlook makes clear that not every use of Scripture is "scriptural." In this instance, for example, the canonical function of Scripture is clearly different from the Bible's function as a source of data. To be sure, the church actually embraces both these functions; and, while neither validates the other, each does reinforce the other. Besides, the point needs to be clear that recognition of the Scriptures as canon has certain hermeneutical consequences beyond those which might derive from the study of the Bible as only interesting literature or history or poetry. In the former instance, as canon, the Bible norms our existence as a people; in the latter instance, as nothing more than literature, the Bible functions only as a source of interesting documentary material.

For Christians, the canon is the story through which Jesus is made present as Christ to the church. Christians cannot ignore, however, that it is precisely the role and function of Scripture as "story" which has given rise to considerable controversy about its meaning and, in the bargain, many questions concerning the importance of hermeneutics or interpreting principles. Who, for example, is going to say which of the several "stories" in the Bible functions as canon? Who is going to say why this "story" is norming and not some other? Who will say what the "story" means, and what interpretive modes will control the hermeneutics? Can anyone else tell me what the "story" means in terms of understanding who I am? How can I claim the "story"; and if I claim it, do I also in some sense own it? All of these questions reflect a problem which appears to be distinctly (although perhaps not exclusively) modern—namely, what account can we give of personal appropriation of a community's story? And what is at stake in giving up personal autonomy in order to share with others a communal vision and self-understanding?

Another, more extended citation from Charles Wood helpfully describes the role and function of the canon in and for the Christian community:

> *The canon . . . functions to show what the Word of God is. This is not to say that the words of the text may be simply identified as "God's words." But when the canon, as such, is properly activated, it norms all other Christian witness—that is, it enables a judgment as to whether or how some other human utterance may also participate in God's self-disclosive word. . . . And because God is not only the chief character but also the author, the story's disclosure is God's self-disclosure. We become acquainted with God as the one who is behind this story and within it.*
>
> *The canon, thus construed, norms Christian witness not by providing sample statements by which to test other statements, nor by providing ideals of some other sort, but by reminding the community of the identity*

of the one whose word they bear. The canon may not contain, explicitly or in nuce, every statement the church may want or need to make in its witness. But the church may and must ask, concerning those words which it is moved to receive or to utter in God's name and concerning those actions which it hopes to interpret or to perform, whether they are indeed consistent with the identity of the God whom the canonical story discloses. That which is "scriptural" or "biblical," in the sense of "authorized by the scriptural canon," is that which does accord with that identity."[13]

This is another way of showing that Scripture, like liturgy and everything else in Christian tradition, is not an end in itself. As the church has recognized through the centuries, Scripture is extraordinarily important to Christians; indeed, it is indispensable to us. But Scripture is vital to Christians principally as a means to hearing the story through which Jesus is made present as Christ to the church.

So Luther taught that the Bible is canon insofar as it displays the Gospel; and he therefore took a dim view of the Epistle of James, with its emphasis on works, and of the Revelation of John, with its otherworldly preoccupations. Both of these writings, in Luther's view, tended to compromise the Gospel teaching of justification by grace alone; and because of this, he insisted that what they teach is neither authoritative nor binding. In sum, they do not display or illumine the Gospel.[14]

Scripture is sacred, for Luther, not because of claims for inspiration and inerrancy that can be asserted about it, but because it unfolds and witnesses to God's story of redemption, the story of God's definitive self-disclosure in the long and arduous pilgrimage of God's people. The canon derives its authority from the true norm of Christian witness: Jesus Christ.

Over the past quarter-century there have been many essays, and not a few books, written by Christian ethicists to account for how the Bible is (or ought to be) used in their work.[15] As we might expect, there is enormous diversity in the approaches advocated and there are broad and serious disagreements among the authors. There are, however, three areas of acknowledged accord, all of which, it turns out, are dissonant problem areas in need of reputably orchestrated harmonization.[16] Virtually all of the modern commentators on the use(s) of Scripture in Christian ethics agree that the *distance between the biblical world and our world* can be a difficult matter, both when we need to deal with questions and issues, and when we need to deal with certain contingent matters of faith, which the Bible does not explicitly address. They agree, furthermore, that the *cultural, authorial, literary, historical, and theological diversity within the Bible itself* poses serious difficulties for using the Bible as an integrated standard and guide. And, finally, they agree that it is far from clear just *how Scripture can and ought to be related to other sources* of knowledge and wisdom, such as the sciences, philosophy, experience, tradition, and the like.

If it is so, as I have argued, that Christian ethics is not a prescriptive code or a series of moral propositions, but a way of life for the people of God, it makes sense that the function of the canon—how it is used in the Gospel's service—is correspondent. The canon is not a codification of do's and don'ts, or a compendium of axioms and postulates and principles. It is, instead, the criterion by which the church's witness is assessed and judged, a criterion which derives its authority entirely from the true norm of Christian witness, Jesus Christ.

I believe that this is congruent with my earlier claim that Christian ethics is *ex hypothese* an aspect of Christology: the moral life of Christians is rooted in an understanding of the person and work of Jesus Christ. This is similarly why the liturgy, from beginning to end, from gathering to sending forth, exalts the name of Jesus. We come in the name of Jesus; we go in the name of Jesus; all that we do is done in his name, for his sake, to his glory, because we are a people who acknowledge that Jesus alone is Sovereign, the source of who we are and the criterion for our identity, our self-understanding, our true and authentic self and story.

If I mean to be a Christian, and if being a Christian means being shaped and formed by a vision of myself and the world which is focused and directed by Jesus Christ, then I must perceive and talk about these matters within and from that perspective, that point of view; because it is only from that orientation that God's story gets displayed and illumined to us in Jesus Christ.

Sometimes, when I have talked this way with students or pastors or laypeople—and emphasized how it is that the Bible is the church's book; and how the canon governs and presides over Christian witness; and how the canon in turn derives its authority from, and is exercised in obedience to, the source of authority which is Jesus Christ—and when I have struggled with this understanding of Scripture as canon, some have wondered aloud whether the Gospel may not be discerned elsewhere, perhaps in noncanonical writings. They are not asking about the *Didache* or the *Shepherd of Hermas*, but about *The New York Times* or Kahlil Gibran's *The Prophet* or Martin Luther King's "Letter from Birmingham Jail."

Employing Luther's hermeneutic, why shouldn't one be able to discern the Gospel in these writings? The clue to the answer is partly in the question: why shouldn't *one?* To be sure, lots of individualist water has swept over the cultural dam in the almost five hundred years since Luther proposed this interpretive principle; but this does not alter the fact that Luther, by all accounts, did not offer this hermeneutic as a manifesto for an individualist interpretation of the Bible. The suggestion that each person is either permitted or entitled to determine for himself or herself the meaning of Scripture is plainly foreign to Luther.

But more to the point, consider how the Lutheran position in the controversy at Worms was formulated by Philip Melanchthon in Article VII, "Of the Church," in the 1530 Augsburg Confession:

> *They teach that the one Holy Church will remain forever. Now this Church is the congregation of the saints, in which the Gospel is rightly taught and the sacraments rightly administered.* [17]

An Anglican version of this interpretive principle is found in Article XIX, "Of the Church," in the *Articles of Religion*:

> *The visible Church of Christ is a congregation of faithful men, in which the pure Word of God is preached, and the Sacraments be duly ministered according to Christ's ordinance.* [18]

What appears unarguably clear in these formulations is that this hermeneutics depends on and derives from ecclesiology. The Gospel cannot be rightly taught, nor the pure Word of God preached, nor the sacraments rightly and duly ministered except in the church, in the congregation of the saints. And that, of course, is an odd if not alien notion in the modern world. A measure of its oddity is reflected in the fact that it is precisely this rather more communitarian notion which receives emphasis, time and again, when the church stands over against its pagan environment.

One of the most important Christian texts of this century emerged, for example, from a synod of the German Evangelical Church in May 1934. It is generally referred to as the Barmen Declaration, and it was composed almost entirely by Karl Barth. Although not without demurrers, it has been widely regarded as a critique of the German Christian church, which had been coopted by the Nazis, and as an attempt to say how the church remains Christ's church even when its leaders steer it astray and its members are wicked and godless.[19] So the third thesis of the Barmen Declaration affirms:

> *The Christian Church is the community of brothers and sisters in which, in Word and sacrament, through Holy Spirit, Jesus Christ acts in the present as Lord. With both its faith and its obedience, with both its message and order, it has to testify in the midst of the sinful world, as the Church of pardoned sinners, that it belongs to him alone and lives and may live by his comfort and under his direction alone, in expectation of his appearing.*[20]

Here the mediation of salvation belongs to those who receive and respond to Jesus Christ in Word and sacrament through Holy Spirit, and who witness to this in their lives in the world. But this is far removed from a simple and uncomplicated identification of a visible church with recognized forms of piety, as something self-contained and complete, as an end in itself. And it is also a far cry from the truth claims of traditional metaphysics and the quest for universal truths in belief and practice. It entails, instead, the complex and risky business of acknowledging that Christians live by the power of God in a world which tries persistently either to push them out toward the periphery or to seduce them to embrace the world's distorted virtues. And it requires the unsettling recognition that we ourselves are not in control, that the written text may actually transform us through our reading of it, and that truth is not a property to be possessed but a pilgrimage toward God's perfection to be practiced and performed.[21]

It has been in this context—of claiming that a hermeneutic of this sort is operative in order to know where (or where not) Christ is to be discerned in the Bible, and what of the Scriptures is therefore canon—that my students and parishioners alike have sometimes asked why they should not be permitted to employ that same principle in order to discern the Gospel in noncanonical writings.[22] They ask what, after all, is or could be so wrong with taking the text for a sermon from Augustine's *Confessions*, or Calvin's *Institutes*, or even *The Gospel According to Peanuts*. This question becomes an invitation to elaborate the claim that this is a communitarian, not an individualist, hermeneutic.

The short answer is that the confession "Jesus is our Savior" only makes sense within a particular story which gets told by a particular community. In this case, such a confession of faith makes sense within an account of who Jesus is, and what it means and how it happens that he is acknowledged and confessed as Savior—an account which can be told only by the company of those who believe this claim and order their lives by it. In other words, this is a declaration which is believable when a speaker can deliver it as an authentic word. And a clear implication which follows is that this word must be delivered to a hearer who is equipped, who is able, to hear it.

To put it another way: unless both speaker and hearer share a common context, they share nothing in common but the words; and it is no secret that mere words can, and do, mean a great many things to a great many people, and that these meanings are not always congenial or compatible. Again, Charles Wood has helped us to see that if there is no context which exercises a norming function, there is no control in principle over the interpretation and use of the text. Indeed, "Only in its scriptural matrix does 'Jesus is Lord' convey the associations which enable it to function as Christian confession."[23]

To test this hypothesis, let me invite you to try for a moment to exegete a somewhat different confession: "Maggie O'Donnell is our mother." This assertion is structurally and grammatically the same as "Jesus is our Savior." Syntatically they look very much alike. But whereas "Maggie O'Donnell is our mother" is (very probably) a nonsensical confession for *you* to make, it is in fact true for *me* to claim that Maggie O'Donnell is my mother. Could it ever be possible for you to say such a thing? Maybe; but unless you are my brother or sister, you would be talking about a different Maggie O'Donnell from the one to whom I refer. The Maggie O'Donnell who was my mother is dead and therefore beyond a relationship with others as mother.

There is no way, in other words, for the Maggie O'Donnell who was *my* mother to be *our* mother. "Maggie O'Donnell is our mother" only makes sense within the circle of those who knew her as mother—her children—

within an account of who she was with which we are acquainted, and which would then permit us to acknowledge and confess her as "mother." But the fact of the matter is that you and I do not participate in that account of who she was, and what maternity meant in relation to her, and how it could happen that she could be "mother." So you cannot make this confession, but her sons and daughter can.

I sometimes (foolhardily) extend the experiment by asking my students whether they can affirm that "Harmon Smith is our teacher" or (with less trepidation) that "the graduate assistants are our teachers." This statement is syntactically identical to "Maggie O'Donnell is our mother," but this time it is also one in which (with allowances for some eccentric reservation) all of us can (more or less) concur.

Of course, the exquisitely interesting question which attends all this is "how come?" or "how is this so?" or "what makes this true?" or "what accounts for why this is so self-evident, beyond the benefit of useful doubt?" And the short answer, again, is that making these claims only makes sense within the shared story of a family, a course of lectures, a set of preceptorials. In this context the characters are displayed as who and what is claimed for them; thus both subject and predicate make compelling sense because they function within a story with which we have organic acquaintance, a story which we commonly share. It would make little or no sense, however, for someone who is not participant, who does not share in this commonality, to make these claims. Now I know that I should not press the analogy too far, because analogies of this sort tend finally to break down. All the same, I hope that this excursion serves to indicate why one cannot readily translate or transfer a hermeneutic which derives its authority *from the canon* with equivalent aptitude to noncanonical writings.

The reason that *The New York Times* and Kahlil Gibran's *The Prophet* and Martin Luther King's "Letter from Birmingham Jail" do not and cannot function to authorize or norm Christian witness is that they are not the church's account of how these words connect us to God's Word, to Jesus Christ, and to the Gospel. They may be accounts acknowledged by certain persons who understand themselves to be Christians; indeed, they may be *your* account or *my* account or *somebody else's* account of the Christian life; and they may be beautifully written and contain lofty and edifying and inspiring principles. But they are not the truth for the church, for Jesus alone is the church's truth; nor are they the church's canon, for the church's canon is the account by which Jesus is made present to the church as Christ.

Because it is the church's story alone which properly norms Christian witness, it is essential to make this point emphatically and unequivocally if we are to keep the norming "horse" before the witnessing "cart." Otherwise there will be lots of essentially pagan stuff which gets offered as Christian witness, in the name of an un-normed tolerance for pluralism or an uncritical embrace of sentimentalism, which thereafter goes unchallenged by careful canonical scrutiny. But there is a further important reason for wanting to nail down this point securely: in order to acknowledge (as we ought) that insofar as they may be authorized by the canon to accord with the identity of the God whom the canon discloses, these noncanonical words just may be among the words which the church is moved to receive and utter in God's name. Even that lofty service, however, does not entitle these writings to function as, or claim the name of, canon. They are not canon, but are only authorized by canon; and this is an important distinction, as we will later have occasion to see again.

Meanwhile, this may be a suitable juncture at which to make explicit a point that has been only tacit thus far—a point that has to do with the place of the Hebrew Scriptures in the Christian canon. Christians cherish the Old Testament because it is the record of God's self-disclosure in the pilgrimage of the people of Israel, and as such it is part of the overall narrative of the canon. But when Christians read the stories of Abraham, Isaac, and Jacob, I believe that we construe them through the eyes of the four evangelists and Paul. Let me try to explain.

The church has clearly profited from the work of disciplines not directly under the umbrella of theology, and perhaps nowhere more dramatically and substantively than in what has come to be known as "lower criticism" and "higher criticism" of the Bible. What is called "lower criticism" consists chiefly in the work of historians, archivists, linguists, and others in establishing the most accurate Hebrew and Greek texts of the Bible. The result, we hope, is a text which is closer to the original writing and, thereafter, translations which are more faithful to these ancient documents.

Beyond this search for accurate texts, however, there is also the effort of "higher criticism" to establish the authorship of a writing, the date of its composition, and the set of historical circumstances which surround its writing. Work of this sort, of course, challenges notions that the Bible is divinely dictated, inerrant and infallible in every "jot and tittle," or to be literally interpreted. But higher criticism need not destroy the Bible as the Word of God or imply that Holy Spirit had no part in inspiring its composition. What it chiefly does is provide a literary and historical frame of reference within which we might better understand what the biblical stories and sayings meant in their original cultural and historical settings.

Having said this, it is important to reiterate that Scripture as a whole is not an end in itself. The parables, hymns, poems, histories, etc., are not freestanding and autonomous. Nor can the whole or any part of Scripture be understood or interpreted without reference to an interpretive norm, a hermeneutic. So, for example, it is a careless error of some advocates of the historical-critical method to suppose that the assumptions of this method are adequate to control a proper understanding of the text. But the problem here is not that this, or some other, method is illegitimate or false; it is only that it claims too much for itself when it supposes that it sufficiently norms Christian understanding of the Bible.

The criterion for Christian understanding and witness derives its authority from the account by which Jesus is made present to the church as Christ. There are no uninterpreted facts; and for Christians, the criterion for interpretation is Jesus Christ. A clear implication of this line of argument is that not everyone can read texts. I cannot read Russian or Chinese texts, and I have painfully discovered that most computer instruction manuals are plainly beyond my comprehension. On the other side, I am beginning to take lessons on the double bass and I am therefore learning the bass clef; so that what remained unintelligible to me all those years that I played instruments in the treble clef is now making perfectly good sense, if not yet good music.

We have thus come full circle: unless the speaker and listeners share a common context, they have nothing in common but the words of the text. And we have seen that appeal to the text is not equivalent to appeal to the Scripture. What Christians appeal to is not a collection of texts which, in their diversity, can yield an embarrassingly arbitrary ethics in an interpretive mine field; what Christians appeal to is Scripture, which exercises a shaping and norming control over the formation and existence in time of the community of those who understand and intend themselves to be disciples of Jesus Christ.

PROCLAIMING THE CANON

Although I indicated earlier that, of course, I appreciate that there are lots of nonverbal ways in which the church proclaims the gospel, and that the Bible knows full well that God is revealed not only through speech but likewise through silence, I also argued that there are times "under heaven" when it is both appropriate and necessary to speak.[24] And among those times when we are obliged to speak, I reckon that preaching is the activity which is most typically employed by the church for saying the good news of the Gospel and acknowledging the Scripture as canon. I am among those who devoutly believe that Word and sacrament belong indissolubly together; all the same, after almost forty years of preaching and celebrating, sometimes regularly and sometimes only occasionally, I discover that I am still intimidated by the preaching office. It is an awesome thing to venture to speak to brothers and sisters in the family on behalf of the parent. So I find it to be excruciatingly hard labor, but it can also be enormously satisfying when Holy Spirit takes over and perfects the scut work. My perduring judgment is that nowhere is authority in the church so much at issue—sometimes tacitly, sometimes explicitly—as when one presumes to preach, to interpret for a particular people in a particular time and place and circumstance what it might mean for them and us together to undertake to be this special people of the new age here and now, where we are, warts and all.

I have learned that it is what is going on in preaching that makes it so intimidating and satisfying. Just as the canon governs and presides over Christian witness, and just as the canon's authority derives from its obedience and fidelity to the Christ of the canon, so it is with preaching: in order for it to be Christian proclamation, preaching must witness to Jesus Christ as the source of its authority. But not all preaching does this.

While R. Taylor Scott was on the staff of the College of Preachers, he identified three "modes" of preaching which, he argued, indicated three different (though sometimes related) purposes of preaching.[25]

Scott called the first mode "rhapsodic," and meant by this the kind of preaching that intends to be uplifting and inspiring to the point of transporting its listeners out of this world. Rhapsodic preaching produces a kind of ecstasy, a rapture, a weightless freedom of spirit which liberates one from the cares and responsibilities of the world. It speaks frequently of "my religious pilgrimage" and of "private journeys," and it elicits individual flights of fancy. It does not point to any blessing in everyday life; indeed, the world as real is rejected in preference for being out of this world. So rhapsodic preaching is basically escapist in its purpose and outlook. And the church, correspondingly, becomes that place where we can get away, literally find sanctuary, from the cares and troubles of the world. Preaching in this mode reduces religion to aesthetics, and provides liberation (however brief) from the nuts and bolts of day-to-day living. A sermon in the rhapsodic mode, says Scott, is what most congregations and preachers take to be a "good sermon."[26]

Virtually the opposite number of the rhapsodic mode is what Scott calls the "rhetorical" mode. Here the listener will not encounter preaching which intends principally to uplift and inspire, but rather exhortation explicitly oriented to deciding and doing. If the rhapsodic mode is escapist, the rhetorical mode is *praxis* through and through. In order to work, preaching of this sort must abandon poetic metaphors in favor of plain talk which is commonly understood. Of course, the warrant for such plain talk obviously cannot be an individual's private religious pilgrimage, so rhetorical preaching assumes a common tradition among listeners; and this common tradition becomes the source of its force and coherence. Listeners are moved, to be sure, but not to aesthetics. They are addressed as real persons, in real places, confronting real moral existences; and they are called to decision. Good and evil are juxtaposed as alternatives, what is right and what is wrong are named, and listeners are called to action. The direction of this preaching is ethical, and its purpose is to exercise moral agency. So it is hardly surprising that if the tendency of rhapsodic preaching is to provide escape from the world, the tendency of rhetorical preaching is to embrace the world with a propensity for ideology. This mode of preaching, says Scott, is prone to be the public expression of the programmatic values of a particular group, put forward as the authoritative program for everyone.

Scott's final mode of preaching, the "liturgical" mode, is inimical to both the escapist motif of the rhapsodic mode and the ideologic aptitude of the rhetorical mode. Liturgical preaching undertakes to help its listeners understand their work in the world as a holy activity, offered as an oblation, and as a manifestation of both their consecration and the world's. It does not provide an escape from life in the world, nor does it serve an ideologic interest of some sort. Of course, it takes place within the liturgy, but this is not what makes it liturgical. Its liturgical character derives from its intention to identify the religious significance of a people's work—a work done in the world as a place of blessing on God's behalf, and offered to God along with money, bread, and wine as oblations which condense and contain the worldly work of God's people. In liturgical preaching, the world and the Word connect. *By God's power & Christ's presence*

I have presumed to summarize and paraphrase this much of Scott's article; now he is entitled to have the last word and speak for himself:

> *In liturgical preaching the world is not a place of curse, or an imprison-ment of spirit, or a theatre of vanity. The world is where religion mat-ters; it is the place of spirit, holy and profane, crushing and liberating, requiring of the people the most serious attention to their condition in society. This preaching does not wish to rhapsodize us into aesthetical transcendance, nor to convince laity to carry out the agenda of the clergy, but to help people present themselves in their difficult worldly con-ditions to be broken and to be blessed. The primary workers, in the lit-urgy itself and in liturgical preaching, are the* people. *This work, we trust, joins us to the liturgy of God, always and everywhere going on.*[27]

Christian proclamation is witness to the gospel of Jesus Christ, and this is why the authority of preaching derives from its obedience and fidelity to the one whose gospel it is. This is also why we cannot preach from the Old Testament alone as though these texts were self-contained. Nor can we adopt a timely topic or a special virtue and moralize some universal truth. The issue of authority for Christians is not whether but what kind. Authority becomes a problem for Christians whenever anything other than the church's story of the gospel of Jesus is permitted to shape the church's proclamation. And authority becomes a serious problem for preaching when the preacher becomes his or her own authority. Christians are a people who read every text and occasion through the eyes of Paul and the Gospel authors.

If I have been right about these things, the function of Scripture in the liturgy is to be the church's story of God's self-disclosing Word, Jesus Christ, through the long pilgrimage of God's people. For those of us who understand and intend ourselves to be disciples of God's Christ, Scripture norms our understanding of how Jesus inaugurates the new age of the kingdom of God, and initiates God's pilgrim people into it through Jesus' resurrection and their baptism. It is from this material that the community has heard the Word of God, and from which it expects to hear it again, because it is this Word of God spoken through the Scripture which constitutes the Scripture as canon and that governs all other Christian witness. In the context of the liturgy, the power of the canon as control and norm is distinct for the authority of preaching, because the principal function of preaching is to witness to Jesus Christ. Thereby we have our true and authentic identity disclosed to us, and learn what we could not discover for ourselves: that God so loved us as to give Jesus for us, and in that self-giving reclaimed both us and the world as his own.

TEST CASES AT THE BEGINNING AND END OF LIFE

Consider the fact that the Bible does not speak either explicitly or in recognizably determinate ways about many matters. Early Lutherans judged that what was not expressly prohibited in or by the Bible was permitted; and Richard Hooker argued that "it is no more disgrace for scripture to have left a number of . . . things free to be ordered at the discretion of the church, than for nature to have left it unto the wit of man to devise his own attire."[28]

Scriptural silence is particularly noticeable in respect of certain modern issues which raise urgent questions. I think immediately, for example, of contemporary biomedical technologies: of tissue and organ transplantation (both inter- and intraspecies); of *in vitro* fertilization and embryo implantation; of genetic interventions of one sort or another; of the means for managing the manner and time of human dying and death; of abortion; of surgeries and pharmacologic preparations for the control of violence, or even hyperkinesis; of human experimentation; of adequate requirements for valid (not merely "informed") consent; and of the fragile business of scarce resource allocation. Among many other matters, these are some of the ones about which the church may want or need to make a witness, but for which we cannot cite a text, a biblical chapter and/or verse, which contains the statement the church ought to make.

The tendency among modern Christians, when confronted by these matters, has been either (1) to look out for the secular policy which seems most congenial in the circumstance (meaning that we accommodate or compromise the gospel in ways that finally make Christian faith a dispensable adjunct of no practical importance for living out who we are in what we do) or (2) to abandon these matters entirely to secular policy on the grounds that the world simply cannot and will not be ordered on virtues and principles which are proper to the church (which means that we abdicate the moral struggle which these matters occasion by making the Gospel disjunctive, in some dualistic or two-tiered way, with life in the world). In the second instance, Christians conveniently abandon the canon, confirming Cab Calloway's famous line that "the things that you're liable to read in the Bible, they ain't necessarily so"; and in the first instance, Christians resort to proof-texting wooden responses to agonizing moral questions.

But if Scripture is canon, and authoritative for Christian witness, neither of these ways provides a viable option for evangelical Christians. To have a canon means that whatever we venture to say on behalf of God (and that, I believe I understand, is an awesome and appropriately frightening prospect) must be assessed by that self-disclosure of God to which the canon attests. The canon, and not our experience or reason, is thus the criterion of our knowledge of God. So to speak of these matters which the Scripture does not directly or explicitly address obliges us to speak in the sense of the canon as a whole. How might we do this?

Consider, for example, that an appropriate tack for the church to take in making statements about human *in vitro* fertilization and embryo implantation, and the management of human dying and death, might be to address the canon's teaching about parenthood and family and the larger community. What does the Scripture say about the kind of people we should be if we understand ourselves to be the "children of God," the "family of God"? Is there a paradigm appropriate to human parenting which derives from understanding God as parent? If the parent-child bond between God and us is not a function of biologic successiveness rooted in an autonomous natural law which translates *imago dei* into a "divine spark" theory in which all of us participate, and if the parent-child bond between

God and us is a vision of who we are which is rooted in God's intention, purpose, and destiny for us, could the church say something about the meaning of parenthood and family which is coherent with the identity of God that the canon discloses? Are there clues in the tradition about what it means to live well and die well? I believe that the canon as a whole responds to these questions; and the following paragraphs discuss some of the issues associated with Christian parenting and Christian dying that I tried to illustrate in a parish setting in early 1987.

A courtroom in Hackensack, New Jersey, was the site of an agonizing landmark case involving custody of a ten-month-old infant whom the court papers called "Baby M." The case was described in the press as "the agonizing dilemma of surrogate motherhood" and, barring a Solomonic decision, the court was expected to decide straightforwardly whether Baby M was to be delivered into the custody of William and Elizabeth Stearn (Mr. Stearn being the putative sperm donor) or to Mary Beth Whitehead (who was inseminated with William Stearn's sperm after signing a contract for conceiving and bearing a child). Of course, there were ethical issues and moral concerns raised by both protagonists and antagonists; but the judicial question before Judge Harvey Sorkow appeared to be whether to treat the case mainly as a contract dispute or as a custody battle.

I believe that Christians ought to have had serious misgivings about the Baby M case for several important reasons. Because the power to describe and name the issues was tantamount to setting the conditions and boundaries for the possible range of responses, we ought to have been extraordinarily careful about whether the grammar in the Baby M case was descriptively accurate. Of course, opinions on whether it was descriptively accurate might vary according to the canons of more than one discipline: what lawyers find interesting about the case may be different from what physicians think remarkable about it, and the opinions of physicians may in turn be different from what moral theologians may take to be ethically significant about it.

So, for example, while others might find it descriptively accurate, Christians ought to find the term "surrogate motherhood" to be a kind of grammatical misfire. I think I understand that the "motherhood" referred to in this term underwrites a kind of biological successiveness, the same kind of relationship which is the natural correspondence between progenitors and progeny. But when human beings (and I would think, surely, when Christians) speak of parenthood, we mean to describe a relationship which, while it may certainly embrace biologic reproduction (although it does not have to, as adoptive parents well know), is neither defined nor exhausted by biologic (or even genetic) successiveness. What we mean to talk about are certain virtues—like caring and loving and long-suffering and responsibility—when we speak of parenthood.

Conception, gestation, and birthing—important as they are—do not begin to comprehend the full meaning of human parenthood. In fact, Christians take our cue for characterizing every human relationship—including this one—from how God has regarded us, loved us, sacrificed for us, reconciled us, and blessed us. And it is on these understandings that we venture to bless marriage and comprehend the meaning of parenthood. This is precisely what is at stake in allowing the adjective to control the noun in the phrase "Christian ethics"; and this is also what is at stake in allowing the adjective to control the noun in a term like "surrogate motherhood." A surrogate is a substitute, and Christians are a people who don't know anything of surrogate mothers. One may be a mother, or one may be "like a mother" to someone, but I don't know anybody who is or can be a *substitute* mother. So the term which alleges to describe this business seems not only enormously misleading, but also misanthropic.

Among other objections to this extraordinary pronatalism, I mention only one more—one that is substantively theological. While all of us are called in the first of it to a vocation of singleness, and while some of us find that this is a life-long vocation, it is given to others of us to marry and, as we say in the Book of Common Prayer, "if it be God's will," to have children. For those of us in this latter group, and on the terms of the account I want to give, parenting is a vocation on behalf of God and the church. We have babies as witness to our belief in God; having babies is not merely a natural instinct for us. And this is the difference between "procreation" and "reproduction."

This is an important difference to acknowledge, because it means that neither disease, nor environment, nor nuclear bomb, nor any other condition of our existence which would suggest that bringing babies into this world is unloving or selfish, is sufficient to deter us. I agree with my colleague Stanley Hauerwas that Christians have babies as witness to our belief that the power of this world is not the norm of our existence, that our lives are normed by the cross of Jesus, and that our willingness to have children is witness to our determination to exist as a people whose life is formed by that cross even though the world denies that such a people can exist.

Having children is, for us, a vocation; but it is not a private or individually insulated vocation. It is, instead, a vocation on behalf of God and the church. So we speak of procreation rather than of reproduction, and when we have babies, we have them on behalf of God and without the analogies of production line and quality control.

The liturgy for Holy Baptism shows that children do not belong to biological parents; Holy Baptism shows that the whole church is parent. So we repudiate in the liturgy the notion that biological and genetic successiveness are essential to parenthood, just as we reject most instances of *in vitro* fertilization and embryo implantation and so-called surrogate parenting because the church itself represents the destruction of the nuclear family as a natural cultural necessity.

Christians break the natural moral necessity of having children—whether in order to continue a genetic inheritance, or to preserve one's identity through posterity, or to have "one's very own child" who will inherit the family business—because we recognize that children do not belong to us. Our children belong to God. So it is right, I believe, that the Book of Common Prayer should remind us of these things, because it is the function of the church's worship, its liturgy and its prayers, to constitute us ever anew around its common memory.

This account helps us to understand why we cannot any longer, if ever we could, speak of human sexuality as though it were merely a function of bodily metabolism. It is this in part, to be sure; but human sexuality also has a telos, an end. Plants and animals exercise their sexuality, so far as we know, as merely natural phenomena: they "throw off," as it were, objective evidence of themselves through sexual reproduction. But there may be at least this much difference between the procreative activity of persons and the reproductive behavior of plants and animals: persons procreate other unique never-to-be-repeated persons, persons incarnate their engendering love, persons are emancipated from natural necessity and act out deliberate intentions.

Especially since the time of the Enlightenment, our (sometimes overwhelming) temptation has been to embrace every scientific and technological innovation because we have supposed these things to be our salvation. We have believed that they will bring us close to unlocking the last remaining mystery of nature, assist us toward becoming entirely self-determining creatures, and ensure that we are the captains of our souls and the masters of our fate. But we ought to have learned by now that discovery and mastery often carry a capacity for evil which is proportionate to their capacity for good, and that sometimes discovery and mastery even carry a disproportionate capacity for doing harm. Dean Inge of St. Paul's, London, once observed that people who become wedded to the spirit of the times are likely to find themselves widowers in the next generation. The truth of that aphorism need not paralyze us, but it should give us appropriate pause.

At the other end of the life cycle, some of us have come increasingly to believe that medicine has too often been at the service of cheating deaths of the meanings they can (and should) have for the persons who undergo them, whose deaths they are. Here again, Scripture does not offer us a direct or explicit comment on this very modern capability of biomedical science and technology; yet the sense of the canon as a whole is quite instructive. I have come to believe that our deaths too often have no meaning because, in ways consistent with the rationale for "surrogate parenting," we do not believe that our lives have meaning beyond sheer biological extension.

As a matter of fact, ours is a time of especially biting irony in regard to dying and death. Our creature comforts far exceed anything heretofore known in human history, yet we are as much or more discontented with our lot than any generation which has gone before us. In all our getting of longer lifespan and postponed death and eased pain, we seem to have managed to master nature better than history, and technics better than ourselves.

A MORAL MINE FIELD

In 1991, Dr. Timothy Quill published his article in the *New England Journal of Medicine* describing how he "made sure that [Diane] knew how to use the barbiturates for sleep, and also that she knew the amount needed to commit suicide."[29] Three years earlier, an anonymous resident allegedly described how he (or she) had injected Debbie, who "was dying of ovarian cancer," with 20 mg of morphine sulfate and stood by her beside until she stopped breathing.[30] In July 1992, Derek Humpries' *Final Exit*, a manual on "how to commit a suicide that is painless, efficient, and not too messy" made the *New York Times* best-seller list. Meanwhile, Dr. Jack Kevorkian was in the news because he had used his "suicide machine" on more than a dozen patients, most if not all of whom were not terminally ill. In this country's only referendum to date on this issue, voters in Washington state defeated Initiative 119, which would have allowed physicians, in certain circumstances, to honor patient requests for deliberate and intentional death.

These are, of course, only among the most recent venturing into this public and professional moral mine field. The most infamous case surely was the T4 program instituted by Adolf Hitler and his chief physician, Karl Brandt, and dramatically described by Bert Honolka in *Die Kreuzelschrieber* (referring to the "red cross"—the death sentence affixed to patient's records) and by Gerhard Schmidt in *Selektion in der Heilanstalt*, which details how patients in sanatoria and asylums were chosen for extermination. The first case involving the T4 *Gnadentod* ("mercy death") program surely evokes empathy: the parents of a blind, deformed, severely retarded child successfully petitioned Hitler to permit its killing.

Our collective recollection of Nazi atrocities appears to be very selective or very dim, but the ugly resurgence of neo-Nazism ought to revive our memory. Consider that it was barely four years after the doctors' trials at Nuremberg that Dr. Hermann Sander was accused in New Hampshire of killing his patient, Abbie Borroto. Since then there have been sporadic but frequent reports of physicians (and sometimes nurses or paramedical personnel) either killing patients or assisting them in their suicide.[31] Until now, no physician in the annals of Anglo-American jurisprudence has been convicted of killing a patient even though several, including Dr. Sander, have confessed that they did actually kill their patients. These physicians have typically been found not guilty on one of two grounds: (1) by reason of temporary insanity, or (2) because the state was unable to prove that the alleged victim was in fact alive at the time of the death-inducing, life-terminating action.

Having said all this, of course, I do not mean to imply that Dr. Quill is a Nazi, or even that his behavior reflects the harshness of a Dr. Brandt or the callous insensitivity of a Dr. Kevorkian. Even so, I do believe that his actions in the case of Diane, however moving and evocative, were not in keeping with either the best traditions of Western medicine or the teachings of the Christian church. I find Dr. Quill's reflections in his essay, and in his subsequent remarks, deeply moving. I have thought of how difficult it would be to imagine a relationship between physician and patient that modeled better the role of medicine described by Ambroise Paré, the fifteenth-century French surgeon, in his famous triplet: *Guérir quelquefois, soulager souvent, consoler toujours* ("To cure sometimes, to relieve often, to comfort always"). And I have thought that anyone reading Dr. Quill's article could not fail to appreciate the concern and compassion that accompanied the step-by-step description of the care he offered and gave to his patient.

THE MORAL TRADITIONS OF MEDICINE

All the same, I also find Dr. Quill's essay and subsequent remarks deeply disturbing. At the risk of being perhaps too candid, too blunt, let me come directly to the point. The ancient traditions of Western medicine obligate physicians to preserve (some say "prolong") life and to relieve pain (some versions include "and suffering"). The Hippocratic Oath specifically includes the pledge that "I will give no deadly drug to any, though it be asked of me, nor will I counsel such." Although American physicians do not universally subscribe to the Hippocratic Oath, this ancient formula is a fundamental part of the moral and professional heritage of Western medicine, and the meaning of the injunction, I daresay, is not only plain enough but is also acknowledged as common sense by the overwhelming majority of both patients and physicians. It means that, although only physicians in our society are authorized to prescribe "poisons," they do so in order to counteract death-dealing and health-threatening diseases, not to cause death. This plain-sense reading of the Oath is, obviously, not now universally shared, but the weight of tradition places the burden of proving that it means something else on those who reject it.

It is the other moral maxim which mandates preservation of life and relief of pain, formulated in a time when the capacities of medicine to intervene in the course of our lives were extraordinarily limited, that at present gives us trouble. In those ancient times, relief of pain and prolongation of life were typically complementary and not antagonistic goals. My friends who are doctors and nurses tell me that nowadays, given the armamentarium of modern medicine, it sometimes happens that life can be prolonged only at great personal distress, or that intractable pain can be relieved only at the eventual expense of life itself. Here is an apparently clear and straightforward case of two duties coming into irreconcilable conflict; here two cherished notions about the proper ends of medicine are mutually exclusive.

Another contrariety that deserves mention and our careful attention is the familiar antinomy between physician paternalism and patient autonomy. When professional medical judgment and patient self-determination collide, which ought to be granted priority and given right-of-way? When his patient indicated that she did not wish to be treated for leukemia, Dr. Quill gave two reasons why he agreed to assist in her suicide: (1) because she had the right to choose death; and (2) because of her "desire for independence" and her decision to "stay in control." Her decision to "take her life in the least painful way made perfect sense"—that is, he believed she was rational and "not in despair or overwhelmed in a way that might color her judgment." Furthermore, as Arthur Dyck has put it, "Quill [was] not satisfied to have the physician's role be that of lessening suffering; the physician's role should be extended to include assistance in the elimination of suffering."[32]

Throughout history the moral justification of Western medicine has rested on its commitment not to abandon the sick. But as Dr. Quill and others have made clear, some believe nowadays that when a patient's perceived well-being is compromised by incorrigible pain, and when the prospect is that the patient's condition will progressively deteriorate, and when, as he puts it in his essay, the patient is unable "to maintain control of herself and her own dignity during the time remaining to her," the physician's duty is to honor the "patient's right to die with as much control and dignity as possible." The issue now is precisely not a choice between life and death; the issue is what kind of death.

INDIVIDUAL AUTONOMY OR COMMON GOOD

In a democratic society, we depend on commitments which we hold in common to ensure reasonable debate; otherwise, we argue from premises which pass each other like ships in the night. So when, as in our time, we have almost no shared vision about the common good, this issue about what kind of death—very like abortion, and capital punishment, and virtually every other significant moral dispute of our time—appears to be rationally irresolvable. Instead of asking how we may work together to achieve our common good and destiny, the preoccupying query of American individualists is rather how each may secure his or her own privately determined benefit with minimal interference from anybody else.

What makes saying "no"—in this instance, "no" to assisted suicide—so very difficult in the present milieu is that, during the past three or four decades, we have celebrated as never before the claims of individual autonomy. As a result, it has become virtually impossible to draw any lines at all based on predicates of a common good. John Stuart Mill set the stage for our current circumstance when he wrote that "the only purpose for which power can be rightfully exercised over any member of a civilized community, against his will, is to prevent harm to others."[33] In very practical terms, this means not only that paternalisms of all sorts (and maternalisms as well) are nowadays more and more taboo, but also that there is increasing resistance to the notion that anybody ought to be able to tell anybody else what they can and cannot, ought and ought not, do.

Daniel Callahan has argued cogently, and I think persuasively, that the debate about physician-assisted suicide is not just one more moral dispute in a very long list, but that "it is profoundly emblematic of three important turning points in Western thought. The first is that of the legitimate conditions under which one person can kill another; [the second] lies in the meaning and limits of self-determination; [and the third] is to be found in the claim being made upon medicine that it should be prepared to make its skills available to individuals to help them achieve their private vision of the good life."[34] I think that Callahan is correct, and that these are the issues now before us. What beliefs underlie them? Is this the proper way to frame the choices? How is it that physicians have an obligation to prevent a difficult and painful death rather than to attend a patient in her dying? Is it arguable that preventing a difficult and painful death ought to be understood on the same terms as the obligation to relieve pain? Can patients or physicians or both make decisions about these matters without regard for implications larger than the immediate individual situation?

THE MEDICALIZATION OF DEATH

In the case described by Dr. Quill, there is also the matter of falsifying a death certificate in order to avoid "a police investigation and probably the arrival of an ambulance crew for resuscitation and the decision to perform an autopsy," because "the family or I could have been subject to criminal prosecution, and I to professional review, for our roles in support of Diane's choices." My seatmate on a recent flight to Washington, D.C., was a lawyer who informed me that suicide is not a crime and that it therefore cannot be a crime to assist in an act that is itself not a crime. "As long as doctors don't break the law," he said, but then his voice trailed off as though I ought to know how to complete his sentence. At the time, I suggested to him that a distinguishing mark of a profession is that it is "above the law" in the sense that it is not defined by the minimalistic requirements of legal morality. Another lawyer has written, however, that "[a]lthough this is an interesting question [why assisted suicide should be a crime when suicide is not], those who pose it this simply demonstrate the extent to which they do not understand how and why the criminal law concerns itself with solicitation, facilitation, aiding or abetting a crime."[35] Whatever the precise legal implications, it should be clear that professional ethical standards are meant (and expected) to be higher than the least sufficient injunctions of the positive law. It is precisely when they are not loftier that third-party intervention is invited.

So we need to be clear that the issue here is not about withholding or withdrawing so-called life support systems. In fact, the issue here is suicide, the medicalization and institutionalization of death, and physicians who abandon both curing and caring in favor of death. Specifically, the issue is whether physicians should help their patients cause their own deaths.

The American Medical Association has formally condemned physician participation in both euthanasia and assisted suicide. The AMA Council on Ethical and Judicial Affairs specifically recommends that: (1) when the patient possesses decision-making capacity, physicians must respect the patient's decision to forgo life-sustaining treatment; (2) there is no ethical distinction between withdrawing and withholding life-sustaining treatment; (3) in fulfilling the obligation to relieve pain and suffering and to respect the autonomy of dying patients in their care, physicians may provide palliative treatment even though it may hasten death; and (4) physicians must not perform euthanasia or participate in assisted suicide.[36]

Formal prohibition, however, even with the articulated reasoning of the AMA, apparently does not satisfy the advocates of physician-assisted suicide. To put the matter starkly, the salient issue for these advocates is with meaningless and purposeless suffering and pain. But *what is* meaningless and purposeless suffering and pain, and how do we perceive it? Because we do not know these things "naturally," as part of the wisdom that we all innately possess, we must ask how we find out what is "meaningless" and "purposeless." What are the resources, what are the referents, what factors control the meanings of "meaningless" and "purposeless"?

CHRISTIAN REFLECTIONS ON SUFFERING AND SUICIDE

Christians have to be trained to know where to look for meaning and purpose, and Episcopalians (of whom I am one) have historically answered questions such as the ones posed above by appealing to Scripture, tradition, and reason, with the clear understanding, as the Lambeth Conference of 1888 put it, that Scripture is "the rule and ultimate standard of faith."[37] Space is short, so I will paint the rest of this portrait with a rather broad brush.

These questions go back to the earliest traditions of Western civilization. Pythagoras, Plato, and Aristotle held suicide to be a crime against the community, and Plato even argued that it was tantamount to a crime against God.[38] Christians later affirmed this position, but for very different reasons, specifically the Christian belief in God's incarnation as Jesus. According to this doctrine, God took on human flesh as Jesus (John 1:14), atoned for the sins of the whole world (1 John 2:1–2), and reconciled the world to himself (Rom. 5–8). Because of this, human life is valuable not because of any human attribution of worth, but because it is invested with God-given value and worth. In baptism, our lives have been given away to God. It is the notion that human life belongs to God that accounts for Christian condemnation of abortion, infanticide, child abuse, war, homicide, and suicide. On these terms, we do not own our lives, nor is the value of human life self-generated. The distinguishing mark of a Christian anthropology is that God, not ourselves, is in control. I believe that it is essential for us to recall these important components of the rhetoric of Christian faith as we undertake to comprehend moral complexities like the one before us. If we believe in God, then what we believe about God— theology—ought to make a difference in how we engage in practical reasoning about matters of this sort.

In the classical world of Greece and Rome, suicide was often idealized as a noble form of death, but from the second century onward, Christian teaching condemned it.[39] The early fathers of the church—Cyprian, Ambrose, Irenaeus, and Athanasius—all contributed to the Christian doctrine on suicide,[40] but it was Augustine who succinctly formulated the Christian position and, specifically addressing the "nobility of suicide" argument, named the three grounds on which suicide is denounced: (1) it violates the commandment "Thou shalt not kill"; (2) it precludes any opportunity for repentance; and (3) it is a cowardly act.[41] In the thirteenth century, Thomas Aquinas gave the conventional Christian position its classical formulation when he wrote that "[s]uicide is the most fatal of sins, because it cannot be repented of."[42]

In his brief but comprehensive account of how the Anglican tradition has treated suicide, David Smith has noted that, while the greater weight of the evidence is on the side of denunciation, it is impossible to say that consent can *never* be given to suicide.[43] Although it may at times be a morally tolerable or even appropriate action, these times are clearly exceptional and not the rule.

To be sure, thoughtful Anglicans, such as Dean Inge, and maybe John Donne, and, at the time he wrote *Morals and Medicine*, Joseph Fletcher, have defended suicide; and Inge and Fletcher endorsed euthanasia, which Fletcher defined as the painless killing of a person whose "life has permanently ceased to be either agreeable or useful [to] himself or another."[44] In fact, Fletcher identified ten moral arguments against suicide and euthanasia, which he then proceeded to dispose of one by one en route to endorsing what he called "voluntary euthanasia" and hinting at his favor (he would later be an advocate) for the "involuntary euthanasia for monstrosities at birth and mental defectives, a partly personalistic and partly eugenic position."[45] He also suggested "with fine simplicity" that the Scriptures *authorized* us to commit suicide,[46] conveniently failing to mention Judas Iscariot and neglecting to acknowledge the sheer tragedy and repugnance that instanced the deaths of Ahithophel (2 Sam. 15–18), Zimri (1 Kings 16:18–19), etc. David Smith's caveat is apropos: "The great moral danger of medical suicide is that it will be egotistical and manipulative, symbolic of an unwillingness to play the role of dependent when it falls to our turn. Theologically it may 'be the expression of a refusal to trust in God, an embracing of death for its own sake, a form of self-justification, a desertion to the enemy.' "[47]

This judicious sensibility is a familiar refrain in the writings of both Richard Hooker[48] and Jeremy Taylor,[49] who echo the conviction that no one can claim a right to death on the ground that their life is their own. Indeed, Taylor made the point explicit by asserting that human life belongs to God and that persons should not presume to choose the cause of their death. The core thread, says David Smith, "is the idea that 'medically indicated' suicide represents a desertion or betrayal of others and an impatient assertion of the self against conditions of finitude that are part of embodied existence. From the Anglican viewpoint the individualism that voluntary euthanasia represents is a mistaken interpretation of reality. Rather than voluntary euthanasia, Anglicanism should support organizations like the Samaritans and hospices."[50]

I think that David Smith is precisely on target in these observations. I also agree with him that it is impossible to say that an action that causes one's death can never be consented to, because I believe that temporal life is not the *summum bonum* for Christians. Precisely because our life belongs to God, we may be forbidden to will its continuation at all costs. We may, in fact, be bidden to expose our lives to various kinds of risk and danger, as Jesus surely did in going up to Jerusalem and to his eventual death. But he did so in affirmation of the necessity of this event. If I am correct in this formulation, as I believe I am, then the urgent question is "What are the risks and dangers for which we should hazard our lives?"

We have some clues to those risks and dangers in the careful distinctions we make, for example, between suicide and heroism. These distinctions already suggest that a hero's death does not renounce life but affirms it, whereas a suicide's death (as Dr. Quill has described Diane's decision, and despite his protestations to the contrary) despairs of life and acts with final sovereignty "to take one's life." This means, in part, that in the exceptional case there may be moral warrants for an appropriate self-sacrifice of one's own life, but it also means that these moral warrants do not extend to the permissibility, much less the duty, to sacrifice the life of another.

CHOOSING OUR RUT

What is urgently, perhaps even desperately, wanted now is serious and sustained conversation about these matters. Daniel Callahan put it right when he wrote that "Euthanasia is not a private matter of self-determination. It is an act that requires two people to make it possible, and a complicit society to make it acceptable."[51]

My grandfather John O'Donnell's house in Mississippi sat beside the washboard road that led from Ovett to Laurel. Laurel is the county seat of the Free State of Jones, and that old road bore lots of traffic. When it rained, the road was badly rutted because only a thin layer of gravel covered the sand and clay base. As a matter of fact, it was so badly rutted that it was dangerous to drive, and cars routinely wound up in ditches along the way. People wanting directions to Laurel frequently stopped by Papa's house for instruction, and his advice—particularly after a heavy rain—was always the same: "Choose your rut well, because you'll be in it for the next twenty-two miles." With a word change here and there, this advice seems well worth taking as we engage the moral gravity of matters like physician-assisted suicide and euthanasia.

"Euthanasia," which literally means "dying well" or "a good death," is a word known to all of us; but we are pathetically unable to agree on what the word means in practice. So we discover that (ordinarily) we cannot say prospectively that a particular death is timely, or appropriate, or good. The exceptions to this otherwise general rule have been war and capital punishment (and many believe that abortion has, in our time, become a third exception), circumstances in which we are prepared to say prospectively that death is appropriate or good. But in the main we have more confidence that we can affirm a particular death "good" in retrospect than in prospect. Why is this so? I want to suggest that we really cannot know what "dying well" means unless and until we have a better common understanding of what "living well" means. If we knew better what it meant to order a good life, we would know better how to orchestrate our deaths along similar lines. *Euzoia* is the companion of *euthanatos*; it means "living well." Can we hope to get agreement on *euzoia* in ways that we have not been able to do with *euthanatos*?

If so, we will need to be able to specify the good toward which living well is directed—or at least be able to look at examples of people whom we think have lived well, and identify the virtues which they have exhibited in their lives that constrain us to call them "good." To ask about these things will illumine the issues about dying and death because they will confront us with what we cherish and value, with what we affirm to be virtuous, with who we are, with our character. And this, in turn, will probably remind us that a virtuous life consists of more than lengthened metabolism.

Christians are a people who have learned that their death is not an unmitigated disaster; Christians are a people who believe that their life has a grander purpose than avoiding death (and frequently at all costs); Christians are a people who have been trained to believe that their service to each other, for Christ's sake, is more important than life itself. And as a result, we have envisioned forms of care for the poor and the sick and the dying which would otherwise be unimaginable and impossible. Consider, for example, the great imaginative invention we call "hospital." This kind of institution could only have been created by a people who, amid all the hurt and injustice and selfishness of the world, thought that they could take time to care for their sisters and brothers. Displaying an outlook which is odd by modern lights, they could care even when they could not cure. But this is altogether intelligible when we remember that Western medicine did not derive its moral justification from its power to cure; indeed, the history of Western medicine until very recently shows that its reason for being came almost entirely from its commitment not to abandon those who are sick and dying.

I mean to suggest in all this—from employing the new reproductive technologies to managing the manner and time of human dying and death—that Christians may well be asked, and expected, to take a more distinctive stand on these matters than we do now. We will need to learn to deny ourselves some forms of high-technology tertiary-intervention extraordinary care; we will need to learn to look some technologies squarely in the eye and say no to them, because we will have come to some acknowledgments about ourselves and our neighbors which accept the notion that service to the least of these is more important than the life of any one of us. We will have to learn that the real enemy is not death but the idolatry of living at severe and extravagant cost to others. We will need to know better than we seem to know why we should not strive to prevent our own death if that would mean that the weaker members of our community would have to go without care.

Christian traditions provide memory and identity; they denote the truth about who we are, and who we are destined to become. Our very attempts to develop understandings of parenthood, or to conceive notions appropriate to living a good life and dying a good death, when abstracted from a deep sense of that community and its traditions, will succumb to a liberal conception of society as enlightened self-serving individuals who are free of any and all tradition, and bound together (if at all) only by ties of convenient egoism.

CHAPTER SEVEN

SENDING FORTH

"Leaving the nest" is an avian metaphor which we humans sometimes use to describe the time when our young are set out on their own. It seems to me an altogether apt phrase. Several decades of observation, in both my own house and others, further suggest that it signifies a traumatic experience of unique dimension and major proportion for children and parents alike. After years of nurturing and training, of comforting and scolding, of growing and maturing, a daughter or a son is finally ready (everybody hopes against hope) to make the break from parental hearth and home; to cut the *in loco parentis* umbilicus; to be, as we say, "henceforth responsible for himself or herself"; in a word, to leave the nest.

This is a move which is shared by children and their parents alike and that, according to many reports, portends to be a difficult and painful adjustment for both. But a charitable assessment of those reports, like the ones that prematurely announced Mark Twain's death, is that they tend to be somewhat exaggerated. They appear to come mostly from parents who cannot or will not remember the real circumstances of their own leaving, or the anxiety-cum-exhilaration which was theirs, now those many years ago, when they were set out on their own.

On the other hand, the exodus of children from hearth and home has always, in my experience, been something of a mixed blessing. The promised parental satisfaction of seeing offspring take flight on their own wings is chastened by fear of the unknown and loss of final responsibility for the fledglings' well-being. In this one fateful transition, a relationship nurtured for a couple of decades is suddenly and finally altered. "Leaving the nest" provokes a lot of parental prayer and patience and prudence. "Is she eating properly?" "Does he get enough rest?" "Is he taking care of his teeth?" "Does she really know enough to buy a car on her own?" "Is he managing his budget and living within his means?" The litany of familiar questions, sometimes unspoken, is well known to parents; and what it signifies is the double-edged sentiment that we are glad to see them try their wings, but are worried that, like Icarus, they might be too bold and come crashing to the ground.

Something very similar to "leaving the nest" should, and regularly does, characterize the dismissal and sending forth that typically concludes our liturgies. And pastors who are serious about the church's mission and their parishioner's well-being regularly testify to a bifocal sense of expectancy and dread when the congregation is sent out "to do the work God has given us to do."

If truth be told, amid the elaborate trappings which ordinarily attend the church's liturgy, "sending forth" is actually a familiar, and maybe even an ordinary and common, experience about which all of us ought to know something. It is what every cultural rite of passage means to signify—from birth, to matriculating at school, to graduation, to recovery from serious illness, to marriage, to any number of other life experiences, including dying and death. It is, in fact, an obvious way to describe what all of human life is about: we are forever being prepared for taking the next step, for running the race with perseverance, for leaving the comfort and security of a familiar "nest" for new adventure in a relatively strange (and sometimes hostile) environment.

It is therefore probably not an astonishing bit of intelligence that going out—or, as we say in the liturgy, being sent forth—into the world is, and ought to be, an excitingly frightening prospect. All the same, it is probably worth a reminder that this is not a one-sided prospect; so if it is not a very scary as well as a deliciously thrilling expectancy, the likelihood is good that something somewhere is severely discordant, out of tune. The liturgy in the Book of Common Prayer recognizes this bifocality and reciprocity, and it provides a poignant acknowledgment of this sensibility in several places, perhaps nowhere more dramatically and forcefully than in the postcommunion prayers and the dismissals which follow the eucharistic rites I and II.

The postcommunion prayers of rite II simply and starkly bespeak the terror of being sent forth:

> *Send us now into the world in peace, and grant us strength and courage to love and serve you with gladness and singleness of heart."*

Or, alternatively:

> *And now, Father, send us out to do the work you have given us to do, to love and serve you as faithful witnesses of Christ our Lord."[1]*

For all their apparent sanity and blessing, these prayers are terrifying to me. The rite II dismissals are more terse, even blunt:

> *Let us go forth in the name of Christ.*
> *Go in peace to love and serve the Lord.*
> *Let us go forth into the world, rejoicing in the power of the Spirit.[2]*

Pastoral experience clearly suggests that most of us tend to say these words insensibly and perfunctorily, oblivious and callous to their common-sense meaning and purpose and power. They have too often become like so much else in a liturgy that is familiar (and, to some extent, domesticated)—they are taken for granted. Of course, I appreciate that being at home with the liturgy—in a profound sense, that being habituated to it—has very positive and desirable connotations. So what I mean to claim here is that to think seriously about entreating God to expel us—from the comfortable coziness of most worship services into a world that not only finds our churchly behavior and language odd but that, more often than not, is frankly hostile toward folks who, as faithful witnesses of Jesus Christ, would challenge the presiding pagan *status quo*—just to offer these petitions is (or ought to be) sobering and fearful and awesome. They easily and rightly fill us with a sense of dread. It is a fearful thing to "leave the nest."

Earlier I cited V. A. Demant's observation that Christian worship, if it is true worship, must be a purposeless act; and I further suggested two senses in which worship *is* and *must be* a purposeless act.

First, worship is a purposeless act in the sense that it is an *end in itself;* that is, it is an action which we perform for God's sake alone. Worship is not an action which is calculated to make us feel better about ourselves or become more moral in our conduct, or to provide us with aesthetically satisfying experiences. It is, as my colleague Geoffrey Wainwright has shown, doxological.[3] True worship is an end in itself; it is its own explanation of itself; it is not undertaken for justification of anything else or as a supporting role for anything else—as in: "I just wouldn't feel married unless I was married in the church."

Second, worship is moreover a purposeless act in that it does not underwrite a practical identification of the world with God. We do not worship in order to hallow human behaviors which are already independently honored in and for themselves—as, for example, we are likely to do on "Boy Scout Sunday" or "Mother's Day" or "Homecoming Sunday."

I also argued that nailing down this point emphatically is alone what allows us to acknowledge, in another and a derivative sense, that worship *is* a purpose*ful* act, an act whose end in itself is a telos which is also a means. In this sense, worship is the means of Christian service in and to the world. We worship truly when we worship *soli Deo gloria*; doxology is worship's true end, goal, purpose. We glorify God in the church; we serve God in the world; and together these constitute our true worship and bespeak the unity of liturgy and ethics. The end of worship is to equip us through the adoration of God to do the work of God in the world; so it makes sense that, at the end of a service of worship, we should be sent out to do the work which God has given us to do.

Of course, the church withdraws from the world in worship. It does this not only in order to praise God, but also so that it can be formed into the kind of people who can be sent out to be God's people; a people who actually can be in the world but not of it. Part of the church's vocation is to help the world to know itself as "world"—that is, to help the world to know itself as God's creature. It is not autonomous, nor is it its own self-generated and self-authenticated meaning and purpose and destiny; but it acts as though it were. Remember that "world" is a metaphor for all those who exercise their freedom *not* to believe that we are God's creation, *not* to believe that Jesus Christ is the power of God to our salvation. This does not mean that God is not sovereign; it just means that these folks do not believe that God is in control.

To be the "world" is thus to rely on one's own resources, to trust in the power of this world—let us say, for example, in education, or perhaps science, or even technology—for salvation and blessedness. This is actually a descriptively accurate and quite serviceable definition, because it accounts for why the world tends to get catatonic when its power (as, for example, in the threat posed by atomic and nuclear bombs, or destruction of the ozone layer) seems to be unrestrained and out of control. The world's sanity and order depend on its being *in control*, which means, theologically, the creature's dominion over the creation. So when the genie escapes (or happens to be released) from the bottle, the peace of the world is threatened. Facile confidence in the secure future of the world perishes because the capacity for controlling command has been taken away.

In the liturgy, quite simply and in sum, we are taught that a power greater than ourselves is in control and exercises sovereign authority. Just learning this, knowing this, is sufficient to shatter the last residual vestige of confidence in the power of the "world" and in our own pretentious capacity to control our destiny.

Remember also that "church," in contradistinction to "world," is a metaphor for all those who exercise their freedom to believe, as John 3:16 puts it, that "God so loved the world that He gave His only-begotten Son, to the end that all who believe in him should not perish, but have everlasting life." Or again, "church" is a metaphor for those who believe, as 1 John 4:9–10, puts it: "In this the love of God was made manifest among us, that God sent his only Son into the world, so that we might live through him. In this is love, not that we loved God, but that he loved us and sent his Son to be the expiation for our sins."

These are the terms on which Christians are both gathered and sent forth: God is in control; God is sovereign; all of creation is under God's gracious care and keeping. In the church, in a word, theonomy has replaced autonomy. Despite these pious affirmations it is clear that an old and niggling question, which has claimed the attention of the church and its theologians virtually from the beginnings of the Apostolic community, challenges Christians anew today: is what we have just rehearsed about "world" and "church" descriptively accurate? And if it is, and God is not the world's adversary but its friend, how can the church serve God in the world? How in the contingent circumstances of the contemporary situation can the *laos theou* honor and praise God? What can those who submissively depend on God's grace alone possibly offer to their rebellious brothers and sisters who insist on asserting their autonomous individualism?

St. Augustine's attempt to answer these questions was the concept of the "two cities"—the city of God and the earthly city—which, he believed, are mixed together in history but distinguishable by their loves. The people of God and the people of the pagan world continue the historical development of their prototypes, which Augustine believed was signified by the separation of the good angels from the evil angels. In fact, he argued that it is precisely *two loves which have created the two cities*: the love of self, to the contempt of God, has created the earthly city; and the love of God, to the contempt of self, has created the heavenly city.[4]

The *civitas terrena huius mundi* is the result of human sin, and is characterized by its "disordered" or "eccentric" love.[5] Augustine insisted that this condition does not represent the absence of love; it is not "*not* love." Even in the pagan world, the hand of God is present and at work. And although the state is erected on the foundations of sinful pride and love of self,[6] "what takes place on earth becomes a preparation for the eternal life."[7] Everything works according to a divine plan, and therefore persons living in the earthly city may use this disordered love in service to their neighbors. Private property, for example, is the result of sin—of greed and avarice and selfishness—but private property is also a remedy for sin inasmuch as it reduces to order that same greed and selfishness.

St. Augustine believed that these two cities live together, intermixed, until the last winnowing and final separation on the Day of Judgment. The earthly city cannot be identified with any organized society because it is not a formal, visible, located society in a given historical moment; it is simply all the "unrighteous" who are living on earth. The secular realm nevertheless has legitimacy as a dyke against sin; and Christian service in particular, he taught, is the work of turning the "earthly" into the "heavenly" city, of redirecting the many partial and disordered loves of the *civitas terrena* to the complete and perfect good which is the *civitas Dei*.

Twelve centuries later, a former Augustinian monk advanced the doctrine of the "two kingdoms" as a way of dealing with the vexing issue of the proper relationship(s) between church and world. In Martin Luther's view, the kingdom is spiritual and invisible, and revealed only to faith; it arises only in response to the Word, only where the Word becomes operative. And this in turn means that the *invisible* church requires a *visible* church which dispenses Word and Sacraments.

So Luther teaches that "invisible" and "visible" are not two churches but different attributes of one and the same church. Indeed, it is this one church called into being by the Word, which is the order of redemption—through prayer, preaching, and administration of the sacraments—in the world. So the church is constituted by the Word of God and realized in the communion of believers; and the Gospel is the church's life and substance.

The state, of course, is also in the world; and Luther believed that it, too, is a creation of God. But Luther also believed that the jurisdictions of state and church must be sharply distinguished. So he argued that they cannot, under any circumstance, be mixed or intermingled. Secular authority has received its power directly from God for a distinct purpose, and that purpose is the ordering of human society. It does this by providing the conditions for civility and culture. The church, arising in response to the Word, produces inner righteousness; and the state, through the coercive power of law, produces external righteousness. If voluntarism is the mark of gospel and church, harsh compulsion is the mark of the state.

By the power it receives from God, the state retards and restrains the power of evil and wickedness. And as God's instrument for ordering human society, Luther teaches that the state—through the "orders" of marriage and family, labor and economics, law and politics, science, art, and education—is a work of love as the "left hand of God's kingdom." In sum, the two kingdoms of church and world, according to Luther, have their separate reasons for being, their separate authorizations, their separate work. They do not mix; they do not overlap; they do not participate in each other. Each is sovereign in its own sphere.

Luther's contemporary, John Calvin, offered yet another answer to our query concerning the proper relationship between church and world—the model of the theocratic state. The church is an institution by divine right, claimed Calvin; and it consists of all the elect in all ages as well as the congregation of believers who gather around Word and sacrament in a particular place and time.

Because the sovereignty of God is to be taken seriously, the role of the state is to see to it that the right kind of doctrine and worship is protected and maintained. The state should therefore conform its laws to divine law; and it follows that officers of the church are thus appropriately judges in affairs of state which involve religion and morals. It may be unsurprising, then, that the state should have responsibility for punishing sins; and indeed it did.[8]

The state, in sum, is endowed with divine authority and must be obeyed so long as this can be done without sinning. In fact, as one distinguished church historian has put it, "the church dictated to the state in matters of religion and morals and demanded that the state help Christianize the world and permeate the social order and the whole civilization with the

ethical principles of Christianity—with force where this becomes necessary."[9] The "holy commonwealth" experiment in the United States was an
attempt to recapitulate the theocratic state in the new world.

As faithful people must, we continue to wrestle with how it can be that
we are citizens of the earthly city who are simultaneously pilgrims of the
heavenly city.

As preface to a judgment he was about to render, one of my colleagues,
now retired, was frequently given to saying, "I am not clairvoyant and only
seldom given to prophecy, but . . ." So now, especially when I venture
thoughts like the following, I remember those acknowledged (and, yes,
sometimes self-serving) limitations.

A small storm has been developing on the theological horizon in recent
years; or maybe it would be more descriptively accurate to change the
metaphor and say that skirmish lines have been forming for an interesting,
potentially important, and even useful engagement between some
increasingly well identified Protestant theologians. There are, as we ought
to know since Vatican II, internal struggles going on, with perceptible
passion, within Roman Catholicism as well.[10]

The principal contention, as I discern it, is not really new. It was
succinctly drawn, however, in a sympathetic review of George Lindbeck's
The Nature of Doctrine: Religion and Doctrine in a Postliberal Age, where it is
claimed that perhaps the most important aspect of Lindbeck's proposal is
his conviction that

> *the viability of a unified world of the future may well depend on coun-*
> *teracting the acids of modernity. It may depend on communal enclaves*
> *that socialize their members into higher particular outlooks supportive of*
> *concern for others rather than for individual rights and entitlements,*
> *and of a sense of responsibility for the wider society rather than for per-*
> *sonal fulfillment. It is at least an open question whether any religion*
> *will have the requisite toughness for this demanding task unless it at*
> *some point makes the claim that it is significantly different and unsur-*
> *passably true.*[11]

We can defer consideration of whether this is, in fact, the most important aspect of Lindbeck's proposal; meanwhile, the reviewers drew the
following conclusion:

*For those who call themselves Christian, the best hope for providing a
unified world of the future is to be found in a recovery of the distinctiveness and integrity of the church. The future of "religion," therefore, does
not rest a la Cox on Christians providing an ethos to sustain western
civilization, but rather on the Christian community being capable of
sustaining its life* in a world in which it is no longer home. *That
is a message with which Cox, the new-right, liberation theologians,
and liberals have yet to come to terms.*[12]

The issue, of course, is only partly *how* the Christian community can any
longer (if ever it could) understand itself to be "in but not of the world."
The logically prior question is *whether* the claims of the "distinctiveness and
integrity of the Church" as "significantly different and unsurpassably true"
from any religion or cultural ideology are such as to foreclose the possibility
of *the church's life* being sustained "in a world which is no longer home."
What do these words mean? Would church *qua* church be any longer
recognizable?

This, of course, is not a novel issue, although its special features and
configurations may be very particular owing to the cultural and historical
setting in which it now gets raised. The primitive church faced exactly the
same issue, but in an environment which was much more explicitly hostile
and politically repressive than ours. In that earlier period, there was
considerable preoccupation, as revealed in both canonical and noncanonical
sources, with how the young Christian communities could manage (1) to
exist and (2) at the same time maintain internal purity and disciplined
fidelity to the Sovereign of the church.

I am among those who believe that the post-Constantinian era is a fine
example of how the church tended to ignore that tension, and of how it
worried more about accommodating itself to the world in order to guarantee its existence than about maintaining the Christian community's internal integrity. Like all generalizations, however, this one will not bear the
full weight of critical scrutiny without some qualification.[13]

It is patently clear that the greater weight of evidence certainly confirms
the church's fascination with and commitment to institutionalization and
various other domestications of grace in the post-Constantinian period;
nevertheless, this era (like all others in the church's history) was not entirely

void of vital piety. Even a cursory reading of the history of Christianity suggests that the rudimentary struggles of our religious forebears has generally characterized, in varying ways and measures, the entire subsequent story of Christian peoples. There is very little, if anything, really new under that sun. Indeed, one way (and I think an essentially correct way) to understand schism and heresy in the church's history is to view them as the attempts by those who are nominated schismatic and heretic to be faithful to the Gospel in ways which are disallowed by a superordinate ecclesial authority. But that is another story.

Just now it is perhaps enough to suggest that, on the whole, it is historically a too-naive and too-simplistic understanding of who we are and where we have come from to suppose that there is some pristine distinctiveness and integrity to which we can lay claim, and which is recoverable from our very complex and confused (and I mean this in the literal sense of being "mixed together") journey over these many centuries. There have always been "accommodationists" in the church; they were a problem for Paul, and Augustine, and Bonaventura, and Luther, and Wesley, and a host of unnamed others the church remembers and honors. There have also always been schismatics and heretics and separatists in the church who, when rightly acknowledged, have not only been judged for error and divisiveness but also remembered (and sometimes even honored) for the important ways in which they contributed to the church's authentic self-understanding.

There are those who nevertheless radically oppose, as "either/or," the Christian community and "a world which is no longer home"; and that weighty claim, in turn, raises many very serious and prominent theological issues, perhaps none more urgent than ecclesiology. Indeed, this contrariety has been extended in an essay co-authored by Stanley Hauerwas and William Willimon. They assert that "to us the church has an independent and intrinsic value" and that "our account of the church is (we admit) more *imperialistic*."[14] The title of a subsequent book by Hauerwas and Willimon, *Resident Aliens: Life in the Christian Colony*, is descriptively accurate of this theological ecclesiology.[15]

The several claims—of "distinctiveness," "significantly different," "unsurpassably true," "independent and intrinsic value," and "more imperialistic"—reflect assumptions not only about the relationship (or lack thereof) between church and world, but also between and among representations of "church." One suspects that among these assumptions is likely one with which the reformers worked, and which continues to exercise considerable influence (if only tacitly nowadays) between and among Protestants and Catholics alike. Tersely formulated, it goes something like this: there can be only one, true church; if Rome is that church, the church of the reformers is not, and vice versa. Luther viewed Catholic Christianity as a "Babylonian captivity" of doctrinal and canonical authority by the papacy; his modern heirs are persuaded that both Catholic and Protestant Christianity are currently in bondage to a "post-Constantinian" accommodation to secular culture. Heresy, schism, deviation—these cannot be suffered in such an ecclesiology. But as I will try to show, there is an alternative to this brittle concept of the visible church.

Maybe this opposition between church and world is offered as a heuristic device in order to provoke us to discover how to separate grain from chaff; but if that is its intention, it compares favorably with the rhetoric of "destroying the village in order to save the people." Maybe it means to acknowledge that there may have been a time when "the world" could have been "home" to the church, and that such a time is no more; but if this is the case, there are large accountings wanted both historically and theologically for how this could once have been but cannot be now. More, much more, is required than merely declaring that the church is always and only a stranger both in and to the world.

Maybe the juxtaposition of church and world is methodologically most urgent, and means to confront Christians with the alternatives of choosing between competing hermeneutics: that is, whether the perceived significance of modern experiences and developments should control or shape theological perspective, or vice versa. But if that is what is at issue, we need to be shown why that conflict carries, *eo ipso*, an essential feature of mutual exclusivity. Maybe the claim is sheer advocacy, and ought to be taken at face value; but if that is what it is, it will sooner or later have to embrace materially what it formally abjures—namely, apologetics.

Even if these several "maybes" do not exhaust the interpretive possibilities of this syntax, my guess is that all of them are operational in perhaps varying measures of significance, by either the intention of the authors or the construal of readers, or by both. If I had to say where I think the priority lies, I would tend to elect the methodological juxtaposition; for this is not only a fundamental issue in itself, but an instructive prolegomenon to the other issues as well.

From the most primitive times onward, and in ways not dissimilar to the "accommodationist/separatist" tension, the church has perennially agonized over whether (and if so, how) (a) "theological perspective should determine the ultimate significance of contemporary developments," or (b) "the world" appropriately sets the agenda for and shapes and forms theological perspective. The options are posed again as mutually exclusive. And while it is commonly conceded that nobody has surpassed the attempt by Thomas Aquinas at synthesizing that tension, the debate continues. In the first half of this century it was marked by the sustained, and sometimes acrimonious, disputes between Karl Barth and Emil Brunner over "nature and grace"; it was a pivotal issue in the earlier "Jesus of history/Christ of faith" controversies; and it now appears before us increasingly as a repristinization, albeit in sophisticated modern ways, of the old and bitter rivalry between "revealed religion" and "natural theology."

It is open to question whether Lindbeck's interpreters have rightly represented him on this methodological issue. True, in the later pages of *The Nature of Doctrine*, Lindbeck judged the failure of modern liberal churches which "primarily accommodate to the prevailing culture rather than shape it";[16] and true enough, Lindbeck further asserts that "When *or if* dechristianization reduces Christians to a small minority, they will need for the sake of survival to form communities that strive without traditionalist rigidity to cultivate their native tongue and learn to act accordingly."[17] But the book ends, as Lindbeck himself acknowledges, "on an inconclusive note."

Despite his confidence that "a cultural-linguistic understanding of religion can be faithful, applicable, and intelligible,"[18] and his hope that "some younger theologians" will in fact pursue this path,[19] Lindbeck grants that "the intratextual intelligibility that postliberalism emphasizes may not fit the needs of religions such as Christianity when they are in the awkward intermediate state of having once been culturally established but are not yet clearly disestablished."[20]

Although Lindbeck is clear (and I think correct) in claiming that liberalism has gotten the cart before the horse by allowing, indeed embracing, "the ultimate significance of contemporary developments" as determinative of theological perspective, his cultural-linguistic approach does not require (although it may permit) the conclusion that church and world are mortal enemies, or that the world is entirely void of God's presence and action. Early on, though not consistently applied in later parts of the book, the language of "leading partner" as theologically descriptive of the relationship between "church" and "world" seems more apt for the Lutheran Lindbeck than the Anabaptist rhetoric of mutual exclusivity.

Of course, I may have misread Lindbeck; but I don't think so, if only because neither withdrawal nor accommodation can be a serious option for a church whose mission (at least in part) is to shape culture. Lindbeck's approach seems to reject (I'd say rightly) those alternatives; and it is when he is most self-conscious about ecumenical conversation that this emphasis is most prominent. In the latter parts of the book, the relation between religion and experience, church and world, reflects old and well-worn Lutheran dualisms and seems to be so heavily weighted toward preserving the identity and integrity of religion and church that experience and world receive scant attention.

Giving him the benefit of doubt, one can view this as an effort by Lindbeck to get the priorities straight rather than as a kind of unchastened triumphalism. Indeed, he said as much at the outset: "The relation of religion and experience . . . is not unilateral but dialectical. It is simplistic to say . . . merely that religions produce experiences, for *the causality is reciprocal.*"[21] Reciprocal, yes; dichotomous, no. One could wish that this seemly reciprocity had been sustained throughout the book.

To speak of reciprocal causality could be another way of acknowledging what I've called the bifocality of the Christian life. We surely are, as 1 Peter describes us, strangers and aliens; but we are these in our own land, within our own homes. What is strange and alien about us is that we are to do God's will here and now, in this world, according to God's intention for both it and us.

Or, remembering the prologue to John's Gospel, what is quite astonishing about the Word becoming flesh is that "he was in the world, and the world was made through him, yet the world knew him not; *he came to his own home, and his own people received him not.*"[22] Surely this is the reason for tension and dialectic and paradox; not because contraries are opposed but because wholeness got fractured. And if this is so, we are—like our predecessors in the Christian faith—locked into moral struggle.

The roots of the word—"re-ligio"—in fact mean to bind back together, presumably what once was whole but is now broken.[23] So if the church finds itself struggling for its identity and integrity, it cannot be because God and the world are adversaries but precisely because, amid this fracturedness, the church acknowledges that this really is God's world and that God is "at home" here despite all the evidences of paganism and secularity to the contrary.

However else biblical theists (and I reckon especially Christians) view the world, it is first of all as of God's making, a world filled with intimations of the incarnation for which it was prepared, modeled on the Word, and designed as its proper receptacle. Christians take this world with utter seriousness because it is God's world. Of course, this is merely an article of faith; but then so are the undemonstrated hypotheses of every human intellectual discipline merely articles of faith.

If the world is thus so fertile, it may also be salvific. If the world contains already rich clues of the One who called it into being, it may also be precisely the place where God's salvation takes place. If the world be vessel into which the Word becomes flesh and dwells, it may also be where God meets us and re-ligates us into a community of brothers and sisters, sons and daughters, who are the *laos theou*, the family of God, the church.

Only Christians know that we are misotheists,[24] God-haters. I learned this point from Karl Barth, via Robert Cushman: it is an arrogant pretension to suppose that Christians can know that we are sinners apart from Jesus Christ. So, far from it being the case (as seems so widely, but erroneously, supposed in some quarters) that original sin is the necessary requisite for incarnation, precisely the converse is true: incarnation is the presupposition of sin. Apart from acknowledgment of Jesus as incarnation of God's word, sin (original or otherwise) is for Christians meaningless and absurd.

Apart from the church and its self-understanding, sin makes no sense for Christians. To put it differently: apart from that perception of "the world" as the company of those who exercise their freedom *not* to acknowledge God, Christians do not know how to perceive fallenness and faithlessless.[25] So Cyprian was right to say that there is no salvation outside the church (*extra ecclesia nulla salus*). He was right, however, not for the institutional reasons that are so often misbegotten and mistakenly alleged, but precisely for the reason Lindbeck gives: "The beginning of damnation, the deliberate opposition to God, is possible only within the church, within the people of God."[26]

It is along these routes, I think, that the skirmish lines are being drawn; and while I agree with Lindbeck that a religion like Christianity "is likely to contribute more to the future of humanity if it preserves its own distinctiveness and integrity than if it yields to the homogenizing tendencies associated with liberal experiential-expressivism," I think that his own conclusion is a telling argument in support of the criticism (which he explicitly rejects) that what he offers us is basically a fideistic (that is, basically a subjectivist and experiential) solution:

> *This conclusion is paradoxical: Religious communities are likely to be practically relevant in the long run to the degree that they do not first ask what is either practical or relevant, but instead concentrate on their own intratextual outlooks and forms of life. The much-debated problem of the relation of theory to praxis is thus dissolved by the communal analogue of justification by faith. As is true for individuals, so also a religious community's salvation is not by works, nor is its faith for the sake of practical efficacy, and yet good works of unforeseeable kinds flow from faithfulness. It was thus, rather than by intentional effort, that biblical religion helped produce democracy and science, as well as other values Westerners treasure; and it is in similarly unimaginable and unplanned ways, if at all, that biblical religion will help save the world . . . from the demonic corruptions of these same values.*[27]

Lindbeck has argued for the claim that religion is the source, not the product, of experience; and while this claim may be normative, it is scarcely simple or unproblematic. Indeed, it is arguable that *the* problem of Western culture is that it is severed from its roots, and that this general cultural rootlessness is evident in the abandonment by much modern Christianity of its historical and traditional sources.[28] An obvious consequence of this state of affairs is that much modern religion is in fact the product of experience. So I think it impossible to express too strongly that the axiology of Francis Bacon's empirical experimental method, or the epistemology of René Descartes' "*Je pense, donc je suis,*" are no more methodologically revolutionary than popular Protestantism's reduction of Christian tradition to individuated experience.

As important as these methodological matters are, we can bracket them just now in order to ask: Why must alternatives be presented so starkly and in such apparent mutual exclusion? What has become of reciprocal causality?

At least since Plato, the relationship between "being" and "doing" has been vigorously argued; and old and familiar discussions of "nature" and "nurture" persist into the present. What needs to be asked is whether these terms must be at odds with one another. Is it at all conceivable that, without doing violence to either, terms like these can be understood as complementary and not as forces conspiring to pull us apart, and can Christian peoples aid and abet moves which are fragmenting rather than reconciling? I think not.

I noted earlier that I have lived long enough now to know that there are some people in this life with whom I am not likely to be reconciled. I say "likely" because I cherish the possibility (however remote by my present lights), and because (one or twice) I've been mistaken about irreconcilability in the past. I view the threat of likely lifelong antagonism as neither happy, nor good, nor even right, but as evidence of the tragic dimension of the human condition. I know that it is my own determined sense of identity and integrity (however perverse) together with the other's obstinacy and ignorance (however invincible) which has produced, and continues to nourish, this awful estrangement.

Moreover, it is clear to me that even a distanced analysis of a problem like this leaves much unclear—not least of all, sorting out what is the "source" and what is the "product" of this incompatibility. The entire business is not unlike the usually futile effort to establish blame and innocence in a divorce. So I am not comfortable about myself and others when I suspect that facile refuge from such alienation both participates in and perpetuates its dilemmatic character—that is, by engaging in a kind of double-talk.

How much happier and less ambiguous and more congenial our common life would be if we were just able to settle our various claims and counterclaims one way or another—to cut this Gordian knot and be done with it! But we do not do it, as Augustine recognized, because we cannot do it. Christians cannot with integrity willingly embrace freedom without responsibility, moral agency without accountability, body without spirit, nature without nurture, and so on. These complementaries require each other. Both are related, are ingredient, to spiritual wholeness and health.

Surely no Christian doubts that "good works of unforeseeable kinds flow from faithfulness." We call this "providential"; and it would be faithless were the people who understand and intend themselves to be disciples of Jesus to say otherwise. But it is precisely because we undertake *both to understand and to intend* ourselves as disciples of Jesus that faith also issues in intentional behaviors, in actions which (even with qualification) we call "good works."

The new right, liberationists, modern secularists, and liberals have programmatically reduced the Gospel to "good works"—"good works" which have been associated with social policy, or Marxist dialectic, or autonomous individualism, or the like. The temptation is great, but this reductionism is not sufficient warrant for seeking refuge in fideism, for abandoning the moral struggle to live as men and women who believe that their pilgrimage is a journey undertaken in faith. We persevere in the earthly city knowing that our ultimate destination is somewhere else. But if we are to talk this way about who we are, where we have come from, and where we are going, we will also have to talk about apparent contradictions which are nevertheless true; that is, we will sooner or later have to talk about paradox. How otherwise can we understand ourselves to be simultaneously in but not of the world, to be *simul iustus et peccator*.

Although the moral analogues are well-known, they bear repeating here. On the side of the accommodationists are those who claim that "I just do the best I can (or the most loving thing) in the circumstance." This is the ethical rendition of Popeye's definition of himself: "I am what I am, and that's all that I am." Here, I take it, is a crude but roughly analogous formulation of Lindbeck's "experiential-expressive" model, where experience is the source—the "given" as it were—and as source, it norms the objectification of common core experience (such as, e.g., religion).

On the other side are the separatists who claim that there is a single normative reading (or hearing) of the Christian story which commands, unequivocally and unambiguously, who one ought to be and what one ought to do. This is roughly analogous to the fall-out from the "cultural-linguistic" alternative, and it is illustrated by the gospel according to *Peanuts*. When Lucy said, "I just hope to goodness that it doesn't rain," Linus responded, "'Hoping to goodness' is not theologically sound."

Lindbeck himself acknowledged early on that "in the interplay between 'inner' experience and 'external' religious and cultural factors, the latter can be viewed as the *leading partners*, and it is this option which the cultural and/or linguistic analyst favors."[29] Because this is descriptively accurate of what actually occurs in the reciprocations of experience and reflection, one could wish that this insight had not receded in impact in later developments of the book.

In some ways, the result can be viewed as yet another argument between empiricism and rationalism in which the latter functions not as a "leading partner" but as a tyrant. But this way of viewing what is at stake here, although tenable, would both miss and obscure the fundamental matter at issue; and this is the question of whether there really are two different realms on earth—one the realm of Christ and the other the realm of the world—that have neither anything in common nor the possibility of intercourse.

The conclusion which Lindbeck reaches (and the one, incidentally, claimed by Hauerwas and Willimon[30]) seems to be an affirmative answer to this question. It is an answer which makes sense in the context of Luther's "two kingdoms" ethics, and an answer which achieves even more rigorous and radical expression in sixteenth-century Anabaptist theology. But it is also a very long way from any kind of partnership, or reciprocal causality, or even conversation, between an experiential-expressive model and its cultural-linguistic alternative.

To be sure, "tags" of various sorts do not serve well in unpacking what is controversial about all this; so I will try to say plainly what is most troubling and troublesome about talking this way. Part of the problem resides in rhetorical exaggeration and excess. This syntax, as I have already suggested, lends itself to more than one reading and interpretation. But more to the point (and sometimes convoluted syntax notwithstanding) the basic issue is ecclesial and epistemic: is it Christianly true to claim that the presence and action of God are *only* within the church? It is worth noting parenthetically that this is a question not dissimilar from the question of whether Christians believe that revelation occurs *only* within the Bible, or *only* within the sacraments, or *only* anywhere.

I have addressed questions of this sort in earlier parts of this essay; so it may be enough just now to observe that "church," "Bible," "sacraments," and "anywhere" are themselves spatio-temporal as well as theologically freighted terms. It is important to remind ourselves that questions like these emerge from presuppositions which are themselves much more interesting to examine. Recognizing this fact, we would be better positioned to deal with these matters *in toto* if we acknowledged doctrine, creed, church, scripture, etc., not as autonomous entities but as (all of them) part and parcel of the Christian tradition.[31]

To be sure, forcing choices between and among these articles of faith is symptomatic of a lack of nerve for facing some tough judgment calls; on the other hand, this is precisely what underlay the formation of canon and creed and doctrine and church, even under the guidance of Holy Spirit. Flannery O'Connor seems to me close to the truth when she wrote to her friend, "A":

> *I think that the church is the only thing that is going to make the terrible world we are coming to endurable; the only thing that makes the church endurable is that it is somehow the body of Christ and that on this we are fed. It seems to me a fact that you have to suffer as much from the church as for it but if you believe in the divinity of Christ, you have to cherish the world at the same time that you struggle to endure it.[32]*

The key to understanding why we should "cherish the world" is not, of course, discoverable in terms of what is salvageable because it is relevant, or the adoption of standards according to human need as defined by prevailing psychological, sociological, and ethical consensus. What is fundamentally at stake is the alternative to human self-affirmation which Christians call worship; and "worship is simply life that, in entire trustfulness, is given back into the hands of Him who gave it."[33]

I have wanted to suggest that it is inappropriate for biblical theists, and especially for Christians, to oppose terms like "church" and "world" as though they were autonomous—and, worse yet, adversarial. And I have argued that one way to distinguish theonomy from autonomy is to acknowledge that it is possible to recognize what it means to live faithfully *kata sarx* because that differentiation is controlled and normed by encounters with life *kata pneuma*.

A similar logic is what invests retelling the Christian story with such urgency and importance: apart from hearing that story, and ourselves being made part of it, we have no way to identify sin or "world" as contrary to God's will and intention as pardon and "church." Talking this way makes theological good sense because the beginning point is not with a dualism constituted of unilateral autonomies. Instead we proceed with a reciprocating relation between religion and experience in which the former is the "leading partner"—perhaps something more than *primus inter pares* but something less than *in loco parentis*.

Without that reciprocation and complementarity, what we would have are doctrines of a God of judgment and redemption, but little or nothing of God's manifest action and presence in creation. And if this were so, Christian theists would surely wonder about such a fissure in the Godhead. On the other hand, this may be more appearance than reality. Lindbeck's anxiety, which is shared by others, is that Christians in modernity either are, or are threatened to become, just like everybody else in all the wrong ways, except that Christians may exhibit an odd (even idiosyncratic) bit of pious talk and behavior now and then—not enough to upset or alter the *status quo*, mind you, but just enough to satisfy sentimental claims which hang on from upbringing by devout parents or the cultural cooptations of religion which define what it means to be a good American.

I believe that there are felicitous ways to own that Christians are participant in the human condition and, with a vision of the *mysterium fascinans et tremendum*, caught (perhaps even trapped) in the tension between the now and the not yet. I also grant that this may appear to some a saccharine *via media*, which is neither hot nor cold. What is urgent and important about all this, however, is not labeling but recognizing God's truth about us, which flows both from the church's account of the Christian story and the human circumstance within which that story gets told and heard and embraced. Christians cannot participate in the world without that story as canon—that is, without that story as controlling and norming. Nor can that story function as canon except in the world—that is, under the conditions of finitude and creatureliness. A suitable way to understand the nature of doctrine is precisely as mediating that tension, as trying simultaneously to be true to the heavenly vision and its imperfect earthly form. Vida Scudder, commenting on the passion of Catherine of Siena, put it this way:

> *Iconoclastic zeal against outworn or corrupt institutions fires our facile enthusiasm. Let us recognize also the spiritual passion that suffers unflinchingly the disparity between the sign and the thing signified, and devotes its energies, not to discarding, but to restoring and purifying that sign.*[34]

I had not read Scudder's commentary on Catherine of Siena when I was pastor to a fledgling (and struggling) congregation in the piedmont of North Carolina, in the halcyon days of the 1950s; but I can appreciate in retrospect how I was beginning to discern the "disparity between the sign and the thing signified." In those days, the big issues had to do with civil rights and manned space flights; but there were other, smaller by comparison, challenges to conventional Christian wisdom and piety. One of these was the effort (eventually successful) to abolish the "blue laws" which prohibited certain commercial activities on Sundays. I believed then, as I do now, that "blue laws" were a dispensable crutch for nominal Christians and that the church ought to be able to assert its claims on the devotion of Christians without having their loyalties shored up by the civil law. I failed, however, to comprehend that modern secular American society is, in fact, *not* religiously and ideologically neutral; I had to be taught that it is, instead, committed to a particular view of the world and our place in it.

We have to learn, says Lesslie Newbigin, "that what has come into being is not a secular society but a pagan society, not a society devoid of public images but a society which worships gods which are not God."[35] What this means for churches and congregations is that we cannot peacefully coexist in a "comfortable concordat between Yahweh and the Baalim" in which Christian faith speaks only to individual and private truth, while secular culture defines public truth. The church must not avoid the public square, because the truth which Christian faith acknowledges is, as Newbigin puts it, "the claim to provide the public truth by which society can be given coherence and direction."[36]

To embrace the world or abandon it are not viable options for the disciples of Jesus; we have to learn somehow that a holy life cherishes the world at the same time that it struggles to endure it.

I embrace the qualification that "I am not clairvoyant and only seldom given to prophecy," and offer this opinion: to ask whether the puzzles associated with "accommodation/separation," "reason/revelation," "nature/nurture," and similar juxtapositions are finally soluble is plainly to ask quite the wrong question. It is not merely that these issues have such a long and tenacious hold on the history of Christianity (although this in itself strikes me as instructive); it is, more importantly, that issues like these are ingredient in the human condition. So, *if I were* clairvoyant or even given to prophecy, I would want to remind us all that Jesus never promised a rose garden in this life and to suggest that, like the poor, the moral struggle to overcome these irresolvable tensions will always be with us.

To understand these things in this wise might have the redeeming grace of enabling us to be definite about certain relationships between church and world without supposing that we are thereby definitive. Indeed, a very large part of Protestant American Christianity's problem in this regard seems to me to be the indoctrination (largely learned from our Teutonic tutors) that "either/or" is always preferable (and perhaps superior) to "both/and," although we are almost never told precisely why. For those of us who cut many of our theological teeth on Karl Barth's writings, this is compellingly the case: that little word "and," he said on more than one occasion, has been the undoing of Christian theology *as* Christian theology.[37]

Barth's splendid insulation of *das Wort* from all worldly taint was and is, I believe, too extravagant in the measure to which it denies any and every "point of contact" with the world (except on what Barth took to be the Word's own and unique terms). It is nevertheless profitable to recognize the truth in his claim and to resist the kind of cozy alliance between the Gospel and secularity which, many moderns claim, is required for the continued viability of religion. If the difficulty with Barth on this point is an intransigent distinction and difference between what has been called "the Christian community" and "a world in which it is no longer at home," the problem with modern pagan liberalism is that any distinction and difference between them gets blurred to the point of vanishing entirely.

The paradox of "being in but not of" the world is, I believe, not reducible to either the separationist or the accommodationist outlook. Neither, to be sure, is this paradox resolved in a fully satisfactory way by commitment to a lifelong moral struggle from which one knows at the outset that there will never be relief (much less extrication) in this life. On the other hand, there is much to commend moral struggle as a virtuous and viable alternative in that it acknowledges and affirms this paradox as paradigmatic of the human situation and of faithful discipleship. It is a cheap grace which forces the either/or choice; but it is a costly grace which embraces the tension.

My children have done me the great service (and honor) of reminding me that the family relationship is a bond which, despite their growing up and moving away, is never completely severed. In the terms of the metaphor which begins this chapter, I take this to mean that when parents and children are properly parents and children to each other, the children never entirely "leave the nest"; they are not, by their leaving, dismembered. So "family," by this limiting condition, is too circumscribed and meager to be "nest" in this comprehensive sense.

Something similar, I believe, is the case with a certain notion of "church": it is also too limited to function as "nest" in this comprehensive sense. Acknowledging this limiting condition, in fact, affords a more apt analog for understanding the church/world dialectic. When we are sent out from the church into the world to do the work God has given us to do, to love and serve God as faithful witnesses of Christ our Savior, we are neither severed from "church" nor setting foot on the alien turf of "world."

My ornithologist friends tell me that some birds "leave the nest," never to return. The old nest is simply abandoned and never used again, even by other birds. The next time that a nest is needed, these birds just start over and make a new one. But I am also told that there are other species which "leave the nest" only temporarily. These birds come back again and again to the same nest; and such new beginnings as they make are always undertaken from this "home base." My guess is that there are perils and promises in both behaviors: in the former, debris and filth tend to accumulate, so periodic cleaning out and some refurbishing are needed; and in the latter, while there is no need to reinvent the wheel, it is probable that familiarity will breed contempt.

Aware that the analogy might be stretched too far, I would reckon that Christians are more akin to birds of the latter sort who treat their nest as simply part of their world. The language of "church" and "world" is rich and varied, as we have seen, and it is pliable in its several meanings. In earlier settings, I suggested that these terms serve as metaphors for our primary loyalties and commitments: "world" represents one's determination to be autonomous and in control, whereas "church" signifies one's submission and subjection to God.

In the present context, however, these words suggest spatial metaphors which define the parameters of the human condition and of human congress. Thus, if we Christians are more like those birds which never abandon the nest, it is owing to God's mighty work in Jesus, which reconciled the world to himself and made the world a hallowed, if not always a friendly, place for us to be. Indeed, "world," in this sense, is for us Christians a metaphor for "nest." Because it is complex and expansive, we may feel threatened and like strangers in some parts of it; but because God has claimed it for himself and has sanctified it with the reconciliation of Jesus' death and resurrection, it is our home, as it were, and we are never completely estranged from it.

This is why we are the kind of people who are not only obligated, but can happily embrace the commission, to go forth in peace in the name of Christ, to love and serve the Lord, all the while rejoicing in the power of the Spirit. Thanks be to God!

NOTES

INTRODUCTION

1. Cf. Donald Juel, *Messianic Exegesis: Christological Interpretation of the Old Testament in Early Christianity* (Philadelphia: Fortress, 1988); and Morna Hooker, *New Wine in Old Bottles: Christological Interpretation of the Old Testament in Early Christianity* (London: University of London, 1984).

2. Cf. 1 Corinthians 4:7b.

3. Cf. 1 Peter 1:18.

4. 1 Corinthians 11:23. Robert Cabie, in a superb essay titled "Christian Initiation," reinforces the claim that the Christian life is something received by observing that when instructions for candidates for baptism in the early church were completed, "the *traditio symboli* took place, that is, the symbol of faith (the Creed) was 'handed over' to them: they were to learn it by heart and be able to recite it publicly at the end of Lent; they would then 'give back' the Creed (the *redditio symboli*), that is, they would profess their personal acceptance of the faith that had been handed on to them. As St. Augustine said: 'In eight days' time you will give back what you have received today. . . .'" See A. G. Martimort, ed., *The Church at Prayer*, vol. III (Collegeville, Minn.: The Liturgical Press, 1988), 28.

5. It is ironic, on this point, to note that Protestantism's emphasis on the communal aspect of worship—as, for example, in its insistence that baptism was to be done during the Sunday service, or that eucharist was not to be celebrated without an assembly—was almost completely lost until the twentieth century renewal of biblical and liturgical studies. It may be that individualism of one sort or another is the constant temptation for Christians in all times and circumstances. "Private" baptisms, as well as "private" marriages and burials, continue to occur not infrequently in Protestantism; and Holy Communion, while never celebrated in strict privacy, has been "set out" on a communion table for a period of several hours so that worshipers could serve themselves at their convenience. Holy Communion is being celebrated more frequently; but frequency alone hardly overcomes the overall observation that so many of these practices are patently individualistic from start to finish. Insofar as this is so, Protestantism has forsaken its own heritage.

6. William J. Wolf, in his introduction to *Anglican Spirituality* (Wilton, Conn.: Morehouse-Barlow Co., Inc., 1982), emphasizes the communal or "common" character of worship, and recalls a comment from Frederick Denison Maurice on the Lord's Prayer which also accentuates the importance of bringing the individual into a corporate context of worship: "When thou art most alone thou must still, if thou wouldest pray, be in the midst of a family; thou must call upon a Father; thou must not dare to say *my*, but *our*." [*The Kingdom of Christ* (London: James Clarke, 1959), vol. II, pt. 3, p. 26.]

7. Cf. the *Didache*, 8:2–3. This ancient catechism (ca. 150 C.E.) includes instruction on both the form and the frequency of prayer: "You must not pray like the hypocrites, but 'pray as follows' as the Lord bid us in his gospel: [hereafter follows the Lord's Prayer]. You should pray in this way three times a day."

8. Cyprian's commentary on the Lord's Prayer (ca. 251–52 C.E.) eloquently reflects this aspect: "Along with His other salutary admonitions and the divine precepts through which He counsels His people for their salvation, He has also furnished a format for prayer. He Himself has told us what to pray for. With the same generosity that deigned to lavish all else on us, He who gave His life has also shown us how to pray, so we may more readily be heard as we speak to the Father in the very words His Son has taught us. . . . As a result, we who have received the Spirit and truth through His sanctification can also worship truly and spiritually through His teaching." Cyprian of Carthage, *The Lord's Prayer*, trans. Edmond Bonin (Westminster, Md.: Christian Classics, 1983), 5–6.

9. *Commentary of Theodore of Mopsuestia on the Lord's Prayer and on the Sacraments of Baptism and the Eucharist*, ed. and trans. A. Mingana (Cambridge, England: W. Heffer and Sons, Ltd., 1933), vol. 6 in the Woodbrooke Studies, 1–5.

CHAPTER I

1. Evelyn Underhill, *Worship* (New York: Harper and Brothers, 1937), 3.

2. I first learned of this lore from Leonel L. Mitchell's *The Meaning of Ritual* (New York: Paulist Press, 1977), and I remain deeply indebted to his work. The material which follows immediately is especially dependent upon the first chapter of Mitchell's work. My initial sense of congeniality with his interpretation of these data has grown over the years as I have confirmed this point of view in my own experience and represented it in my teaching. An alternative approach suggests that Christian ritual, ceremony, and liturgy are unique, or perhaps only discontinuous or unrecognizable in relation to pre-Christian worship; but these positions seem to me historically untenable and theologically naive, and in a variety of ways I undertake to show that this is so throughout this essay.

3. Johannes Maringer, *The Gods of Prehistoric Man*, trans. Mary Ilford (London: Weidenfeld and Nicolson, 1960), 27ff.

4. Ibid., 33.

5. Ibid., 37. Cf. 42.

6. Ibid., 41.

7. Cf. Mitchell, 3.

8. Johannes Maringer and Hans-Georg Bandi, *Art in the Ice Age* (New York: Frederick A. Praeger, 1953), 112.

9. Among these are Deuteronomy 12:23, "the blood is life," and Leviticus 17:14, "the life of all flesh is the blood thereof." Christians ought to be especially sensitized to this awareness, and I will say more about this later; but it cannot go unnoticed at this point that Aidan Kavanagh is precisely on target in reminding us that there is nothing nice or pretty about crucifixion, and that we must not allow sacramental knowledge of Jesus' sacrifice to become repressed or obscured through sentimentality: "For to know Christ sacramentally only in terms of bread and wine is to know him only partially, in the dining room as host and guest. It is a valid enough knowledge, but its ultimate weakness when isolated is that it is perhaps too civil." See Kavanagh's *The Shape of Baptism* (New York: Pueblo Publishing Company, 1978), 160. Cf. Mitchell, 6.

10. Mircea Eliade, *Rites and Symbols of Initiation* (New York: Harper and Row, 1958), x.

11. Mary Douglas, *Natural Symbols* (London: Barrie and Jenkins, 1970), 19.

12. Ibid., 20.

13. Ibid., 21.

14. Marianne H. Micks, *The Future Present: The Phenomenon of Christian Worship* (New York: Seabury Press, 1970), ix.

15. Mircea Eliade, *Images and Symbols: Studies in Religious Symbolism* (New York: Sheed and Ward, 1961), 12.

16. Mircea Eliade, *The Sacred and the Profane* (New York: Harcourt, Brace and World, 1959), 11–18.

17. Cf. J. A. Jungmann, *The Early Liturgy: To the Time of Gregory the Great* (Notre Dame, Ind.: University of Notre Dame Press, 1959), 12–13. Citing Gregory Dix (*The Shape of Liturgy*) for support, Jungmann claims, "It was precisely their [the early Christians'] attendance at worship which constituted their great crime in the eyes of the pagan state. Anyone and everyone could *believe* what he pleased, but that the Christians should shun the official state worship in favor of their own cult—that was the reason for the persecution. . . . Even at this early period, the Christians must have had the same thought that was expressed by the martyrs of Abitina during the Diocletian persecution: We cannot survive with the Eucharist: *Sine Dominico (esse) non possumus*. The Eucharistic celebration cannot be superseded: *Intermitti Dominicum non potest*."

18. *Didascalia Apostolorum, XIII*, ed. R. H. Connolly (Oxford: Clarendon Press, 1929), 124. The *Didascalia* includes extensive textual fragments from even earlier instructions, including the *Apostolic Constitutions* and the *Didache*, both of which emphasize the importance of assembling the faithful for worship. Thus, for example, there is this prayer-directive in the *Didache* (9:4) for giving thanks for the bread at the eucharist: "As this piece [of bread] was scattered over the hills and then was brought together and made one, so let your Church be brought together from the ends of the earth into your Kingdom. For yours is the glory and the power through Jesus Christ forever." (Cyril C. Richardson, ed., *Early Christian Fathers* [Philadelphia: The Westminster Press, 1953, vol. I, 175.) This citation from the *Didache* is also, coincidentally, part of the text of the second stanza of Hymn #302: "Watch o'er thy Church, O Lord, in mercy, save it from evil, guard it still, perfect it in thy love, unite it, cleansed and conformed unto thy will. As grain, once scattered on the hillsides, was in this broken bread made one, so from all lands thy Church be gathered into thy kingdom by thy Son." (*Hymnbook 1982* [New York: The Church Hymnal Corporation, 1982], #302.)

19. I will say more of this in chapter 2, "Liturgy and the Christian Life," where I cite and discuss the particularly apposite essay by M. Francis Mannion, "Liturgy and the Present Crisis of Culture," *Worship*, vol. 62 (March 1988): 98–123.

20. Augustine, Sermon 227. The Latin text is in J. P. Migne, *Patrologia Latina* (Rotterdam: Soc. Editr. De Forel, 1952), vol. 38, 1099–1101. The English translation is in *The Fathers of the Church* (New York: Fathers of the Church, Inc., 1959), vol. 38, 195–98. This sermon is similar, in several ways, to Sermon 6; and owing to their complementary compositions, I have taken the liberty of interpolating parts of that homily into this one. The English translation of Sermon 6 is in *The Fathers of the Church*, vol. 11, 321–26.

21. The Book of Common Prayer (New York: The Church Hymnal Corporation, 1979), 306.

22. Ibid., 363. Italics added.

23. Thomas J. Talley, "The Work of Ritualization," in H. Barry Evans, ed., *Prayer Book Renewal* (New York: Seabury Press, 1978), 79.

24. Cf. Raymond E. Brown, *The Anchor Bible: The Gospel According to John (i–xii)* (Garden City, N.Y.: Doubleday and Co., 1960), 374–75. Brown comments: "While the former blind man is gradually having his eyes opened to the truth about Jesus, the Pharisees or 'the Jews' are becoming more obdurate in their failure to see the truth" (p. 377). Brown further suggests that verses 22–23 may be related to verse 34 for contrast: verse 34 almost surely does not mean excommunication but merely "ejection from their presence," whereas verses 22–23 "refer to the attempt around A.D. 90 to drive out from synagogues Jews who had accepted Jesus as the Messiah" (pp. 375, 380).

25. Cf. O. Casel, *The Mystery of Christian Worship, and Other Writings*, ed. B. Neun-

heuser (Westminster, Md.: Newman, 1962), 87: "The liturgy . . . from the very beginning, from the time when the Lord made bread and wine the elements of the mass, has given nature its part to play."

26. Brown, *Anchor Bible: John*, 381. Of particular help in comprehending this Gospel has been two classic monographs on John, both of them not only scholarly but also profoundly devotional: one of these is E. C. Hoskyns's *The Fourth Gospel*, 2d ed. rev. (London: Faber and Faber, 1947), 402–22; and the other is William Temple's *Readings in St. John's Gospel*, 2 vols. (London: Macmillan and Co., 1940), 153–61. I have also found very useful the more contemporary treatment of critical issues associated with the setting, sources, and theology of this gospel in D. Moody Smith's *Johannine Christianity* (Columbia, S.C.: University of South Carolina Press, 1984).

27. Ibid. In the Eastern church, candidates for baptism were called *photizomenoi*, connoting that they were destined for illumination.

28. Frederick Denison Maurice, *The Kingdom of Christ*, 2 vols. (London: James Clarke and Co., Ltd., 1959). Maurice's method in these volumes is to carry on a dialogue with various contending "systems" that claim universality (either to have achieved it or to have a recipe for it!). As Richard Norris has put it: "Maurice chooses . . . to believe that in the creed of every party and movement there is some fundamental affirmation which must be taken seriously, and yet at the same time every such creed has its 'dark side.' " [See his essay "On Theology," in F. McClain, R. Norris, J. Orens, *F. D. Maurice: A Study* (Cambridge, Mass.: Cowley Publications, 1982), 8.] In his conversations with "Quakerism," "pure Protestantism," "the Romish system," and other parties and schools, Maurice challenges and rejects what he perceives to be false and acknowledges and affirms what he discerns to be true. These judgments are made on the basis of a statement's participation, or lack of it, in what Maurice calls "reality"; and "reality" is God and the givenness of the constitution of all that is. So the theological task is not invention but discovery of the order of things as God intends. Because reality is the presupposition of all that is, what is "true" tends to be expressions which testify to a speaker's direct involvement with "reality"; and what is "false" is typically an attempt to explain or account for the reality testified to.

29. Norris, "On Theology," 14.

30. Ivan Illich was a co-founder of the widely known and controversial Center for Intercultural Documentation (CIDOC) in Cuernavaca, Mexico. This comment about iatrogenic illness refers to his book *Medical Nemesis* (1975).

31. Sermon 227, *Saint Augustine: Sermons on the Liturgical Seasons*, vol. 38 of *The Fathers of the Church* (New York: Fathers of the Church, Inc., 1959), 195. See further *Saint Ambrose: Theological and Dogmatic Works*, vol. 44 in *The Fathers of the Church* (New York: Fathers of the Church, Inc., 1963), 5–28; *The Works of Saint Cyril of Jerusalem*, vol. 64 in *The Fathers of the Church* (New York: Fathers of the Church, Inc., 1970), 153–203; *St. John Chrysostom: Baptismal Instructions*, trans. P. H. Harkins, in J. Quas-

ten and W. J. Burghardt, eds., vol. 31 in *Ancient Christian Writers—The Works of the Fathers in Translation* (Westminster, Md.: Newman Press, 1963); and *Commentary of Theodore of Mopsuestia on the Lord's Prayer and on the Sacraments of Baptism and the Eucharist*, ed. and trans. A. Mingana (Cambridge, England: W. Heffer and Sons, Ltd., 1933), vol. 6 in the Woodbrooke Studies. For a recent examination of the content and method of the mystagogical lectures of Ambrose, Cyril, John Chrysostom, and Theodore, see Enrico Mazza, *Mystagogia: A Theology of Liturgy in the Patristic Age*, trans. M. J. O'Connell (New York: Pueblo Publishing Co., 1989).

32. Cited in A. G. Martimort, ed., *The Church at Prayer* (Collegeville, Minn.: The Liturgical Press, 1986), vol. 1, pp. 10–11.

33. V. A. Demant, "The Social Implications of Worship; and the Necessity of Specific Acts of Worship," in P. T. R. Kirk, ed., *Worship: Its Social Significance* (London: The Centenary Press, 1939), 107–8.

34. The Book of Common Prayer (New York: The Church Hymnal Corporation, 1979), 857.

35. Augustine, *The City of God*, bk. VIII, chap. 17, in vol. 14 of *The Fathers of the Church* (New York: Fathers of the Church, Inc., 1952), 53.

CHAPTER 2

1. Cf. p. 69 in the 1979 Book of Common Prayer. See also p. 324. See further Matthew 22:36–40, Mark 12:28–31, and Luke 10:25–28.

2. See Marion J. Hatchett, *Commentary on the American Prayer Book* (New York: Seabury Press, 1981), 319. The 1789 revision of the Book of Common Prayer was the first to include the Summary of the Law; even so, it was included for optional use following the decalogue. When the Prayer Book was revised in 1892, the Decalogue was permissibly omitted from the liturgy except for one service each Sunday, and the revision of 1928 required its use on only one Sunday a month; in both of these revisions, the Summary was required when the decalogue was omitted. Again in the 1979 revision, the rubrics for Rite I direct that the Summary is optional; and in Rite II the Summary functions rather like *primus inter pares* among optional scripture sentences in the Penitential Order (p. 351) and may be said prior to the general confession.

3. Will Herberg, *Protestant-Catholic-Jew: An Essay in American Religious Sociology* (Garden City, N.Y.: Doubleday and Co., 1955).

4. Ibid., 126.

5. Ibid., 247.

6. Alasdair MacIntyre, *After Virtue* (Notre Dame, Ind.: University of Notre Dame Press, 1981), 2.

7. Nolan B. Harmon, *Understanding The Methodist Church* (Nashville: The Methodist Publishing House, 1940), 21–22.

8. M. Francis Mannion, "Liturgy and the Present Crisis of Culture," *Worship*, vol. 62 (March 1988): 98–123.

9. Robert N. Bellah, et al., *Habits of the Heart* (Berkeley: University of California Press, 1985), 334.

10. Mannion, "Liturgy and the Present Crisis of Culture," 107.

11. Richard Sennett, *The Fall of Public Man* (New York: Vintage Books, 1978), 219.

12. Ibid., 259.

13. Bellah et al., *Habits,* 219ff.

14. Mannion, "Liturgy and the Present Crisis of Culture," 113.

15. Ibid., 114.

16. Ibid., 119.

17. There is also an insistent strand in the church's history which claims that a complete separation of church and world is reductionistic and naive; and of this we must say more later.

18. Maurice Merleau-Ponty, *Phenomenology of Perception* (London: Routledge and Kegan Paul, 1962); see esp. pp. 174–99.

19. The 1549 Prayer Book formulated the classical "causes for which matrimony was ordained" as follows: "One cause was the procreation of children, to be brought upon in the fear and nurture of the Lord, and praise of God. Secondly, it was ordained for a remedy against sin, and to avoid fornication, that such persons as be married might live chastely in matrimony, and keep themselves undefiled members of Christ's body. Thirdly, for the mutual society, help, and comfort that the one ought to have of the other, both in prosperity and adversity. Into which holy estate these two persons present come now to be joined." An accessible modern reference is Marion J. Hatchett, *Commentary on the American Prayer Book* (New York: Seabury Press, 1981), 432.

20. Harmon L. Smith, "Decorum as Doctrine: Teachings on Human Sexuality," in *The Crisis in Moral Teaching in The Episcopal Church*, eds. T. Sedgwick and P. Turner (Harrisburg, Pa.: Morehouse Publishing, 1992), 15–40.

21. Stanley Hauerwas, *Truthfulness and Tragedy* (Notre Dame, In.: University of Notre Dame Press, 1977), 151.

22. For a remarkably brief yet superb exposition of the history, theology, and observance of Sunday as the principal day for celebrating the central event of Christian salvation history, see P. Jounel, "Sunday and the Week," in A. G. Martimort, ed., *The Church at Prayer*, vol. IV in *The Liturgy and Time* (Collegeville, Minn.: The Liturgical Press, 1985), 11–29.

23. Robert Cabie, *The Eucharist*, in A. G. Martimort, ed., *The Church at Prayer* (Collegeville, Minn.: The Liturgical Press, 1986), v. II, p. 173.

24. For examples of contemporary liturgical texts, see the very useful collection selected and introduced by Bard Thompson, *Liturgies of the Western Church* (Cleveland:

World Publishing Co., 1962), esp. pp. 27–224. Included are Latin and English versions of Pius V's *Missale Romanum*, Luther's *Formula Missae* and *Deutsche Messe*, Zwingli's *Liturgy of the Word* and *Action or Use of the Lord's Supper*, Bucer's *Psalter, with Complete Church Practice*, and Calvin's *The Form of Church Prayers* for both Strassburg and Geneva.

25. Cabie, *The Eucharist*, 175.

26. For the English translation of the new order of the mass, see *The Sacramentary*, revised according to the second typical edition of the *Missale Romanum*, March 27, 1975 (Collegeville, Minn.: The Liturgical Press, 1985).

27. For a different view of this matter, see Michael Warren's *Faith, Culture, and the Worshiping Community* (New York: Paulist, 1989), which takes the position that eucharist is not a formative act but is only approached and understood following Christian formation. Indeed, Warren suggests that what he calls "cultural formation" may in fact provide the dominant interpretive grid which informs the approach to and understanding of eucharist.

28. Commenting on John 6:56 ("He that eateth my flesh and drinketh my blood, abideth in me and I in him"), William Temple made this point succinctly: "Those words express in completeness the substance and the goal of the Christian life. . . . It is not the momentary eating but the permanent abiding that is of primary importance; the sacramental communion is an end in itself so far as it is communion, but a means to an end so far as it is sacramental. The sacrament is normally necessary; but it is the communion alone that is vital." [William Temple, *Readings in St. John's Gospel*, vol. I (London: Macmillan and Co., Ltd., 1940), 95.]

29. Cf. Matthew 26:26–28; 1 Corinthians 11:23–26.

30. Mary Douglas, *Natural Symbols* (New York: Pantheon Books, 1970), 1.

31. Cf. Thompson, *Liturgies of the Western Church*, 129.

CHAPTER 3

1. Massey H. Shepherd, Jr., *The Oxford American Prayer Book Commentary* (New York: Oxford University Press, 1950), 83–84.

2. Cf. p. 366. The postcommunion prayer which follows Rite I is grammatically closer to the 1549 prayer; but there is a remarkable structural and substantive constancy over these almost 450 years.

3. This is called the "Collect for Purity," and it reads: "Almighty God, to you all hearts are open, all desires known, and from you no secrets are hid: Cleanse the thoughts of our hearts by the inspiration of your Holy Spirit, that we may perfectly love you, and worthily magnify your holy Name; through Christ our Lord. Amen." Book of Common Prayer, 355.

4. Indeed, the adverb "immediately" (Gr. *euthus*) occurs eleven times in Mark 1—

from Jesus *immediately* seeing the heavens opened and the Spirit descending upon him when he came up out of the water of his baptism; to Jesus' being *immediately* driven into the wilderness by the Spirit; to Simon, Andrew, James, and John *immediately* leaving their nets to follow Jesus; to a leper being healed *immediately* when Jesus touched him and ordered him to be made clean—and many times more in the remainder of the Gospels.

5. The phrase "the world" is a familiar one in Christian rhetoric; and its meaning can range across a broad spectrum from prosaic to paradisal. I intend and use it here as a metaphor for all of God's creation which has exercised, and continues to exercise, its freedom *not* to believe in God and have its life ordered accordingly.

6. I should indicate at this point that, in contradistinction to "world," I use the word "church" here as a metaphor for all those who exercise their freedom to respond to God's gathering and who, thereby, have their lives ordered accordingly.

7. Ernst Troeltsch, *The Social Teaching of the Christian Churches*, trans. Olive Wyon (New York: The Macmillan Co., 1931).

8. "In opposition to the exclusive and doctrinaire application of this [Marxist] method, however, the whole of this survey has shown that all that is specifically religious, and, above all, the great central points of religious development, are an independent expression of the religious life. Jesus, Paul . . . Luther, Calvin: as we study their thought and their feeling we realize that it is impossible to regard them as the product of class struggles and of economic factors" (ibid., 1002). Interestingly, this same point was made at the outset: "In order to understand the foundation principles of Christianity as a whole, in its relation to social problems, it is of the utmost importance to recognize that the preaching of Jesus and the creation of the Christian Church were not due in any sense to the impulse of a social movement. To put it quite plainly: Christianity was not the product of a class struggle of any kind; it was not shaped, when it did arise, in order to fit into any such situation; indeed, at no point was it directly concerned with the social upheavals of the ancient world" (ibid., 39).

9. Ibid., 993.

10. Ibid., 994.

11. Ibid., 994.

12. H. Richard Niebuhr, *Christ and Culture* (New York: Harper and Brothers, 1951). Niebuhr develops five historical types of Christian response to the polar tensions between Christ and culture. In sum, the relations between them are described as: (1) Christ against culture, (2) the Christ of culture, (3) Christ above culture, (4) Christ and culture in paradox, and (5) Christ the transformer of culture.

13. Cf. Leviticus 4:1–4 (if an anointed priest sins); 13–21 (if the whole community of Israel sins); 10:1–7 (the excommunication of Nadab and Abihu); 11:1ff (laws of purification and atonement), 23–25 (touching a "winged creature with four legs" makes unclean); 17:10–12 (prohibition against eating blood).

14. Cf. re: excommunication 1 Corinthians 5, 1 Timothy 1:20, and Titus 3:10–11; and re: reconciliation and restoration to the community 2 Corinthians 2:5–11 and 1 Timothy 5:19–22.

15. Cf. e.g., L. Bieler, *The Irish Penitentials* (Dublin: Dublin Institute for Advanced Studies, 1963). For a sense of Anglican appropriation of penance, see Hubert S. Box, ed., *The Theory and Practice of Penance* (London: Society for Promoting Christian Knowledge, 1935), and Francis George Belton, *A Manual for Confessors—Being a Guide to the Administration of the Sacrament of Penance for the Use of Priests of the English Church* (London: A. R. Mowbray and Co., Ltd., 1936).

16. Cf. Marion J. Hatchett, *Commentary on the American Prayer Book* (New York: Seabury Press, 1981), 450–51 and 309–10. The quotations from the prayer books are taken from Hatchett.

17. Cf. Gunnar Myrdal, *An American Dilemma: The Negro Problem and Modern Democracy* (New York: Harper and Brothers, 1944), 2 vols.

18. Cf. John 20:23: "If you forgive the sins of any, they are forgiven; if you retain the sins of any, they are retained"; and Matthew 18:18: "Truly, I say to you, whatever you bind on earth will be bound in heaven, and whatever you loose on earth will be loosed in heaven."

19. *Commentary of Theodore of Mopsuestia on the Lord's Prayer and on the Sacraments of Baptism and the Eucharist*, ed. and trans. A. Mingana (Cambridge, England: W. Heffer and Sons, Ltd., 1933), vol. 6 in the Woodbrooke Studies, 120–23.

20. "If we say we have no sin, we deceive ourselves, and the truth is not in us. If we confess our sins, he is faithful and just, and will forgive our sins and cleanse us from all unrighteousness. If we say we have not sinned, we make him a liar, and his word is not in us."

21. T. Jackson, ed., *Wesley's Works* (London: John Mason, 1829), vol. V, 55.

22. Cf. H. Lindstrom, *Wesley and Sanctification* (London: The Epworth Press, 1946), 84f.

23. Paul made this point emphatically, but with reference to the role of law and commandment in the epistle to the Romans. Cf. esp. Romans 7:1–12.

24. This dependency upon Jesus as God's self-revelation, and as the presupposition for the intelligent development of Christian accounts and arguments, is more fully considered in the chapter on "Greetings: Peace." My claim, in sum, is that when "Christian" modifies a word or phrase, it becomes controlling for nuanced meaning. So, if we speak of a "Christian understanding of sin," we are bound to refer *ex hypothese* to the adjective which, presumably, gives the concept "sin" this "Christian under-standing" rather than some other understanding. Otherwise, it would be altogether sufficient to speak of "sin" without particularity or differentiation. What we discover, however, is that it is not sufficient to speak of "sin" in this way; and hence the indispensability of a modifier.

25. William Ernest Henley, "Invictus," in Frances Parkinson Keyes, ed., *A Treasury of Favorite Poems* (New York: Hawthorn Books, Inc., 1963), 253.

26. John Stuart Mill, *On Liberty* (London: John W. Parker and Son, 1859), 24. A complementary observation at the other side is offered by Robert Browning: "There are those who believe something, and therefore will tolerate nothing; and on the other hand, those who tolerate everything, because they believe nothing."

27. Immanuel Kant, *Religion Within the Limits of Reason Alone*, trans. T. M. Greene and H. H. Hudson (New York: Harper and Brothers, 1960), 107–9.

28. Alasdair MacIntyre, *Whose Justice? Which Rationality?* (Notre Dame, Ind.: University of Notre Dame Press, 1988), 2.

CHAPTER 4

1. In the following section, I have excerpted and emended some paragraphs from my essay "Language, Belief, Authority: Crises for Christian Ministry and Professional Identity," *Pastoral Psychology* 23 (April 1972): 15–21.

2. Paul Van Buren, *The Secular Meaning of the Gospel* (New York: The Macmillan Company, 1963), 103.

3. Cf. "The Shape of the Liturgy," supra.

4. See David C. Steinmetz, "The Superiority of Pre-Critical Exegesis," *Theology Today* 37 (1980): 27–38.

5. Timothy E. O'Connell, *Principles for a Catholic Morality* (New York: The Seabury Press, 1976); see esp. chap. 4, pp. 30–41.

6. Ibid., 34–36.

7. William Temple, *Nature, Man, and God* (London: Macmillan and Co. Ltd., 1960), 246–300.

8. Ibid., 298.

9. Roland Bainton, *Christian Attitudes Toward War and Peace* (New York: Abingdon, 1960), 15ff.

10. Emil Brunner, *The Divine Imperative* (Philadelphia: Westminster, 1958), 132ff.

11. Cf. Sissela Bok's entertaining and instructive book *Lying: Moral Choice in Public and Private Life* (New York: Pantheon, 1978).

12. Augustine, *The Enchiridion on Faith, Hope, and Love*, trans. J. F. Shaw (South Bend, Ind.: Regnery/Gateway, Inc., 1961), 28–30.

13. Literally, a calling to mind or recollection, as reflected in the phrase which institutes the Holy Communion: "this do in remembrance of me."

14. *Baptism, Eucharist, and Ministry* (Geneva: World Council of Churches, 1982).

15. A form of this prayer for Holy Spirit to indwell the bread and wine of the sacrament is the following from *The Book of Common Prayer*: "We pray you, gracious God, to send your Holy Spirit upon these gifts that they may be the Sacrament of the

Body of Christ and his Blood of the New Covenant." Cf. Rite II, Eucharistic Prayer B, p. 369.

CHAPTER 5

1. Cf. the extended quotation from V. A. Demant's essay "The Social Implications of Worship; and the Necessity of Specific Acts of Worship," cited in Chapter 1.

2. Cf. E. O. James, *Origins of Sacrifice* (London: J. Murray, 1937); W. O. E. Oesterley, *Sacrifices in Ancient Israel* (London: Hodder and Stoughton, 1937); and Gary A. Anderson, *Sacrifices and Offerings in Ancient Israel: Studies in Their Social and Political Importance* (Atlanta: Scholar's Press, 1987).

3. For example, the Hittite Instructions for Temple Officials.

4. Henry Fairlie, *The Seven Deadly Sins Today* (Notre Dame, Ind.: University of Notre Dame Press, 1979), 67.

5. M. Merleau-Ponty, *The Phenomenology of Perception*, trans. Colin Smith (London: Routledge and Kegan Paul, 1962), esp. chap. 5, "The Body as Expression, and Speech," 174 ff. Merleau-Ponty puts the point this way: "A thought limited to existing for itself, independently of the constraints of speech and communication, would no sooner appear than it would sink into the unconscious, which means that it would not exist even for itself. . . . Thus speech, in the speaker, does not translate ready-made thought, but accomplishes it" (177–78).

6. Immanuel Kant, *Religion Within the Limits of Reason Alone*, trans. T. M. Greene and H. H. Hudson (New York: Harper and Brothers, 1960), 107–9.

7. Dietrich Bonhoeffer, *The Cost of Discipleship*, trans. R. H. Fuller (New York: The Macmillan Company, 1963), 45–48.

8. Cf. Stephen Sykes, *The Identity of Christianity* (Philadelphia: Fortress, 1984). Sykes's thesis is that different views of Jesus himself, together with the relationship of his life, death, and resurrection to the preaching of primitive Christianity, were inseparable from the actual form and content of Christian origins. Whatever unity there is in the New Testament is therefore best understood as "contained diversity." So Sykes understands the "identity of Christianity" to consist "in the interaction between its external forms [institutional embodiments, propositions, rites, etc.] and an inward element [piety, prayer, praise, etc.], constantly maintained by participation in communal worship" (282–83). On Sykes's terms, the external forms and the inward element are dialectically related and require each other for intelligibility: "The context of communal worship permits doctrinal dispute. But dispute is not an end in itself; rather it is a means of drawing all things into a unity with Christ" (286).

9. Cf. Romans 5:6–11.

10. Cf., e.g., Mark 10:45; Romans 5:8–10; Ephesians 2:13; 1 Peter 2:24; Hebrews 9:28.

11. Cf. Romans 8.

12. Cf. Ephesians 2:13–20.

13. Cf. Ephesians 2:4–9; Romans 3:21–26.

14. Cf. Hebrews 10:19–22.

15. Cf. John 14:25–27; Romans 5:1; Ephesians 2:14–20.

16. Cf. 2 Corinthians 5:14–21; Romans 8:1–2.

17. Cf. Luke 22:25–27 and Matthew 20:25–28.

18. Quoted in *The North Carolina Independent*, 20 July–2 August 1984.

19. See Peter Berger, *The Precarious Vision* (Garden City, N.Y.: Doubleday, 1961), esp. 85ff, 113ff, and 193ff.

20. *Church Dogmatics*, vol. 3, no. 4, p. 447 (1961).

CHAPTER 6

1. Cf. Luke 24:28–35 and John 21:1–14.

2. Cf. Acts 2:38–42.

3. Cf. Acts 20:7, 11.

4. Our usual count is 39; but this is a *scroll count*—that is, all of the minor prophets are considered one scroll or book.

5. The place of the *Apocrypha* in the canon is another important and instructive story, but there is neither space for nor purpose in pursuing it here. "Apocrypha" means "hidden (books)" and refers to a collection of fourteen or fifteen books (or parts of books) that have stood between the Old Testament and the New Testament in English Bibles. They were not included in the Hebrew Scriptures as finally canonized by the Council of Jamnia. Readers interested to pursue this matter are referred to James H. Charlesworth, *The New Testament Apocrypha and Pseudepigrapha: A Guide to Publications, with Excursuses on Apocalypses* (Metuchen, N.J.: Scarecrow Press, 1987).

6. William Temple, *Nature, Man, and God*, 307–8.

7. Karl Barth, *Church Dogmatics* (Edinburgh: T. & T. Clark, 1936), I/1, 124ff.

8. Walker Percy, "The Message in the Bottle," in *The Message in the Bottle* (New York: Farrar, Straus, and Giroux, 1975), 119–49.

9. I think, for example, of a broad range of slogans: "Get right with God," "Jesus loves me, this I know," "The family that prays together stays together," etc.

10. Cf. the article by Edmund Pincoffs, "Quandary Ethics," *Mind* 80 (October 1971): 552–71, for an insightful analysis of the "indefensibly narrow conception" of an ethics rooted in and defined by dilemmas.

11. "Ethology" is the term used to describe the study of how an animal experiences its world and organizes its environment. "Human ethology" is similarly concerned with how the human animal interacts with and locates itself in its social and cultural environment. It is useful to recall that the earliest use of the term "ethos" signified a

shed or stall in which horses stood for shelter. Our modern usage continues to carry a sense of the protective cultural ambience in which persons find significance and security for their lives.

12. Charles M. Wood, *The Formation of Christian Understanding* (Philadelphia: Westminster Press, 1981), 84.

13. Ibid., 100–101.

14. Whether the canon is closed and inviolable continues, through the centuries, to be an issue for some. There has been recent debate, for example, about whether to amend the canon by the addition of certain contemporary materials, among them Martin Luther King's "Letter from Birmingham Jail." On the other side, in recent years the Episcopal Church in the United States has debated whether to omit certain of the psalms from the Psalter because some think them offensive; and Thomas Jefferson, who considered himself an Episcopalian, did in fact cut out from his Bible certain portions (the passion and resurrection narratives) which he thought unsuitable. An Anglican view similar to Luther's, published at the request of the Archbishop of Canterbury in 1922 as part of the "Report of the Commission on Christian Doctrine," stated that as it is the church's duty to interpret "the relative spiritual value of different portions of the Bible, the standard is the mind of Christ."

15. Cf. Charles E. Curran and Richard A. McCormick, eds., *Readings in Moral Theology, No. 4: The Use of Scripture in Moral Theology* (New York: Paulist Press, 1984); David H. Kelsey, *The Uses of Scripture in Recent Theology* (Philadelphia: Fortress Press, 1975); and William C. Spohn, *What Are They Saying About Scripture and Ethics?* (New York: Paulist Press, 1984).

16. I am indebted to my former graduate teaching assistant, Dr. Paul Lewis, for suggesting these problem areas in a finely crafted lecture.

17. Henry Bettenson, ed., *Documents of the Christian Church* (New York and London: Oxford University Press, 1947), 298.

18. The Thirty-Nine Articles of 1563 were a revision of the forty-two articles of Edward VI. They became binding in the Anglican Church in 1571 and, with a few minor changes, were adopted by the Protestant Episcopal Church in the United States in 1801. Cf. the Book of Common Prayer (1979), 871. John Wesley revised the *Articles of Religion* and reduced their number to twenty-five; but this one remains among them, as Article XIII, for United Methodists.

19. Trutz Rendtorff has argued, contrary to much popular sentiment, that the church and the resistance to Nazism did not coincide. "What is forgotten," he claims, "is that an explicitly stated condition for the meeting of the synod at Barmen and for the passage of the theological declaration was that there, in that situation, no political resistance against the Nazi state was intended. On this point complete unanimity ruled among the assembled laity, church leaders, and theologians at Barmen." Even

Karl Barth was to comment some time later that "It was a minimal opposition on a very thin line against the whole National Socialist regime as such." What actually generated the will and power to issue the Barmen statement, according to Rendtorff, was "a concern to preserve the spiritual and confessional independence of the church, together with the organizational and institutional autonomy corresponding to it." Despite this preoccupation, Barmen did, however, make it possible to connect political and ecclesial resistance; so Rendtorff's judicious point, in the end, is that the value and courage of the Barmen declaration "should not be celebrated uncritically." See Trutz Rendtorff, "More Than Resistance: What We Need to Learn from the German Church Struggle," in *Confession, Conflict, and Community*, ed. Richard John Neuhaus (Grand Rapids, Mich.: Eerdmans, 1986), 49–66.

20. Karl Barth, *Texte zu Barmer Theologischen Erklärung*, ed. M. Rohkramer (Zurich: TVZ Verlag, 1984), 223–24.

21. Cf. Claude Geffre, *The Risk of Interpretation: On Being Faithful to the Christian Tradition in a Non-Christian Age*, trans. David Smith (New York: Paulist Press, 1987).

22. I ought to observe in this context that the question is related to, but not the same as, whether couples ought to be permitted to compose their own marriage vows, or whether parents should be allowed to write the baptismal liturgy for their children. We will need to address these matters later.

23. Wood, *The Formation of Christian Understanding*, 103.

24. See chapter 4 of this book, "Greetings: Peace."

25. R. Taylor Scott, "Preaching: Rhapsodic, Rhetorical and Liturgical," *College of Preachers Newsletter* 30 (winter 1985): 1–3.

26. Perhaps no preacher in twentieth-century America has exceeded Norman Vincent Peale as an exponent of rhapsodic preaching, and Scott is not the first to criticize this mode. When Adlai Stevenson was asked, during his second presidential campaign, his opinion of Dr. Peale, he responded: "I find Paul appealing, and Peale appalling." Stevenson's candor, among other things, cost him the election.

27. Scott, "Preaching," 3.

28. Richard Hooker, *The Laws of Ecclesiastical Polity* (London: George Routledge and Sons, 1888), III/4, p. 185.

29. T. E. Quill, "Death and Dignity: A Case of Individualized Decision Making," *New England Journal of Medicine* 324 (1991): 693–94.

30. Anonymous, "It's Over, Debbie," *Journal of the American Medical Association* 259 (1988): 272.

31. Harmon L. Smith, *Ethics and the New Medicine* (Nashville: Abingdon Press, 1970), 135ff.

32. Arthur Dyck, "Physician-assisted Suicide: Is It Ethical?" *Trends in Health Care, Law, and Ethics* 7 (1992): 20.

33. John Stuart Mill, *On Liberty* (London: John W. Parker and Son, 1859), 23–24.

34. Daniel Callahan, "When Self-Determination Runs Amok," *Hastings Center Report* 22 (1992): 52.

35. G. R. Scofield, "Physician-assisted Suicide: Part of the Problem or Part of the Solution?" *Trends in Health Care, Law and Ethics* 7 (1992): 16.

36. Council on Ethical and Judicial Affairs of the American Medical Association, "Decisions Near the End of Life," *Journal of the American Medical Association*, vol. 267, no. 16 (22–29 April 1991): 2229–33.

37. The Book of Common Prayer, 877.

38. Plato, *Laws*, ix, 873 C; Aristotle, *Politics*, 1335 b, 19ff.; for Pythagoras, cf. Cicero, *Cato Major* 20 (72 sq.) and *De Officiis*, i.31 (112). Cited in J. Fletcher, *Morals and Medicine* (Princeton, N.J.: Princeton University Press, 1954), 177.

39. D. W. Amundsen and G. B. Ferngren, "The Early Christian Tradition," in R. L. Numbers and D. W. Amundsen, eds., *Caring and Curing: Health and Medicine in the Western Religious Traditions* (New York: Macmillan Publishing Company, 1986), 50ff.

40. Cf. Cyprian, *De Charitate Inter Fratres* (C.S.E.L. 4, p. 737); Ambrose, *In Psalmum enarrato*, XXXVI (P.L. 14, p. 975); Irenaeus, *Advers. Haereses*, XXVII (P.G. 18, p. 729); Athanasius, *De Operibus Charitatis* (P.G. 18, p. 880).

41. Cf. Augustine, *City of God*, Bk. I, chaps. XV–XXVI, specifically XIX, p. 4.

42. Thomas Aquinas, *Summa Theologica*, II-II, q. 64, art. 5.

43. D. H. Smith, *Health and Medicine in the Anglican Tradition* (New York: Crossroads, 1986), 63 ff.

44. Fletcher, *Morals and Medicine*, 172.

45. Ibid., 207.

46. Ibid., 178.

47. Smith, *Health and Medicine in the Anglican Tradition*, 64.

48. R. Hooker, *Laws of Ecclesiastical Polity* (Oxford: Leble, 1874), V.46.2.

49. J. Taylor, *Holy Living and Holy Dying* (New York: Oxford University Press, 1988), vol. IV, i; vol. III, ix.

50. Smith, *Health and Medicine in the Anglican Tradition*, 66.

51. Callahan, "When Self-Determination Runs Amok," 53.

CHAPTER 7

1. The Book of Common Prayer (New York: The Church Hymnal Corporation, 1979), 365–66.

2. Ibid.

3. Geoffrey Wainwright, *Doxology, the Praise of God in Worship, Doctrine, and Life* (New York: Oxford University Press, 1980).

4. Augustine, *The City of God*, trans. John Healey, ed. R. V. G. Tasker (London: J. M. Dent, 1945), bk. XIV, chap. xxviii.

5. "This then is the mischief: man liking himself as if he were his own light turned away from the true light, which if he had pleased himself with, he might have been like." Ibid., bk. XIV, chap. xiii.

6. Ibid., bk. XIV, chap. xxviii.

7. Ibid., bk. XXI, ch. xv.

8. For an authoritative analysis of Calvin's polity, see William J. Bouwsma, *John Calvin: A Sixteenth-Century Portrait* (New York: Oxford University Press, 1988), esp. 210–13.

9. J. L. Neve, *A History of Christian Thought* (Philadelphia: The Muhlenberg Press, 1946), vol. I, p. 286.

10. Much of what immediately follows first appeared in my essay "On Cherishing the World and Struggling to Endure It," *Anglican Theological Review* 68 (January 1986): 27–39.

11. George A. Lindbeck, *The Nature of Doctrine: Religion and Theology in a Postliberal Age* (Philadelphia: Westminster, 1984), 127.

12. Stanley Hauerwas and L. Gregory Jones, "Seeking a Clear Alternative to Liberalism," *Books and Religion* (January 1985), 7; emphasis mine. The reference to "Cox" is to Harvey Cox, and specifically to his book *Religion in the Secular City*.

13. By "post-Constantinian" I mean to suggest only that serious distinctions between church and empire got blurred and eroded when the extent of accommodation and cooperation between church and empire produced a virtual union of these two. The phrase serves as a prominent metaphor in the theology of John Howard Yoder, but his meaning is more than metaphorical; he means also to convey certain historical claims about the pre- and post-Constantinian eras which I do not accept. I do not agree, for example, that the evidence supports Yoder's claim that pre-Constantinian Christians were pacifists and refused to participate in the military. For a fuller critical assessment of this and related matters, cf. Philip LeMasters, *The Import of Eschatology in John Howard Yoder's Critique of Constantinianism* (San Francisco: Mellen Research University Press, 1992), esp. chap. 3.

14. Stanley Hauerwas and William H. Willimon, "Embarrassed by God's Presence," *Christian Century* (30 January 1985): 99.

15. Stanley Hauerwas and William H. Willimon, *Resident Aliens: Life in the Christian Colony* (Nashville: Abingdon, 1989).

16. Lindbeck, *Nature of Doctrine*, 133.

17. Ibid., 133–34; emphasis mine.

18. Ibid., 134.

19. Ibid., 135.

20. Ibid., 134.

21. Ibid., 33; emphasis mine.

22. John 1:10–11; emphasis mine.

23. There is some disagreement among etymologists about the origins and historical development of the word "religion," but it is a disagreement which is substantively inconsequential. If "religion" derives from *re-legere* ("to reread"), the function signified would seem to be to re-tie (*religare*) the reader to the message of the text; so, in either case, the word denotes connection, presumably between what is otherwise disconnected.

24. Although I have never before seen or heard this word, I think that its transliteration from Greek roots is comparable to other, familiar words which share a similar etymology; for example, misogamy, misogyny, misology, etc.

25. Cf. Paul's discussion of the role of law in both the occasion for and the knowledge of sin in Romans 7:1–12: "if it had not been for the law, I should not have known sin. . . . But sin, finding opportunity in the commandment, wrought in me all kinds of covetousness. Apart from the law sin lies dead . . . but when the commandment came, sin revived and I died; the very commandment which promised life proved to be death to me."

26. Lindbeck, *Nature of Doctrine,* 59.

27. Ibid., 128.

28. Two recent attempts to argue this thesis, but from different perspectives and methodologies, are Alasdair MacIntyre, *After Virtue* (Notre Dame, Ind.: University of Notre Dame Press, 1981), and Robert Bellah et al., *Habits of the Heart* (Berkeley: University of California Press, 1985).

29. Lindbeck, *Nature of Doctrine,* 33–34; emphasis mine.

30. Cf. further Stanley Hauerwas and William H. Willimon, "Embarrassed by God's Presence," 98–100.

31. I appreciate that this claim requires considerable explication and argument. Perhaps I could say tersely that the familiar trilateral (reason, scripture, tradition) and quadrilateral (reason, scripture, tradition, experience) formulae lump together criteria that are, in fact, incommensurate in both substance and function. A good deal of our confusion and uncertainty regarding authority derives from failure to discriminate the tradition from its constituents.

32. Flannery O'Connor, *The Habit of Being,* ed. with an introduction by Sally Fitzgerald (New York: Vintage Books, 1980), 90.

33. Robert E. Cushman, *Faith Seeking Understanding: Essays Theological and Critical* (Durham, N.C.: Duke University Press, 1981), 193.

34. Vida D. Scudder, *Catherine of Siena as Seen in Her Letters* (New York: E. P. Dutton, 1927), 16.

35. Lesslie Newbigin, *The Gospel in a Pluralist Society* (Grand Rapids, Mich.: Eerdmans, 1989), 220.

36. Ibid., 223.

37. To Barth's credit, he devoted considerable attention to this matter, especially in writings which antedate the *Church Dogmatics*.

BIBLIOGRAPHY

Ambrose. *In Psalmum enarrato* XXXVI, P.L. 14.

———. *Saint Ambrose: Theological and Dogmatic Works*. Vol. 44 of *The Fathers of the Church*. New York: Fathers of the Church, Inc., 1963.

Amundsen, D. W., and G. B. Ferngren, "The Early Christian Tradition." In *Caring and Curing: Health and Medicine in the Western Religious Traditions*, edited by R. L. Numbers and D. W. Amundsen. New York: Macmillan Publishing Co, 1986.

Anderson, Gary A. *Sacrifices and Offerings in Ancient Israel: Studies in Their Social and Political Importance*. Atlanta: Scholars Press, 1987.

Anonymous. "It's Over, Debbie." *Journal of the American Medical Association* 259 (1988): 272.

Aquinas, Thomas. *Summa Theologica* II-II, q. 64, art. 5.

Athanasius. *De Operibus Charitatis*, P.G. 18.

Augustine. *The City of God*. Bk. I, chaps. XV–XXVI; Bk. VIII, chap. XVII (in vol. 14). In *The Fathers of the Church*. New York: Fathers of the Church, Inc., 1952.

———. *The City of God*. Bk. XIV, chap. XXVII, trans. Jean Healey, ed. R. V. G. Tasker. London: J. M. Dent, 1945.

———. *The Enchiridion on Faith, Hope, and Love*, trans. J. F. Shaw. South Bend, Ind.: Regnery/Gateway, Inc., 1961.

———. Sermon 6, English translation. In vol. II of *The Fathers of the Church*, 321–26. New York: Fathers of the Church, Inc., 1959.

———. Sermon 227. Latin text in J. P. Migne, vol. 38 of *Patrologia Latina*, 1099–1101 (Rotterdam: Soc. Editr. De Forel, 1952); English translation in *Saint Augustine: Sermons on the Liturgical Seasons*, vol. 38 of *The Fathers of the Church*, 195–98. New York: Fathers of the Church, Inc., 1959.

Bainton, Roland. *Christian Attitudes Toward War and Peace*. New York: Abingdon, 1960.

Baptism, Eucharist, and Ministry. Geneva: World Council of Churches, 1982.

Barth, Karl. *Church Dogmatics*. Vol. I/1. Edinburgh: T. and T. Clark, 1936; Vol. III/4, 1961.

251

————. *Texte zu Barmer Theologischen Erklarung*. Edited by M. Rohkramer. Zurich: TVZ Verlag, 1984.

Bellah, Robert N., et al. *Habits of the Heart*. Berkeley: University of California Press, 1985.

Belton, Francis George. *A Manual for Confessors—Being a Guide to the Administration of the Sacrament of Penance for the Use of Priests of the English Church*. London: A. R. Mowbray and Co, Ltd., 1936.

Berger, Peter. *The Precarious Vision*. Garden City, N.Y.: Doubleday, 1961.

Bettenson, Henry, ed. *Documents of the Christian Church*. New York and London: Oxford University Press, 1947.

Bieler, L. *The Irish Penitentials*. Dublin: Dublin Institute for Advanced Studies, 1963.

Bok, Sissela. *Lying: Moral Choice in Public and Private Life*. New York: Pantheon, 1978.

Bonhoeffer, Dietrich. *The Cost of Discipleship*, trans. R. H. Fuller. New York: Macmillan Co., 1963.

The Book of Common Prayer. New York: The Church Hymnal Corp., 1979.

Bouwsma, William J. *John Calvin: A Sixteenth-Century Portrait*. New York: Oxford University Press, 1988.

Box, Herbert S., ed. *The Theory and Practice of Penance*. London: Society for Promoting Christian Knowledge, 1915.

Brown, Raymond E. *The Anchor Bible: The Gospel According to John (i-xii)*. Garden City, N.Y.: Doubleday and Co., 1960.

Brunner, Emil. *The Divine Imperative*. Philadelphia: Westminster, 1958.

Cabie, Robert. "Christian Initiation." In *The Sacraments*, vol. III of *The Church at Prayer*, edited by A. G. Martimort, 11–100. Collegeville, Minn.: The Liturgical Press, 1988.

————. *The Eucharist*, vol. II of *The Church at Prayer*, ed. A. G. Martimort. Collegeville, Minn.: The Liturgical Press, 1986.

Callahan, D. "When Self-Determination Runs Amok." *Hastings Center Report* 2 (1992): 52.

Casel, O. *The Mystery of Christian Worship, and Other Writings*, ed. B. Neunheuser. Westminster, Md.: Newman, 1962.

Charlesworth, James H. *The New Testament Apocrypha and Pseudepigrapha: A Guide to Publications, with Excursuses on Apocalypses*. Metuchen, N.J.: Scarecrow Press, 1987.

Chrysostom. *St. John Chrysostom: Baptismal Instructions*, trans. P. H. Harkins. Vol. 31 of *Ancient Christian Writers—The Works of the Fathers in Translation*, edited by J. Quasten and W. J. Burghardt. Westminster, Md.: Newman Press, 1963.

Council on Ethical and Judicial Affairs of the American Medical Association. "Decisions Near the End of Life." *Journal of the American Medical Association* 267, no. 16 (April 22–29, 1991): 2229–33.

Curran, Charles E., and Richard A. McCormick, eds. *Readings in Moral Theology, No. 4: The Use of Scripture in Moral Theology.* New York: Paulist Press, 1984.

Cushman, Robert E. *Faith Seeking Understanding: Essays Theological and Critical.* Durham, N.C.: Duke University Press, 1981.

Cyprian of Carthage. *De Charitate Inter Fratres.* C.S.E.L., 4.

———. *The Lord's Prayer,* trans. Edmond Bonin. Westminster, Md.: Christian Classics, 1983.

Cyril. *The Works of Saint Cyril of Jerusalem.* Vol. 64 of *The Fathers of the Church.* New York: Fathers of the Church, Inc., 1970.

Demant, V. A. "The Social Implications of Worship; and the Necessity of Specific Acts of Worship." In *Worship: Its Social Significance,* edited by P. T. R. Kirk. London: The Centenary Press, 1939.

Didascalia Apostolorum, XIII, edited by R. H. Connolly. Oxford: Clarendon Press, 1929. (The *Didascalia* includes extensive fragments from the *Apostolic Constitutions* and the *Didache*).

Douglas, Mary. *Natural Symbols.* London: Barrie and Jenkins; New York: Pantheon Books, 1970.

Dyck, Arthur. "Physician-assisted Suicide: Is It Ethical?" *Trends in Health Care, Law, and Ethics* 7 (1992): 20.

Eliade, Mircea. *Images and Symbols: Studies in Religious Symbolism.* New York: Sheed and Ward, 1961.

———. *Rites and Symbols of Initiation.* New York: Harper and Row, 1958.

———. *The Sacred and the Profane.* New York: Harcourt, Brace, and World, 1959.

Eucharistic Prayer Book, Rite II.

Fairley, Henry. *The Seven Deadly Sins Today.* Notre Dame, Ind.: University of Notre Dame Press, 1979.

Fletcher, J. *Morals and Medicine.* Princeton, N.J.: Princeton University Press, 1954.

Geffre, Claude. *The Risk of Interpretation: On Being Faithful to the Christian Tradition in a Non-Christian Age,* trans. by David Smith. New York: Paulist Press, 1987.

Harmon, Nolan B. *Understanding the Methodist Church.* Nashville: The Methodist Publishing House, 1940.

Hatchett, Marion J. *Commentary on the American Prayer Book.* New York: Seabury Press, 1981.

Hauerwas, Stanley. *Truthfulness and Tragedy.* Notre Dame, Ind.: University of Notre Dame Press, 1977.

Hauerwas, Stanley, and L. Gregory Jones. "Seeking a Clear Alternative to Liberalism." *Books and Religion* 7 (January 1985).

Hauerwas, Stanley, and William H. Willimon. "Embarrassed by God's Presence." *Christian Century* (January 30, 1885): 98–100.

————. *Resident Aliens: Life in the Christian Colony*. Nashville: Abingdon, 1989.

Henley, William Ernest. "Invictus." In *A Treasury of Favorite Poems*, edited by Frances Parkinson Keyes. New York: Hawthorn Books, Inc., 1963.

Herberg, Will. *Protestant-Catholic-Jew: An Essay in American Religious Sociology*. Garden City, N.Y.: Doubleday and Co., 1955.

Hooker, Morna. *New Wine in Old Bottles: Christological Interpretation of the Old Testament in Early Christianity*. London: University of London, 1984.

Hooker, Richard. *The Laws of Ecclesiastical Polity*, III/4 (London: George Routledge and Sons, 1888); V.46.2 (Oxford: Leble, 1874).

Hoskyns, E. C. *The Fourth Gospel*. 2d ed. rev. London: Faber and Faber, 1947.

Hymnbook 1982, #302. New York: The Church Hymnal Corporation, 1982.

Irenaeus. *Advers. Haereses* XXVII, P.G. 18.

Jackson, T., ed. *Wesley's Works*, vol. V. London: John Mason, 1829.

James, E. O. *Origins of Sacrifice*. London: J. Murray, 1937.

Jounel, P. "Sunday and the Week." In *The Liturgy and Time*, vol. IV of *The Church at Prayer*, edited by A. G. Martimort, 11–29. Collegeville, Minn.: The Liturgical Press, 1986.

Juel, Donald. *Messianic Exegesis: Christological Interpretation of the Old Testament in Early Christianity*. Philadelphia: Fortress, 1988.

Jungmann, J. A. *The Early Liturgy: To the Time of Gregory the Great*. Notre Dame: University of Notre Dame Press, 1959.

Kant, Immanuel. *Religion Within the Limits of Reason Alone*, trans. T. M. Greene and H. H. Hudson. New York: Harper and Brothers, 1960.

Kavanaugh, Aidan. *The Shape of Baptism*. New York: Pueblo Publishing Co., 1978.

Kelsey, David H. *The Use of Scripture in Recent Theology*. Philadelphia: Fortress Press, 1975.

LeMasters, Philip. *The Import of Eschatology in John Howard Yoder's Critique of Constantinianism*. San Francisco: Mellen Research University Press, 1992.

Lindbeck, George A. *The Nature of Doctrine: Religion and Theology in a Postliberal Age*. Philadelphia: Westminster, 1984.

Lindstrom, H. *Wesley and Sanctification*. London: The Epworth Press, 1946.

MacIntyre, Alasdair. *After Virtue*. Notre Dame, Ind.: University of Notre Dame Press, 1981.

————. *Whose Justice? Which Rationality?*. Notre Dame, Ind.: University of Notre Dame Press, 1988.

Mannion, Francis M. "Liturgy and the Present Crisis of Culture." *Worship* 62 (March 1988): 98–123.

Maringer, Johannes. *The Gods of Prehistoric Man*. Translated by Mary Ilford. London: Weidenfeld and Nicolson, 1960.

Maringer, Johannes, and Hans-Georg Bandi. *Art in the Ice Age*. New York: Frederick A. Praeger, 1953.

Martimort, A. G., ed. *The Church at Prayer*, 4 vols.: *Principles of the Liturgy*, vol. I, 1987; *The Eucharist*, vol. II, 1986; *The Sacraments*, vol. III, 1988; *The Liturgy and Time*, vol. IV, 1986. Collegeville, Minn.: The Liturgical Press.

Maurice, Frederick Denison. *The Kingdom of Christ*, 2 vols. London: James Clarke and Co., Ltd., 1959.

Mazza, Enrico. *Mystagogia: A Theology of Liturgy in the Patristic Age*. Translated by M. J. O'Connell. New York: Pueblo Publishing Co., 1989.

Merleau-Ponty, Maurice. *The Phenomenology of Perception*. Translated by Colin Smith. London: Routledge and Kegan Paul, 1962.

Micks, Marianne H. *The Future Present: The Phenomenon of Christian Worship*. New York: Seabury Press, 1970.

Mill, John Stuart. *On Liberty*. London: John W. Parker and Son, 1859.

Mitchell, Leonel L. *The Meaning of Ritual*. New York: Paulist Press, 1977.

Myrdal, Gunnar. *An American Dilemma: The Negro Problem and Modern Democracy*. New York: Harper and Brothers, 1944.

Neve, J. L. *A History of Christian Thought*, vol. I. Philadelphia: Muhlenberg Press, 1946.

Newbigin, Lesslie. *The Gospel in a Pluralist Society*. Grand Rapids, Mich.: Eerdmans, 1989.

Niebuhr, H. Richard. *Christ and Culture*. New York: Harper and Brothers, 1951.

Norris, Richard. "On Theology." In *F. D. Maurice: A Study*, edited by F. McClain, R. Norris, and J. Orens. Cambridge, Mass.: Cowley Publications, 1982.

The North Carolina Independent. July 20–August 2, 1984.

O'Connell, Timothy E. *Principles for a Catholic Morality*. New York: The Seabury Press, 1976.

O'Connor, Flannery. *The Habit of Being*. Edited by Sally Fitzgerald. New York: Vintage Books, 1980.

Oesterley, W. O. E. *Sacrifices in Ancient Israel*. London: Hodder and Stoughton, 1937.

Percy, Walker. "The Message in the Bottle." In *The Message in the Bottle*. New York: Farrar, Straus, and Giroux, 1975.

Pincoffs, Edmund. "Quandary Ethics." *Mind* 80 (October 1971): 552–71.

Quill, T. E. "Death and Dignity: A Case of Individualized Decision Making." *New England Journal of Medicine* 324 (1991): 693–94.

Rendtorff, Trutz. "More Than Resistance: What We Need to Learn from the German Church Struggle." In *Confession, Conflict, and Community*, ed. John Neuhaus, 49–66. Grand Rapids, Mich.: Eerdmans, 1986.

Richardson, Cyril C., ed. *Early Christian Fathers*, vol. I. Philadelphia: Westminster Press, 1953.

The Sacramentary, revised according to the second typical edition of the *Missale Romanum*, March 27, 1975. Collegeville, Minn.: The Liturgical Press, 1985.

Scofield, G. R. "Physician-assisted Suicide: Part of the Problem or Part of the Solution?" *Trends in Health Care, Law, and Ethics* 7 (1992): 16.

Scott, R. Taylor. "Preaching: Rhapsodic, Rhetorical, and Liturgical." *College of Preachers Newsletter* 30 (winter 1985): 1–3.

Scudder, Vida D. *Catherine of Siena as Seen in Her Letters*. New York: E. P. Dutton, 1927.

Sennett, Richard. *The Fall of Public Man*. New York: Vintage Books, 1978.

Shepherd, Massey H., Jr. *The Oxford American Prayer Book Commentary*. New York: Oxford University Press, 1950.

Smith, D. H. *Health and Medicine in the Anglican Tradition*. New York: Crossroads, 1986.

Smith, D. Moody. *Johannine Christianity*. Columbia, S.C.: University of South Carolina Press, 1984.

Smith, Harmon L. "On Cherishing the World and Struggling to Endure It." *Anglican Theological Review* 68 (January 1986): 27–39.

———. "Decorum as Doctrine: Teachings on Human Sexuality." In *The Crisis in Moral Teaching in the Episcopal Church*, ed. T. Sedgwick and P. Turner, 15–40. Harrisburg, Pa.: Morehouse Publishing, 1992.

———. *Ethics and the New Medicine*. Nashville: Abingdon Press, 1970.

———. "Language, Belief, Authority: Crises for Christian Ministry and Professional Identity." *Pastoral Psychology* 23 (April 1972): 15–21.

Spohn, William C. *What Are They Saying About Scripture and Ethics?* New York: Paulist Press, 1984.

Steinmetz, David C. "The Superiority of Pre-Critical Exegesis." *Theology Today* 37 (1980): 27–38.

Sykes, Stephen. *The Identity of Christianity*. Philadelphia: Fortress, 1984.

Talley, Thomas J. "The Work of Ritualization." In *Prayer Book Renewal*, ed. H. Barry Evans. New York: Seabury Press, 1978.

Taylor, J. *Holy Living and Holy Dying*, vol. III, ix; vol. IV, i. New York: Oxford University Press, 1988.

Temple, William. *Nature, Man, and God*. London: Macmillan and Co. Ltd., 1960.

———. *Readings in St. John's Gospel*, 2 vols. London: Macmillan and Co., 1940.

Theodore of Mopsuestia. *Commentary of Theodore of Mopsuestia on the Lord's Prayer and on the Sacraments of Baptism and the Eucharist*, ed. and trans. A. Mingana, vol. 6 in the Woodbrooke Studies. Cambridge, England: W. Heffer and Sons, Ltd., 1933.

Thompson, Bard. *Liturgies of the Western Church*. Cleveland: World Publishing Co., 1962.

Troeltsch, Ernst. *The Social Teaching of the Christian Churches*, trans. Olive Wyon. New York: Macmillan Co., 1931.

Underhill, Evelyn. *Worship*. New York: Harper and Brothers, 1981.

Van Buren, Paul. *The Secular Meaning of the Gospel*. New York: Macmillan Co., 1963.

Wainwright, Geoffrey. *Doxology: The Praise of God in Worship, Doctrine, and Life*. New York: Oxford University Press, 1980.

Warren, Michael. *Faith, Culture, and the Worshiping Community*. New York: Paulist, 1989.

Wolf, William J. *Anglican Spirituality*. Wilton, Conn.: Morehouse-Barlow Co., Inc., 1982.

Wood, Charles M. *The Formation of Christian Understanding*. Philadelphia: Westminster Press, 1981.

Subject and Name Index

Scriptural Index